Adoption Detective

9/27/11

Nikki —

May this book open new
horizons for you!
Enjoy —

Judith Hand

(signature)

Adoption Detective

Memoir of an Adopted Child

JUDITH AND MARTIN LAND

Adoption Detective: Memoir of an Adopted Child

Published by Wheatmark®
610 East Delano Street, Suite 104
Tucson, Arizona 85705 U.S.A.
www.wheatmark.com

ISBN: 978-1-60494-571-3 (hardcover)
ISBN: 978-1-60494-570-6 (paperback)
Library of Congress Control Number: 2011932715

To my husband and coauthor Martin,
without whose loving support and assistance
this book could not have been written

Contents

PART 3
Epilogue

Introduction

THE PRACTICE OF ADOPTION is as old as recorded civilization. The Bible addresses this topic. Fearing for Moses's life, Jochebed places her baby in a watertight basket and floats it among the reeds along the bank of the Nile. Pharaoh's grown daughter discovers the babe, takes pity on him, and decides to adopt him as her own.

Adoption was a common practice among Romans in the upper senatorial class during the imperial period for ensuring a smooth succession. The emperor took his chosen successor as his adopted son. During Republican times, Augustus Caesar was the most famous Roman adoptee. Tiberius, Caligula, Nero, Trajan, Hadrian, Antoninus Pius, and Lucius Verus all became emperor through adoption.

In the Koran, Muhammad instructed adoptive parents to refer to their adoptive children by the names of their biological parents. Adopted parents were to be the guardians and foster parents of the child. Adopted family members were not considered blood relatives, and it was okay for them to marry. Inheritance remained separate from the biological family. If an adoptee inherited wealth from a birth parent, the adopted family was commanded to act as trustee and not to combine that property or wealth with their own.

Conscripting or enslaving children into armies and labor pools often occurred as a consequence of war or pestilence when many children were left parentless. Abandoned children then became the ward of the state, military organization, or religious group. When this practice happened en masse, it had the advantage of ensuring the strength and continuity of cultural and religious practices in medieval society.

Foundlings were commonly abandoned on the doorstep of churches, thus forcing clergy to draft rules governing the exposing, selling, and rearing of abandoned children who were without legal, social, or moral advantage. As a result, many of Europe's abandoned and orphaned became alumni of the Church, which then took the role of adopter. This trend marked the beginning of a shift toward institutionalization, eventually bringing about the establishment of foundling hospitals and orphanages. From these locations, children were doled out as cheap labor. Children were indentured to families who took them in as laborers and household servants.

In many countries, European law reflects an aversion to adoption. English common law did not permit adoption because it contradicted the customary rules of inheritance. For the ruling classes, bloodlines were paramount to sustaining a dynasty. The lack of a natural-born heir apparent usually meant automatic termination and replacement. Baby farming in the Victorian era was the taking in of a child for payment, but baby farmers were often unscrupulous and many orphans suffered neglect and death. The destiny of most orphans was a lifetime of squalor, poverty, and crime. English families considered it short-sighted to take into their midst a child whose pedigree was absolutely unknown when there was a strong probability that he or she would show poor and diseased stock and his or her offspring would be degenerates if a marriage should take place between that individual and any member of the adopted family.

Most societies paid little care or attention to orphans until several stories about the personal lives of adoptees captured the imaginations of the populace and stirred public opinion about their plight in society. Charles Dickens' second novel, *The Parish Boy's Progress*, commonly known as *Oliver Twist*, is the subject of numerous film and television adaptations and the basis for a highly successful musical. Orphaned by his mother's death in childbirth and his father's unexplained absence, Oliver is brought up with little to eat and few comforts. The story is printed in many languages, and people around the world love it.

Little Orphan Annie became a highly popular daily comic strip, radio show, and successful Broadway musical simply known as *Annie*. Little Orphan Annie escapes from an orphanage and makes her way in the world by hard work and a cheery disposition. She has a mop of curly red hair, a red dress, and vacant circles for eyes. She has only two friends, her doll Emily Marie and dog Sandy.

Heidi is a novel about the events in the life of an orphaned girl in the Swiss Alps. The *Heidi* books are among the best-known works of Swiss literature and film adaptations are popular all over the world. Five-year-old Heidi is left with her grandfather, who at first resents her arrival. Eventually the girl manages to penetrate his harsh exterior and subsequently has a delightful stay with him. When she is removed from his care, she becomes very homesick, and her only diversion is learning to read, write, and help others.

The largest migration of children in history took place in the United States between 1854 and 1929. Over two hundred thousand orphans were forced onto railroad cars and shipped west, where any family desiring their services as laborers, maids, and servants used and abused them. Orphan trains were highly popular as a source of free labor. The sheer size of the displacement and degree of exploitation that occurred gave rise to new agencies and a series of laws that promoted adoption rather than indenture.

Almost all children without parental care in the United States were in orphanages or foster arrangements until President Theodore Roosevelt declared the nuclear family was best able to serve as primary caretaker for the abandoned and orphaned. Inspired by his leadership, forces against institutionalization gathered momentum, and the practice of formal adoption gained popularity.

Eventually, adoption became a quintessential American institution, embodying faith in social engineering and mobility. By 1945, adoption was formulated as a legal act with consideration of the child's best interests. The origin of the move toward secrecy and the sealing of all adoption and birth records began when Charles Loring Brace introduced the concept to prevent children from the orphan trains from returning to or being reclaimed by their parents. Brace feared the impact of the parents' poverty and their Catholic religion, in particular, on the youth. Progressive reformers later carried on this tradition of secrecy when drafting American laws.

The legalization of artificial birth control methods and abortion resulted in a sudden drop in the number of babies available for adoption. As concerns over illegitimacy began to subside in the early 1970s, social welfare agencies began to emphasize that, if possible, mothers and children should be kept together. Societal opinions and adoption laws continue to evolve and vary by state. In safe haven states, infants may be left anonymously at hospitals, fire departments, or police stations within a few days of birth. While some states allow for open adoptions, others impose strict secrecy laws to protect identities.

Advanced biological, genetic, social, and psychological research in recent years has greatly enhanced public knowledge about the symbiotic relationship between birth mothers and infants.

The perception of similarities between adoptive parent and child appears important to successful parenting. In relationships marked by like personalities and appearances, both adult adoptees and adoptive parents report being happier with the adoption. For this reason, Native Americans and many other cultural and ethnic groups consider it very important to keep adoption within the child's ancestral population. There are several reasons for this, including the wish for a more complete genealogy, the child's curiosity about his or her relinquishment, a desire to pass on information to his or her children, and a need for biological and medical information. Although a third party could communicate this information, adoptees who express a need to actually meet biological relatives generally reject this information from others.

Reunions can be a beneficial experience for most adoptees who desire to learn about their biological and ancestral backgrounds, but this is not to imply that the goal of reunions is to establish ongoing relationships.

Authors' Note

ADOPTION DETECTIVE IS A true story with fictitious names. Judith Land's reunion with her birth parents and extended family opened a new chapter in her life. She was blessed because her family displayed unconditional love toward her. Consequently, she has more people to love today and more people to love her. Her tale and path to glory is likely to inspire other adoptees to do the same. Mothers and fathers everywhere in the world need to understand children are forever and always.

Acknowledgments

To EVERYONE WHO PLAYED a major role in my life: adopted parents Anthony and Rosella; cousins Jimmy and Barb; foster parents William and Priscilla, and foster sister Mary, who has the heart of an angel; my birth parents and family whose unconditional love and acceptance changed my life; members of the First Lilac Club, Judi, Kathy, Rene, and Diane, with whom I shared intimate childhood secrets; my wonderful classmates at Dominican High School for setting high standards and good personal examples that made my teenage years enjoyable and productive; and surrogate parents Leo and Helen; Hans and Eleanor; and Dorothy and Dan, who were wonderful neighbors and good role models.

Jim and Penny Hassell provided the catalyst to write my story. Terrie Drake's editing was invaluable. Jean Paton, founder of the Adoption Reform Movement, was a personal mentor. Sheila Mincer's enthusiastic endorsement and emotional support brought hugs and tears of joy.

Mike and Kathy Brandis, Rich and Jennifer Cooper, Fred and Millie Logan, and Dr. Judith Green shared insights and understanding. I am grateful to Judi Comstock, Bert and Ronny Martin, Maya Trysil, Jack Nason, Louise Netherton, Lois Martin-Orr, Cis Hawk, and Rhoda Serrin for their advice and assistance; Nicholas Martin for his editorial comments; and Peggy James for her heartfelt songs. I received spiritual inspiration from Dave Pearson, senior pastor at Mountain View Church, and Brother Thomas at St. Benedict's Monastery.

Adoption Detective

PART I

Childhood

Memories, Dreams, and Fantasies

"Everything that ever happened lingered in my imagination. Separation from my biological roots encouraged visions of my birth mother inspired by obscure memories, mystical dreams, and childhood fantasies." –Judith Romano

Conception

Dear Mom, I am the quintessence of your heart and soul. I was conceived in your womb last night as the result of two young, passionate spirits mystically combined in erotic love and beauty. You were sprinkled with magical stardust, and the arrow of Cupid, god of love and son of Venus and Mars, pierced your heart. You sleep with a prayer for your beloved in your heart and a song of praise on your lips, for love has no other desire than to fulfill itself. The strings of the violin are separate, but they quiver together with the music to create the birth of a soul in a new body. It is the pleasure of the bee to gather the honey of the flower, but it is also the pleasure of the flower to yield its honey to the bee, for, to the bee, a flower is the fountain of life, and, to the flower, a bee is a messenger of love. And to both, bee and flower, the giving and receiving of pleasure is a need and an ecstasy. The conflict of reason and passion are the sails and rudder of seafaring souls. Without one or the other, the danger of hasty action has doomed lovers since the beginning of time. You have lovingly but recklessly left your seed to be dispersed by the wind to an unforeseeable future. Love, Baby

BRUNO HELD REBECCA TIGHTLY in his arms and pulled her down on the blanket beside him. She was nervous. She sensed his youthful passion, intensity, and enthusiasm. He touched the smooth skin on her arms with his fingertips and caused goose bumps. A cold chill traveled down her spine. She felt the warmth of his body. His skin was moist. She liked the warm feel his breath made on her neck. She felt secure and loved.

It was a sultry evening in August. Waterlogged air from Lake Michigan jacketed the city of Milwaukee. The Mills Brothers song "I Love You So Much It Hurts" was playing on the radio in the background. "Don't Have to Tell Nobody" by Frankie Lane followed.

Bruno was strong, and Rebecca felt protected and comfortable in his arms. The good feelings that he produced in her heart and soul enraptured her. She looked into his eyes as he leaned forward and kissed her. Their embrace was mutual, and the memory of that evening was burned into their souls forever. They were high school seniors and madly in love.

REBECCA LOVED BEING AROUND Bruno and hanging out in the neighborhood where he lived, known as Little Italy. It was a vibrant part of the city with many street parties and constant activity. The excitement of being with Bruno's family and friends contrasted greatly with her own cultural and family life. The higher level of consideration, communication, and love between members of the Italian families made Rebecca naturally gravitate toward them. She loved their friendliness and the support they gave her. She enjoyed the fact that they were passionate about nearly everything, especially the foods they prepared and the stories they told about each other. Laughter prevailed, and lighthearted humor glowed throughout the family household.

She felt welcome and bonded easily with Bruno's mother, Flora, who was open-minded and interested in her as a person. Rebecca's mother, Bertha, was an entirely different sort of person. She was a strict disciplinarian, and she did not express the same feelings of genuine warmth and understanding that Rebecca experienced in the Italian community.

Bruno and Rebecca had had a mutual affection for each other ever since they were children. Over time, their youthful exuberance and puppy love matured into a feeling of mutual respect. Their relationship was overflowing with genuine passionate love for one another, and they spent more time together as the years progressed. They liked to picnic in the park and go on double dates with other couples. They loved holding hands while munching on toffee caramel crunch ice cream. They had great times together and hated to be apart. They were an attractive couple with cheeks that dimpled when they smiled.

They continued to be sweethearts throughout their high school years. Bruno made Rebecca feel special by carrying her books home after school, and Rebecca reciprocated by helping Bruno with some of his homework assignments. Rebecca took violin lessons after school, and she would walk past the football field after her lessons so she could catch a glimpse of Bruno practicing. She admired his physical strength and his muscular body, which were unsurprising given that he was the star fullback and linebacker. Her friends teased her and called him "Rebecca's Italian stallion." After every Friday night game, they would go out with friends for milk shakes or just hang out at somebody's house.

Rebecca loved it when her hero hugged her tightly and kissed her, and she wanted him to be hers forever. Bruno was popular with the girls, but he chose Rebecca because he loved her beauty and charm. Rebecca also loved to ride in Bruno's black convertible and looked forward to weekends when they could spend time together. Bruno enjoyed watching Rebecca's shiny brown hair blowing in the wind and later straightening the tangles with his fingers when they stopped.

During their senior year of high school, Rebecca wondered if Bruno would eventually propose to her. On their first date in eighth grade, they had held hands and promised to be faithful to each other forever, and neither one of them had ever dated anyone else.

Despite all this, Rebecca's parents did not approve of Bruno and discouraged her from seeing him. They intentionally filled up all of her free time with music lessons and adjusted her schedule in every way possible to keep them apart, but Rebecca was not dissuaded. On the contrary, Rebecca's and Bruno's love continued to intensify.

Rebecca was alarmed and confused when she missed her period for the first time, and Bruno was equally concerned. Regardless of how hard they rationalized their experience that exotic, sultry night on the shore of Lake Michigan, they were unprepared to deal with the circumstances that followed. The inevitable happened. Rebecca became pregnant.

Booth 2 Hill

Dear Mom, Have you noticed that loud, unfamiliar noises make me jump and rouse me to kick and squirm inside of you? Can you feel my heart beating? It calms me when I feel your hands massaging my back, and I like it when you listen to quiet music and rhythmically move from side to side. The fear and shame you feel about me is triggering chemical changes in your body, and your emotions are affecting my sleep patterns. Anticipation of the big day is making you tense and worried because you are not looking forward to my birth. I am growing larger every day. It is six weeks before my expected birth date, and your parents are embarrassed to be seen with us in public. Love, Baby

REBECCA'S PARENTS WERE FURIOUS when they discovered their teenage daughter was pregnant. They had openly anguished about her relationship with Bruno Rossi and repeatedly warned her to stay away from him, but their worst fears had finally come true. They had done everything in their power to keep Rebecca occupied and away from her boyfriend, but their attempts had been in vain. Their daughter had been careless and disobedient, and they admonished her severely for her transgression. The sin she had committed had permanently ruined her life and brought shame to her parents.

In their eyes, Bruno Rossi was an evil man, and Bertha would never forgive him for what he had done. Her cultural bias was strikingly evident when she expressed her negative opinions about his Italian heritage. She felt vindictive toward his entire family and intended to make them pay all medical and legal expenses.

Ben and Bertha Meyer were frustrated, angry, and unforgiving toward their daughter for her poor judgment. What had happened had emotionally devastated Rebecca, and her parent's unsympathetic attitude forced her to internalize her shame. Her agitated state of mind left her feeling unstable, fearful, and dependent on her parents because she did not have the knowledge or finances to act on her own. Rebecca desperately wanted to avoid embarrassment and return to society as quickly as possible without besmirching her reputation.

Ben and Bertha did not feel empathy or offer comfort or sympathy to their daughter in response to her predicament. They considered concealment as the best method for addressing the problem. They kept her pregnancy secret from everyone except Father Hennen, Rebecca's school counselor and spiritual advisor. He listened to the entire story without interruption.

"I have a personal connection with Catholic Social Services Adoption Agency. I suggest Rebecca disappear for a while at a home for unwed mothers and let CSS handle the adoption," Father Hennen suggested politely.

Ben and Bertha concurred. They were angry and aggressively unforgiving. The only way to deal with the situation was to get rid of the baby. Out of sight, out of mind.

Rebecca was forbidden to speak with friends, and her relatives were kept in the dark about her condition. In Bertha's mind, there was no debate about what to do with the baby. Her decision was irrevocable and unchallengeable, thus leaving no choice other than to give up the baby for adoption.

"You have done a terrible thing. You must do as I say because you are not old enough to raise a baby and have no money to support yourself. Bruno would not make a good husband or father. I don't like Italians, and I don't want you hanging around with anyone associated with the Mafia. You need to stay away from Bruno permanently and never see him again. Your baby will be better off raised by strangers," Bertha said assertively.

Rebecca could hardly bear the thought of never seeing her boyfriend again. She loved Bruno and didn't want their relationship to end this way, but her mother was her legal guardian and the ultimate decision-maker. She was a minor. She wasn't old enough to marry the father without her parents' permission or determine the fate of her own baby.

Rebecca was a shapely five-foot-seven. As the weeks passed and she grew rounder around the middle, she was able to disguise her condition by wearing baggy, loose-fitting sweaters to conceal her slightly protruding stomach. None of her classmates seemed to notice her increase in weight or change in physique.

During the third trimester of her pregnancy, Bertha kept Rebecca home from school and instructed her to tell friends and family that she had a bad kidney infection.

BEN'S HEAVY DRINKING CONTRIBUTED to his anger. In a fit of rage, he initiated a lawsuit that forced Bruno's parents into court.

"I'll be damned if I'm going to pay for the high cost of delivery, medical bills, adoption fees, and legal expenses for Bruno's child," Ben exhorted drunkenly.

Brando and Flora Rossi had difficulty speaking English and used their oldest daughter Nina as their interpreter. It was difficult for them to understand the purpose of the court proceedings and what they were being asked to do. They were incapable of mounting a defense or suggesting a compromise. In the end, they were assigned full responsibility for court costs, medical expenses, and extended care of the baby. These costs would continue indefinitely until the baby was legally adopted. The judge scolded them for being irresponsible grandparents and threatened to fine them if they didn't comply with his orders.

They were unhappy with the judge's decision because they didn't understand why their son Bruno and Rebecca couldn't get married and keep their baby. The entire Rossi family supported the idea of keeping the baby. Nina had even offered to raise the baby herself, but the judge ignored her plea.

BERTHA PACKED A SUITCASE for Rebecca and drove her to the Booth Hill Home for Unwed Mothers in Wauwatosa, Wisconsin, where Father Hennen had reserved a private room for her. During the sign-in process, Bertha made certain financial responsibility was assigned to Brando and Flora Rossi. Rebecca was ordered to remain hidden and avoid making any telephone calls until her baby was born while Bertha continued to spread the lie that her daughter had a severe kidney infection.

A new shift of harried, overworked nurses arrived every eight hours to robotically complete their daily rounds. They occasionally checked her physical condition, but never inquired about her mental health, asked about the father, or suggested she keep her baby. Rebecca was unaware of normal childbirth protocols and didn't consider her condition or confinement unique.

Worried and lonely, she was preoccupied with feelings of guilt. She had faith in Father Hennen and never thought about challenging his authority, but her animosity toward her parents was growing deeper each day. Bertha ignored her pleas for emotional support. The controls her mother had exerted over her irritated Rebecca. Her own inadequacies and inability to defend herself frustrated her. Her parents were highly demanding, and she responded to their wrath by readily acquiescing for appeasement.

Rebecca concentrated on the present and wasted little time thinking about her cloudy future, which was thoroughly unsettled. Quarantined from all things familiar, she was thoroughly cut off from all of her friends, relatives, and beloved boyfriend Bruno. She was a pregnant, unwed mother lacking intimate companionship or parental support, and her emotions were sent into turmoil each time her baby kicked or turned inside her.

Her need for self-fulfillment, accomplishment, and recognition weighed heavily on her mind. She had been optimistically looking forward to playing with the Milwaukee Symphony Orchestra after graduation, but her dream had been shattered. She felt like a failure, and her baby was hanging around her neck like a scarlet letter. She was eager to get the birth over and move on with her life. She had resigned herself to her fate with no recourse other than letting others make decisions for her.

"Your father and I are your legal guardians. We will never give you permission to marry Bruno Rossi or keep his child. He is too mature for you. He would never make a good husband. You must pretend this event never happened before you ruin your life for good. You have sinned against the church and humiliated your parents. You have no choice. Someone other than you is going to raise your baby."

Rebecca cried. She knew how wrong she had been to allow this terrible thing to happen. She was losing Bruno and her baby. She longed for the simple way her life used to be. She was depressed knowing she would miss the senior prom, graduation celebrations, yearbook signing, and graduation dance.

REBECCA TURNED OFF THE light, hugged her pillow tightly, and closed her eyes. She dreamed about wearing a beautiful, long-flowing dress and attending the prom with Bruno in his tuxedo until the image of a shadowy figure in the doorway suddenly startled her dream.

Bruno stealthily entered her room, reached out to touch her silky brown hair, bent down, and kissed her on the lips and whispered to Rebecca, "You remind me of Sleeping Beauty with your eyes closed and long, brown hair flowing across the pillow."

Rebecca wiped away her tears of joy and beamed with happiness. She wrapped her arms around his neck and pulled him closer. Her pink lips and smooth complexion smote Bruno. He looked directly into her warm, brown eyes glowing with happiness. She returned his amorous glance and knew immediately that Bruno still loved her. They wrapped their arms tightly around each other and sobbed in unison. Bruno could feel the hard bulge in Rebecca's abdomen kicking. He reached out and touched the baby with his hand.

"What's going to happen to our baby?" he asked.

Circumstances were too emotional for them to verbalize how they felt about each other. Holding hands and hugging was the purest way of communicating their love for each other.

"Do your parents know about our baby?" Rebecca inquired softly.

"Yes, they know. They want us to get married and keep our baby. They offered to help us, but your mother wouldn't allow it. My oldest sister Nina offered to adopt our baby, but your parents didn't want anything to do with her. They sued my parents to make them responsible for the baby's expenses until it is adopted. That is how I found out where you were staying. None of our classmates knows the truth. Everyone thinks you are quarantined because you have a kidney infection. I'm sorry for what happened, but I still love you," Bruno whispered softly into her ear.

His explanation startled Rebecca because marriage had never been discussed with her parents or Father Hennen. They would have automatically rejected these ideas.

Bruno reached into his jacket pocket, slid out his music player, and handed it to Rebecca. She was overcome with emotion knowing that Bruno still loved her. She was grateful he had come to see her when she was feeling blue and isolated from everyone she loved. She attached the earphones and listened to the words to the song "The Things We Did

Last Summer" by Georgia Gibbs. Tears ran down her cheeks as she tightly grasped Bruno's warm hand.

A mutual fear and sadness was in their hearts. Rebecca wished Bruno would lie down beside her and hold her all through the night. She never wanted to be separated from him again. She pondered his words in her heart about getting married and keeping the baby, even though she knew it was too late.

"I joined the marines today. No matter where they send me, I will never forget how beautiful you look tonight," Bruno said stoically as he wiped the tears from his cheeks.

He smiled and waved good-bye as he cautiously backed out of the room, trying not to be observed. Knowing he would soon be going off to war left Bruno with the same fears, emotional heartaches, and feelings of uncertainty that Rebecca was already experiencing.

Birth

Dear Mom,

I can feel your hands touching me. It is crowded in your stomach and becoming more difficult for me to turn around. The time for my birth must be near because I sense you are worried. You seem lonely and afraid of the physical pain and life-threatening complications that may occur during the birthing process. Love, Baby

I T WAS CLOUDY AND damp and drizzling outside. The grass was wet. Small puddles of water were settling in the low spots on the sidewalk leading to the front door of Martha Washington Hospital. The atmosphere inside was gloomy. The color of the interior walls was a nauseating yellowish-green.

The irregular contractions Rebecca was having about every half hour reminded her of extreme menstrual cramps. It was difficult to relax, and it was uncomfortable to remain in one position. Nurses came in periodically to check on her progress. The estimated birth would take place sometime after midnight.

Rebecca tried to read a magazine, but she could only look at the pictures. It was difficult for her to concentrate. Her contractions were too painful and distracting. She felt panicky and imagined her muscle contractions as being too irregular or too far apart. Only recently had the nurses explained to her about most of what was happening. Bertha had never talked to her about sex, the consequences of an accidental pregnancy, or what to expect during the birthing process.

Rebecca was suddenly afraid of what was happening to her. She knew something might be going terribly wrong. The pain was increasing with every contraction, and she was beginning to wonder if the nurses would hear her cries for help. The realization she would never be allowed to hold her baby in her arms was finally giving her remorse.

At two o'clock in the morning, her dilation was almost full term, and her water finally broke.

"Nurse, nurse, my baby!" Rebecca screamed hysterically.

Two nurses rushed in from the hallway and wheeled Rebecca into the birthing room. The doctor immediately gave her a sedative to relieve the pain. The doctor used forceps because Rebecca was not coherent enough to push the baby through the birth canal. As soon as it was born, it was whisked out of the delivery room and placed in an incubator. It was a baby girl.

In her mind, the birth of a first child for married couples was an exciting memorable event, but it was a heartbreaking experience for Rebecca because she didn't have a spouse to reassure or praise her. When she awoke, nobody was there to congratulate or comfort her. There were no flowers, cards, or balloons. She simply lies on her back with an intravenous needle stuck in her arm and fell asleep.

She spent the next two weeks at the hospital to recuperate from the birth of her baby and overcome her grief. Bertha had been adamant that Rebecca not be given an opportunity to view or hold her baby after it was born. She had given the nurses strict instructions to remove the baby from the birthing room as quickly as possible and make sure it disappeared permanently. She wanted to make sure that Rebecca had no memory of her baby and foil any opportunities for mother-and-child bonding. Bertha reasoned that, the less Rebecca remembered, the easier it would be for her to start a new life after her baby was born. Doctors complied by giving Rebecca large amounts of drugs that left her sleepy and confused.

Bertha repeatedly exerted her authority by telling Rebecca to forget about Bruno's baby, but Rebecca could not rest peacefully until she knew the answer to one lingering question.

"Was my baby a boy or a girl?" she humbly requested to know.

Bertha furled her brow, stuck out her chin, and scowled. Her eyes squinted as she angrily snapped back, intentionally lying to Rebecca when she responded tersely through tightly clenched teeth. "You had a baby boy," she said sarcastically.

Rebecca buried her face in her pillow and prayed for her child. Bertha always referred to the baby as "it" because, in her mind, acknowledgment of the gender legitimized the child's presence. She was mean-spirited and purposefully deceitful. She rationalized that her lies would discourage Rebecca from ever thinking about her baby as a real person

The callousness of her decision did not move Bertha, and she was unconscionably willing to abandon her first grandchild to an uncertain fate.

Bonding

Dear Mom, I cried when you left me. Why didn't you hold me, kiss me, or say good-bye? Is there something wrong with me? I have a basic need to nurse from your breast and be cuddled, hugged, and cooed. Instinctively, I need you for sustenance, comfort, and warmth. I have your genes in my blood, and, like you, I have brown hair, brown eyes, smooth skin, and dimples on my cheeks. I am programmed to bond with you as my mother, but you never gave me a chance. You simply abandoned me, and now I have no one to care for me. Wide-eyed and hungry, I look into the eyes of every stranger and hope it is you. A different nurse feeds and cares for me every eight hours. The louder I cry, the more attention I receive, but nobody comes when I cry sometimes. Each day, new people come and go at different times of the day and night as shifts change. Their faces are never the same. Some nurses smile and talk baby talk to me. Others do their job quickly and efficiently and ignore the hugging and holding part that I enjoy so much. I have learned that, the more I smile and clutch the nurses' hair or fingers, the longer each stranger holds me. I cry when I am hungry or uncomfortable or when nobody is there to comfort me. I cry because I miss you and when I am left all alone. Sometimes, nobody is there to hear me cry. I wish I had your arms around me to reassure me that I am safe and secure. I want to smell your skin, your breath, and your hair. I want to hear your calming and soothing voice to let me know everything is all right. On the first day of my life, you cast me aside as an illegitimate orphan. I am a displaced person, but war, pestilence, disease, or human tragedy did not cause my circumstances. I was simply born at a time that was inconvenient to others. I hope that—someday and somewhere—somebody will love me. I am only a baby. I don't remember exactly when I was born, but, deep in my core brain, the separation from you at birth has altered my consciousness and changed me forever. Over time, as I grow older and become more aware of my surroundings, I think I will forever retain a deep sense that I am missing something. That something is you. In the future, there will be nobody to tell me about you or anything at all about my past. I have no way of ever knowing you or my father. I will have no roots, biological family, or information about my beginnings. I will not know my grandparents or have any sense of my real place in the world. I will not know the geographic parts of the world where my parents came from or their nationality. I will have no way of knowing your personal habits and family customs or learning about your occupation, interests, and hobbies. I will not know what kinds of foods you like, your musical preferences, or talents. I won't even know what you look like. Before I was born, it was your decision to have someone else care for me other than you. In my little undeveloped brain, I sensed you were afraid because I could feel your tension and emotional stress. Maybe you were lacking the emotional support of others and didn't view a future together as positive. Did your parents convince you that I was too great a burden and suggest it was best to leave me behind? Did they make you feel ashamed, say you were too young to care for a baby of your own, and convince you that a stranger could raise me better than you could? They are wrong. If I could talk, I would tell you that I am not ashamed of you. You are my mother, and I want to be with you. I don't want to be left alone. I will miss you passionately when you leave the hospital. I will think of you often and hope you will think about me, too. When I get older, I will fantasize about the day you turned your back on me at the hospital. I hope I will learn to handle difficulties and problems caused by separation from you because my abandonment will affect how I feel about others for the rest of my life. Who will want me? I am only a helpless baby. I don't even have a name. Love, Baby

R EBECCA'S UNNAMED BABY SCREAMED for attention. "I'm hungry. Feed me. Hug me. I need comfort. Cover me. I'm cold. I'm wet. Change my diaper."

Babies in the front row of the nursery had a distinct advantage over the ones in the back because they received more attention. Nurses made more eye contact with them, tickled them under their chin, made cooing sounds, and fluffed up their blankets more often than the others. Rebecca's baby was haplessly placed in the last row, and her life passed slowly as she struggled to live. Her life was fragile and entirely dependent on strangers for nourishment and basic human needs. To survive, it was mandatory she gain enough strength to learn how to accept nourishment from a baby bottle. It was a slow process at first. Without her mother there to guide her, she struggled to master the mechanics of sucking. By the third week, she had gained only four ounces.

Each nurse had a different bedside manner and held her in their arms with a different technique. Some rocked her back and forth. Some did not hold her at all. Each one warmed the bottle to a slightly different temperature and held the baby bottle at a different angle. One nurse was left-handed. The height, weight, and facial expression of each person were unique. The actions of some were slow and deliberate as they spoke tenderly with a soft voice and touched her face with their fingertips. Others quickly removed the bottle from her mouth when she paused and wiped her face with a cold washcloth. Each nurse had a unique smell and voice inflection. Some were quiet and shy. Others were bold and talked loudly and frequently. Some nurses looked directly into her eyes and talked to her. A few sang, hummed, or recited short poems. They occasionally went out in the hall to drink a cup of coffee, eat a donut, smoke a cigarette, or chat with the other nurses.

A different group of assistants fed and changed her diapers at different times of the day. Three times each day, the assembly line of nurses taking care of her rotated. A new set rushed in to replace the old team at the beginning of each eight-hour shift. Each nurse would review what the previous nurse had written on the clipboard before semi-accurately scribbling her own notes, recording the time of her visit and the number of ounces of milk each baby consumed and other observations.

On the sixteenth day, something unique happened. Nurse Kathy Brenner came in to the newborn ward carrying official release papers that transferred responsibility for Rebecca's baby from the hospital to the state of Wisconsin. Paternal grandparents Brando and Flora Rossi were named as the financially responsible parties and billed for all the hospital expenses. According to court records, they would continue paying until the baby was legally adopted.

Rebecca had secretly spent an entire month at the Booth Hill Home for Unwed Mothers to conceal her pregnant condition from others before giving birth to her baby. The nursery was operating at full capacity, and other babies with the most serious postnatal conditions were given priority. There was a shortage of cribs and not enough doctors or nurses to care for so many orphans. Despite the difficulty

Rebecca's baby was having with gaining weight, the head nurse decided with the stroke of a pen to transfer her out of the hospital to make room for other newborns.

Unless an adoption was prearranged to take place, legal responsibility was automatically transferred to the state. Rebecca's baby was desperately in need of a permanent home, but there were no pending requests for adoption. Nurse Brenner prepared the legal paperwork, classifying the child as a homeless orphan and assigning responsibility for its care to the state.

Official documents contained the name of the birth mother, date of birth, current address, parents' names and addresses, names of siblings, occupations of mother and grandparents, nationality, and religious preference. Each document required the legal name of the baby to be shown on the first page. Nurse Brenner was used to taking charge, making quick decisions, and operating efficiently. Without serious deliberation, she took the liberty to fill in the blanks herself. "Over the Rainbow" by Judy Garland was playing on the radio at her duty station. The song inspired her, so she smiled.

"Judy is a suitable name for this baby," she said aloud for the benefit of the other nurses.

With an air of self-assurance and confidence, she jotted down the name "Judith Ann" on the cover of the manila file folder containing the baby's medical records and on each line of the release form, medical certificate, legal papers, and official cover letter. Within the blink of an eye, based solely on the whims of a stranger, Rebecca's baby had been assigned a new identity with no links, clues, or connections to her birth mother.

Whereas natural parents often anguished over the selection of names to honor their ancestors, parents or grandparents, cultural preferences, or origins, the official naming of Judy by a stranger was a secrecy equivalent to individuals assigned to the federal witness protection program. Her name provided no clues to her real identity or relationship to her birth parents. Her birth certificate and other official links to her biological past were intentionally deleted. It was ironic that her true identity would only be known in the future to social workers and state bureaucrats. The ability of Judy to find her real mother in the future was permanently concealed.

Conversely, the lack of a paper trail now made it impossible for

Rebecca to find her own biological child, even if she later changed her mind. All legal documents containing the baby's true identity were officially sealed and placed in the vault for the protection of the parents, grandparents, and everyone else concerned. It was now impossible for Rebecca and her baby to ever be reunited again in the future.

Nurse Brenner completed the forms in triplicate: one for the hospital records, one for the state of Wisconsin, and one for Booth Hill. She placed the original copy in her file, set a duplicate in her outbox to be mailed to the state, and handed the third copy to the social worker for her files before calling for the baby. It was a routine business transaction.

A young nurse named Heather, who was shy and completely lacking in self-confidence, brought the baby in from the nursery. She checked the bracelet on its arm three times to make sure this was the right one. Heather was an albino with poor vision, skinny arms, and white hair. She was deathly afraid she might accidentally select the wrong baby.

"Here is the child you requested," Heather stuttered haltingly as she nervously attempted to hand Judy to Nurse Brenner.

Nurse Brenner stepped backward, deflecting the infant directly into the outstretched arms of a social worker as skillfully as a matador giving the bull the brush-off while matter-of-factly escorting both of them out the door and into the hallway. The transfer of authority was simply a cordial routine business transaction.

Bruno Rossi and Rebecca Meyer were officially pardoned and released by the church and state of all moral responsibility. They would never know anything about the destiny of their child or if a family living in a foreign country would adopt her. They wouldn't even know her name. All legal connections with their child had been as coldly and skillfully severed as the cutting of the umbilical cord.

Foster Parents

Dear Mom, You are gone, but your spirit lingers on. I am sixteen days old and struggling to gain weight. In your absence, many different nurses have been feeding me and changing my diapers. Yesterday was unique because, after I finished my warm bottle of milk, a nurse gave me a special bath and rubbed my head and face with a towel and dressed me in a soft pink baby bunting. I was excited by all the attention the nurses gave me. They said I looked cute and called me Judy before saying good-bye and wishing me luck. After that, I was bundled in blankets and handed to a stranger. The hallway was a very busy place with many people walking around. I heard new sounds that startled me. The temperature outside was much colder than it was in the nursery. I don't know where they are taking me. Love, Judy

O N THE WAY OUT of the hospital, social worker Gertrude Schweinhaus clutched the baby a little too tightly, causing it to cry. Gertrude slid into the front seat of a gray, four-door Chevrolet. She cradled the baby in her arms and carelessly brushed its head against the car door, causing her tiny pink bonnet to twist to one side and drop down over her eyes.

"Take me to the home of William and Priscilla Engelmann on South Layton Boulevard in South Milwaukee," Gertrude commanded her driver, Ron Madunic. He ran a comb through his long white hair and dyed mustache, snuffed out his sweet smelling chocolate wrapped cigar, and admired his reflection in the rearview mirror before starting the engine, "Buckle your seatbelt mamma."

Miss Schweinhaus took her responsibilities seriously and exerted her authority by providing a thorough set of instructions to foster parents specific to each baby. A key part of her job was to inspect and approve the condition of each foster home to check for hazards. She was very picky and possessed the habit of finding fault to emphasize her self-worth and authority. If she uncovered any conditions she deemed unsafe, she required those elements to be fixed. She never hesitated to threaten to remove a baby from a foster home if a perceived discrepancy wasn't corrected immediately.

She callously read her prepared speech to William and Priscilla, reminding them of the limited role of foster parents and unsympathetically concluded her remarks with the following statement. "Foster parents provide a temporary fix to one of society's urgent problems. Your responsibility is to provide a base level of interim care until this child is adopted into a permanent home. You are to avoid becoming attached to any children placed in your care."

Miss Schweinhaus handed the baby to Priscilla and spontaneously set about conducting a meticulous inspection of her house. She boldly opened cupboard doors and peered into closets to search for insecticides, poison, sharp objects, and other materials hazardous to children. She walked into the baby's room, tested the stability of the baby crib, and smelled the cleanliness of the bedding materials. Finding nothing wrong, she suspiciously eyed Priscilla's other daughters for signs of mischievousness.

She paused to be certain that she had William and Priscilla's undivided attention before reciting a lengthy list of doctor's instructions, agency requirements, protocols, legal arrangements, responsibilities, and financial elements of their contract. She concluded her remarks by threatening them with future unscheduled inspections in their home to check on the health and welfare of the baby. Finding nothing else to do, she whirled around on her heels and abruptly departed.

Priscilla held the baby softly in her arms and rocked her gently from side to side. Judy opened her eyes briefly. William stared affectionately at her. He was surprised at how much she resembled his own daughters. Her eyes were big and brown, and she was very cute. He was happy knowing that his family had an opportunity to make a difference in this little orphan's life.

Their four girls were thrilled with their new baby sister. Mary, Shirley, Barbara, and Therese had been eager to help their mother clean the house and prepare the nursery for their new guest. The entire family wanted to give the social worker a good first impression. The girls were dressed in their Sunday clothes and sat passively on the living room couch until the front door closed. The sound of the door closing was their signal to jump up and down and shout with glee.

"Yay! It's a baby girl named Judy."

Mary and Barbara took the initiative to dress Judy in a soft, new outfit purchased for this special occasion. The unfamiliar presence of strangers and her new surroundings startled her. Priscilla was aware from previous experiences that Judy's nervous condition was a trait common to most babies raised in orphanages who lacked early bonding.

Judy cried frequently and spit up the formula she was fed. According to her pediatrician, she was colicky due to a lack of maternal bonding and the emotional stress caused by the abrupt change in surroundings. The lengthy bouts of screaming she exhibited were the result of not enough holding and touching. He recommended Priscilla hold her frequently, preferably sitting in a rocking chair while rubbing her back. He recommended soothing classical music and any routine that provided hands-on human contact to help make the baby feel loved and attached.

By the end of the first month, some bonding was evident. Judy cried less often and showed signs of being more content and less colicky. Routine smiles and lots of attention backed with genuine tender loving care by the entire family helped calm her and reduce her bouts of screaming. There was no shortage of arms willing to hold and touch her. Priscilla and William unselfishly took turns during the night feeding and changing her diapers, rubbing her back, and rocking her in their arms.

Their household was a good fit for Judy. The whole family settled into a routine schedule based around the baby's needs. After school, Barbara and Mary took turns pushing her in the baby stroller while Therese and Shirley followed behind, pushing their little, white dog in the doll carriage.

Priscilla wisely assigned each daughter a separate role to make each girl feel responsible for some portion of Judy's welfare. Mary was the oldest. She helped with the more difficult tasks, such as feeding. The others helped with dressing, cleaning, playtime, and reading.

Judy gradually assimilated with all members of her new foster family. She responded with big smiles and demonstrations of excitement by waving her arms and kicking her legs. Each day, the girls looked forward to playing with Judy and helping their mother. By the time Judy was six months old, most of her colicky systems were gone.

Priscilla prepared a baby book for Judy. She recorded her length and weight, physical characteristics, preferences, and unique individual traits. She pasted in a few baby pictures and her original hospital bracelet. Priscilla smiled and recalled the day of Judy's baptism as she carefully recorded the date in the baby book. It was a special day dedicated to Judy, one of her most vivid recollections and favorite memories of her foster child.

The whole family had gathered around the baptism font in the vestibule of Saint Lawrence Catholic Church. The baby was dressed in a beautiful, long, white, lacy dress with a frilly white bonnet. She was wrapped in a soft, white, cuddly blanket. Priscilla held Judy in her arms as the priest removed her bonnet. Father Hennen carefully poured holy water over her head and slowly prayed the words for the sacrament of baptism. The day had been bright and sunny. Pink apple blossoms, yellow forsythia, and red and yellow tulips added color to the spring landscape. The sky was deep blue with white cumulus clouds intermittently drifting slowly across the horizon. Birds were chirping, and several squirrels chased each other across the church lawn. Priscilla was grateful for the opportunity to play a positive role in the raising of this child, and she reflected on the occasion fondly as a beautiful experience because, in her mind, it was the day her foster child became a child of God.

Priscilla always referred to her as "Dearest Judy" because she was special. She had developed a deep feeling for this baby because she was similar to her own daughters in appearance and temperament. Judy's positive responses to her kindness seemed to demonstrate that she was reaching out to Priscilla with her eyes and hands as well as her heart. She smiled and cooed in response to Priscilla's soothing voice and loving touches when held and hugged. Judy smiled and looked into Priscilla's eyes. Priscilla could read her mind and know that Judy was saying, "I feel so comfortable with you. Thank you for loving me."

Most evenings, the family lingered at the dining room table after the meal to entertain Judy. The girls gave her little rattles to play with and stuffed animals to hold. They drew her picture, held her hand, recited nursery rhymes, and even sang to her. One evening, Priscilla presented Judy with a baby bracelet. It was a pink, plastic wristband with a baby blue Scotty dog and small chain for decoration.

Judy responded well to all the attention she received by grinning to show her contentment. She became accustomed to her regular feeding times, the routine smells of baking and cooking, and Pricilla's perfume. She reacted positively to the voices of her foster sisters and other children in the neighborhood. She was less jumpy, and noises made by the vacuum cleaner, the little dog barking, toilets flushing, and cars passing by outside no longer startled her. She anticipated the daily routines of the Engelmann's home and responded positively to each girl's facial expressions.

William and Priscilla were exceedingly happy with Judy's progress and requested permission to adopt, but Gertrude Schweinhaus intentionally dragged her feet. Her policy of delaying every adoption in her district had significantly swollen her annual budget and justified an increase in salary for herself, even though there had been fewer adoptions. As long as Judy remained in foster care, Brando and Flora Rossi were required to continue making their monthly child support payments.

William and Priscilla were adamantly opposed to haphazardly transferring orphans from one foster home to another at the whim of the social agency. They were firm in their belief that every change in parents caused mental stress to children. They were particularly concerned that Judy might become a victim of this hapless policy. She had already been with the Engelmanns for nearly an entire year, and she was progressing normally. In their minds, it was time to formalize her adoption, but Gertrude's only response had been to ask a lot of annoying personal questions.

"What nationality are you and your wife? What is your annual income? How much money do you give Catholic charities? How many children do you have? What are their ages?" she had repeatedly demanded to know.

"We have four girls aged sixteen, thirteen, eleven, and nine. My annual income is average. We are practicing Catholics and donate regularly to the church. Our ancestors were German," William robotically responded for the third time.

Gertrude Schweinhaus' procrastination irritated him, but he had no recourse other than to wait for the bureaucracy to grind out the legal paperwork. From a positive standpoint, his payments from the state for Judy's care could continue as long as he remained a foster parent, but Brando and Flora Rossi were upset because the cost of caring for the baby had become a significant drain on their family budget

JUDY'S FAVORITE TOY WAS a small, roly-poly doll from Russia. Her first words were "Dada" and "Baby." In November, she had started crawling, and her first teeth had protruded through her gums. In January, she had pulled herself into a standing position by tightly clutching a living room chair with her tiny, little fingers. By her eleventh month, she was walking. Her favorite words were "Barbara" and "Mary," and her vocabulary was increasing every day. She was comfortable and thriving in the environment William and Priscilla had provided. Judy responded positively to her foster sisters. They enjoyed her presence and treated her tenderly.

THE TELEPHONE RANG. BARBARA picked up the receiver. Miss Schweinhaus' authoritative voice intimidated her as she listened in fear to her demands.

"I am coming to pick up your foster sister at eight o'clock tomorrow morning. Make sure she is bathed, fed, and dressed before I arrive. Don't bother packing any of her toys or clothes because I don't want her to be reminded of her foster family after she leaves. Her adopted parents will buy her new clothes and toys of their own choosing. Your parents will receive another foster child to replace this one as soon as she is gone."

"What do you mean?" Barbara whispered. Her voice haltingly disappeared.

Miss Schweinhaus' stinging words hung in the air as Barbara hung up the receiver. Her stomach acids churned. A slowly rising sensation of nausea welled up in her stomach. She was terribly distraught, afraid for her baby sister, and uncertain what to do. She decided to keep silent because her parents had taught her not to talk to strangers, especially ones who might want to harm her. She had listened very carefully to what Miss Schweinhaus had said, and now she was terrified. The loss of her baby sister was an appalling thing to imagine.

Barbara became introverted and withdrew into a psychological shell. She looked pale and afraid, as if she had seen a ghost. She played quietly by herself in the corner, which was completely out of character from her usual bubbly personality. A sense of doom overcame her. She lost her appetite, picked at her food at the dinner table, and remained remarkably sullen and withdrawn from her sisters.

Barbara awoke in a cold sweat. She was having a nightmare. She had dreamed that a wicked witch was dragging her baby sister into a dark forest, and she was powerless to stop her.

Kidnapped

Dear Mom, Something is wrong. I heard Barbara screaming my name in her sleep, and she has been holding my hand and crying all morning. The dog has been barking, too. I wonder if an earthquake or natural disaster is going to happen. I am very happy here. William and Priscilla are kind and caring foster parents, and they have four wonderful daughters. We have fun and laugh together. We smile, talk, go for walks outside in the park, and play games. My sisters read stories and recite nursery rhymes to me. Sometimes they put doll clothes on their little dog to make it look silly. I like my family and appreciate what they do for me. I want to stay with the Engelmanns forever. Love, Judy

N EW SNOW WAS STICKING to every tree branch and telephone wire. Drivers throughout the city were cautiously navigating the slippery streets on their way to work. Miss Schweinhaus arrived at her office one hour early to pick up paperwork and meet her driver, Ron Madunic. She had been assigned responsibility for the Engelmann adoption case, and she was eager to complete her mission as efficiently and expeditiously as possible.

A single woman who had never dated, she was tall and physically strong and fanatically defined herself by her religious viewpoints. She was a strong-willed person of German heritage who believed in precisely following instructions and enforcing regulations exactly as written. Her bold, intimidating, and cynical character more than made up for her lack of experience. Her employer described her as a trustworthy, energetic, and competent professional with her only weaknesses being a lack of sympathy for children and an inability to empathize with others, neither of which were requirements for the job.

The snow compressed under the tires as her driver pulled the car into the Engelmann driveway. Clouds heavy with moisture made the sky dark and foreboding. Sacred Heart Sanitarium for the mentally insane was directly across the street. On a snowy morning under dark skies, the building projected an eerie impression of being haunted.

Miss Schweinhaus did not wear makeup or perfume. She twisted the rearview mirror to view her reflection, licked her fingers, and forced the hair on her wiry eyebrows to point straight up because that was how she liked them. She wore a long, gray business dress with a starched collar under a gray wool coat with a plain collar. Her hair was pinned back in a bun and hidden under a gray felt hat.

She was the dominant force in charge of this adoption case. Challenges to her authority were unacceptable. She had been milking child support payments from the paternal grandparents, Brando and Flora Rossi, for nearly a year while ignoring their protests.

She exited the car stiffly and walked rapidly with long strides to get out of the cold and snow quickly. Vapors from her breath hung in the air as she swung her arms from side to side and breathed heavily. She clenched her fist and pounded on the front door, startling the inhabitants inside.

The brass door knocker clanged loudly in the cold air. Priscilla opened the door, and she was surprised to find Miss Schweinhaus standing on her doorstep in the snow. A blast of cold air entered the house as Miss Schweinhaus barged straight into the living room, seemingly unconcerned about the snow she was tracking into the house. She was on a mission and prepared to carry out her obligations. Barbara kept her chin down and stepped to the back of the room as far from Miss Schweinhaus as possible. She feared to look up and kept her eyes focused on Judy, who was fussing with her shoelaces. Miss Schweinhaus sidestepped the other children without acknowledging them and advanced toward Judy.

"My doll had a baby," Therese stated matter-of-factly.

Miss Schweinhaus showed her impatience with the little girl. "Only married dollies have babies. Didn't your mother teach you that? Some women like me have important jobs to accomplish instead of having babies," she stated emphatically with an air of superiority.

Shirley held Judy's hand and carefully walked her up to Miss Schweinhaus. Judy frowned and turned her back. The girls were proud of their baby sister, and they had many positive things to say about her. Except Barbara didn't say anything.

"Judy is our baby sister. Today is her first birthday. She can already walk, talk, and say our names. We are planning a big celebration with fancy dresses, balloons, hats, games, and a big angel food cake with chocolate frosting and homemade vanilla ice cream," Shirley said proudly.

"Judy is not your sister. I'm giving her to a married couple that doesn't have any children. Your family already has too many girls," Miss Schweinhaus said sternly, speaking down to the children.

Therese hugged her mother's skirt. "Oh, Mommy, is it true? I don't like Miss Schweinhaus or what she is saying. Judy is our baby sister. She has been with us since she was born. Miss Schweinhaus is a wicked person." Therese had a worried, contorted expression on her face.

Priscilla Engelmann was in her midforties. She was a hard worker and active parent who supported the girls in all of their activities. She was quick to smile and respond to their needs in a positive way and give her daughters the individual attention and confidence they needed.

"Good morning, Miss Schweinhaus. You are up early on a very snowy morning. I thought you had completely forgotten about us. It has been nearly six months since we applied to adopt Judy. I'm glad you are finally here to complete the adoption process." William concealed his impatience with the ineffectiveness of the bureaucracy. He was a warm, friendly individual who was kindhearted and good at dealing with people.

"Sit down," Miss Schweinhaus ordered launching into her formal narrative. Her posture was rigid. She sat erect on the edge of her seat with her shoulders pulled back, her chin extended, and her elbows on the table. The hair on her eyebrows was sticking straight up. The formality of her introductory remarks bewildered William and Priscilla.

"My decision regarding the disposition of your foster child is legal and binding. It is based on the official statutes of the state of Wisconsin and the will of and furthermore as determined by the board of directors of CSS of which I, Gertrude Schweinhaus, am the official representative," she stated. Her bureaucratic terms were unintelligible to Priscilla and William. "I have decided to give Judy to another couple who are a perfect ethnic match and major financial contributors to the church. They are unable to conceive children of their own. For those reasons, I have selected them as the appropriate parents for this child. My decision is final. I rejected your request to adopt this child because you already have enough children, and I want you to continue your valued role as foster parents. I will arrange for another foster child to be brought to your home next week," she stated coldly. She expected William and Priscilla to automatically support her decision.

Gertrude intentionally omitted any mention of the telephone call she had received from Father Hennen requesting this child be given to a major financial contributor who had been inflexible in his demands. He had offered Father Hennen a blatant financial bride that he couldn't refuse to adopt the specific child he wanted.

Priscilla was indignant and insulted. She clutched Dearest Judy tightly to her breast as tears welled up in her eyes. She was resistant to letting her baby go and stated so emphatically. "I will not allow Judy to leave this house on her birthday. We have a big celebration planned for her this afternoon. It is her special day. We have been looking forward to celebrating this event for many weeks." She fought back her tears.

William stood up, clenched his fists, and gritted his teeth. He was indignant, and he had trouble speaking. He was unaccustomed to challenging authority, facing adversity, or speaking in anger. "This is a terrible mistake and a very bad decision for Judy. We applied to adopt her six months ago and assumed you were taking care of the legal paperwork for us. She is attached to my daughters. It would be unwise and tragic for everyone if you remove Judy from our home. During the last twelve months, we have raised her from a tiny, colicky infant struggling to accept nourishment from a baby bottle into a happy, healthy child. She is one of us. We are closely bonded with her, and she is very content in our home. This is where she belongs. She is my youngest daughter and a full member of my family. This is a very poor decision that should be overturned immediately. I vehemently disagree with your logic to give our child to another couple just because they can afford to buy her with their cash donations to your church. You are corrupt. Your policies and priorities should consider what is best for the child. Staying here with us is where she belongs and the only acceptable solution from the child's point of view," William pleaded passionately. He was furious and finding it difficult to regain his composure and speak in a civil tone. "You shouldn't be influenced by some obscure married couple who has never seen this child. Why do they want this particular child? My wife and I are the most qualified parents for Judy. How can anyone disagree with logic? You need to give us some time to work this out. This is a very bad decision. You are going to break my daughters' hearts because they believe Judy is their true sister. I need to talk to your superiors before I can allow you to take our child out of this house. You will have to come back another time."

In his mind, Gertrude's decision was unconscionable because she had never expressed any doubts about their qualifications as adoptive parents, but Gertrude turned her back and ignored his frustrated pleas for mercy and common sense.

The four girls sat on the edge of their seats and stared at the wall without saying a word. Barbara felt horrible. She was still and silent because she had already experienced a premonition about the unfortunate situation that was unfolding in her living room

Miss Schweinhaus relished her position of authority. "Fetch some winter clothes for the baby," she demanded. Mary ran into the bedroom and returned with Judy's red snowsuit. Gertrude forcefully shoved both of Judy's legs into the bottom half of the snowsuit as they dangled down from Priscilla's arms. Judy resisted as much as she could. Her face turned red as she kicked and fussed. Miss Schweinhaus awkwardly jerked the zipper upward until it pinched the skin under her chin. Judy wailed loudly in pain and wrapped her arms tightly around Priscilla's neck.

"Here is the legal paperwork terminating your responsibilities as the foster parents of this child." She rudely slammed the contract down on the kitchen table.

Gertrude rose to her feet, lurched forward, and forcefully pried Judy out of Priscilla's arms. Judy violently kicked and screamed, and she tried to twist away from the stranger who was terrorizing her. Her panicky actions were scaring her sisters, who simultaneously burst into tears. Judy turned and made one last unsuccessful attempt to grab Priscilla's apron strings, but to no avail. It was too late. Clutching the baby, Miss Schweinhaus twirled around and headed straight out the front door. Judy was scared out of her wits at the thought of being separated from her family. She bawled loudly and waved her arms, hoping someone would come to her rescue.

"Barbara ... Mary ... Dada," she shrieked between panic-stricken gasps for air and a frightening display of tears.

Her chilling pleas for assistance lingered in the air and echoed off the ceiling. She twisted her head around and peered over Miss Schweinhaus' shoulder, hoping for one last look at the only familiar faces she had ever known.

Chills ran down the spines of every member of the Engelmann family as they, standing still, huddled together. Nobody spoke. What had happened bewildered everyone, and they were crying big crocodile tears in quiet astonishment at the sudden, unexplained loss of their dearly beloved baby sister.

Miss Schweinhaus vanished without saying good-bye or even giving a backward glance. Judy's screams hung in the air and resonated in the hearts of the entire Engelmann family. They felt violated. Their baby sister had been kidnapped right before their eyes in their own home, and the incomprehensible way it had taken place was outrageous. Barbara's tears were contagious. She cried the loudest because she had the most emotional stress bottled up inside of her, and she could no longer contain it. She wailed loudly as she unburdened her guilt by mumbling something incomprehensible about the wicked witch with the big, ugly nose who was planning to eat Hansel and Gretel and her baby sister Judy, but her babbling confession was unintelligible to the others.

It was bewildering how the entire event had evolved so suddenly and unexpectedly. Judy's disappearance had happened so quickly and without warning that William and Priscilla had no time to think clearly or react appropriately. It bothered William that he had done nothing to stop her. He had allowed his daughters to watch in horror as Miss Schweinhaus snatched Judy out of Priscilla's arms and coldly marched his foster child out of his house. The sobbing girls were devastated and covered in tears. There had been no warning and no time to prepare. One minute, Judy was giggling, singing, and amusing the girls. Then suddenly she was gone forever. It was a traumatic incident beyond their control.

JUDY'S CHERISHED PINK BABY blanket lay silently on the floor beside the couch, never to be picked up again. The security blanket had made her feel safe as long as it was in her possession. It was a stinging reminder that Judy was gone forever. The little stuffed bunny that she clutched in her tiny hands every day was sitting upright in a living room chair, exactly where she had left it. Its dark, glassy, little eyes were staring back at the family as a powerful symbol of Judy. A dozen birthday presents wrapped with silky ribbons sat idly on the kitchen table beside a cold, partially decorated angel food cake, a package of colored balloons, and one large, pink birthday candle.

A dreadful woman had walked into their home and taken away their baby sister. They would never see her again. It was an emotional catastrophe. William and Priscilla feared for Judy's mental health because they believed this incident would seriously traumatize her, but they had no legal standing because Judy was not their child. Miss Schweinhaus had been very blunt and discourteous when she had stated that it was important for Judy to make a permanent and terminable separation from their home. She had stated that the newly adopted parents should decide what their child should wear and which toys were appropriate. She had a blunt, authoritative way of callously communicating her opinions because she viewed foster parents who became excessively attached to their foster children as weak-minded and spineless. In her mind, it was inappropriate for them to do anything other than take care of the child's basic survival needs.

The Engelmann household was silent other than an occasional sob or whimper from one of the girls. The girls did not understand what had happened or why. Their collective emotional outbursts were comparable to a death of a close family member. When one of the girls cried, it started a sympathetic response from the others, resulting in more sobbing and hugging. Tears streamed down Barbara's cheeks.

Her chest heaved as her confession suddenly burst from the heart. "Miss Schweinhaus telephoned yesterday to tell me she was coming to take Judy away, but I was afraid to tell you," Barbara said disparagingly. She blamed herself for what had happened.

Priscilla hugged her. "It wasn't your fault honey." William didn't want the girls to see his lips quivering or tears in his eyes. It was the most traumatic moment of his life. His entire family was in shock and powerless to do anything. William looked down at the sweet, sad faces of his four daughters and cried openly for the first time in his life. His whole body trembled. In his hands, he held Judy's soft, pink baby blanket and fuzzy, little bunny rabbit that she had loved so much. He touched the soft blanket to his cheeks and wiped the tears from his eyes. The entire Engelmann family huddled together and wept openly as they watched the large, black car with the darkened windows drive away.

William's eyes were glossy and dazed, like an injured boxer struggling to crawl up from the canvas and gather his senses before the count of ten. The clock was ticking, and time was running out quickly. Suddenly, every second was important, and he impulsively knew what he had to do next.

WILLIAM GRABBED HIS CAR keys off the kitchen counter and dashed out the door. He slipped on the snow and tumbled onto the sidewalk as he went. He gathered himself up, holding his injured left elbow, and limped to his car. He recklessly slammed the car into reverse, causing it to jump the curb and veer to one side. It smacked into his neighbor's garbage can, which went flipping and noisily rolling across Layton Boulevard. The lid became detached and rolled wildly in front of an oncoming car, causing it to violently swerve to one side to avoid a collision.

He crammed the accelerator to the floor. The rear tires spun wildly in place, creating smoke and squealing loudly as he recklessly aimed the car north. He nearly lost control on the snow-covered street. He was in hot pursuit. Judy Ann belonged with his family, not strangers. She was walking and talking, and she had bonded nicely with every member of his family. He knew he must act quickly before it was too late.

He was furious that his wife and children hadn't been able to properly say good-bye or even celebrate Judy's first birthday together. They weren't given the courtesy of sharing a last meal together, say a special prayer together, or take Judy to the church where she had been baptized. It made him furious when he realized that Miss Schweinhaus was ignoring the mental health of the baby. The trauma that was certain to affect her was being ignored and ominously missing from her list of decision criteria for deciding what was best for the baby. He was infuriated. The primordial sound of Judy wailing as she was being dragged away to an uncertain future kept echoing in his mind. The innocent way she had looked at him with her big, brown eyes when she twisted her neck around to look back at him was the saddest image he had ever seen. He was haunted by a lingering vision of his youngest child terrorized and covered in tears and grasping for his assistance as she was being forcefully taken away against her will.

He recklessly sped north on Layton Boulevard until he eventually spotted the large, black car making a left turn two blocks ahead. The streetlight had already changed to red when he made a hasty decision to pass through the intersection and race three more blocks ahead before turning left onto Wisconsin Avenue. His plan worked perfectly, and he pulled in right behind them.

Judy had refused to settle down. She was kicking and screaming, and she was crying hysterically. She had no comprehension about where she was going or why these strange people had taken her away from her family. She had never been separated from them before. Miss Schweinhaus and the strange man with the long, white hair and big mustache scared her. Miss Schweinhaus turned around to look behind her and immediately realized what was happening. "Speed up, and ditch William." Both cars increased speed and repeatedly changed lanes as they recklessly moved in and out of traffic without using their turn signals. The dark car tried to get away by speeding through red lights. Each time this happened, William tightly closed the gap and tailgated them through the intersection while completely ignoring traffic signals. He could tell they were no longer heading in a direct route toward their original destination because they were now indiscriminately turning left and right and racing through downtown Milwaukee on snow-packed streets.

Regrettably, William became confused about which black car he was following and attempted to intercept them by driving a short distance down a one-way street, only to find out it was the wrong car. He continued driving around the downtown area for a full hour, hoping he would be lucky enough to spot Miss Schweinhaus on the street or find the location where the driver had parked the car.

It was midafternoon when William finally returned home. Teary-eyed and quiet, everyone was waiting for him in the living room. He came in looking dejected and despondent in a weakened emotional state. He was sad, depressed, angry, emotionally exhausted, and confused. The girls had never seen their father look so distraught.

It was a snow day. After what had happened, the four girls had been allowed to stay home from school. They spent the morning sitting in the living room and looking out the window at the dark, gray sky. The warm, glowing, homey feeling that normally permeated the atmosphere of the Engelmann house was gone. The air felt chilly and damp. Sitting in a stationary location in a cold and dreary house was boring and depressing. There was nothing for the girls to do or say other than hope and pray that their father would return with their baby sister.

Until today, none of them had ever experienced the traumatic loss of a loved one.

Priscilla looked around the room. Judy's stuffed animals, toys, baby books, and clothes were scattered all over the living room. The house was uncharacteristically quiet. The high chair was empty. Cans of baby food filled the refrigerator and pantry. Baby pictures were on the refrigerator door and living room walls. The washing machine contained diapers. Baby clothes hung like pale ghosts on the clothesline in the basement. Everyone dearly loved Judy, and she was surely going to be missed. Her abrupt and unexpected departure had created an instant void and emptiness in the pits of their stomachs. It was the first time the girls had ever seen their father cry.

William regained his composure and broke the silence. "Social services has made a horrible mistake. Judy is your baby sister. She doesn't belong with strangers. I'm going to bring her back." William clenched his fist and released his emotions by lashing out against the establishment.

Adopted

Dear Mom, I was kidnapped and whisked away, kicking and screaming because I didn't want to leave my foster family. The people who took me drove very fast and almost got into several car accidents. I miss my parents and sisters, Barbara, Mary, Therese, and Shirley. I wonder if they miss me, too. Love, Judy

D RIVER RON MADUNIC NEARLY scraped the side of the courthouse building as he frantically steered the vehicle into a service entrance and concealed it behind a brown delivery truck. Miss Schweinhaus grabbed the baby and rushed through the unmarked rear door of the courthouse. Judy was scared and cranky, and she refused to stop fussing and wiggling. Miss Schweinhaus clutched her with both arms to prevent her from escaping.

Mario and Rosella Romano were waiting anxiously on the second floor when she arrived. They were first-time parents and uncertain what to expect. Rosella had green eyes and pale, flawless, white skin that contrasted with her bright pink lips and medium blonde hair. She had been one of twelve children born on a small farm in Iowa that generated a very small income. There were no luxuries. Most of the food they ate was raised on the farm. Rosella blossomed in the church environment as a teenager and viewed the experience as a way to escape the trappings of her home life. With the encouragement of her grandmother, she joined Saint Joseph's Convent in Milwaukee, but she was forced to accept a job two years later as a night attendant with the Milwaukee Sanitarium due to severe budget constraints at the convent. For the next ten years, Rosella worked hard and saved most of the money she earned.

At age twenty-nine, Rosella turned over her bank account and all of her savings to her boyfriend Mario Romano, even though he was still legally married to his first wife Ruth. Father Hennen granted Mario a divorce and gladly performed their wedding ceremony following receipt of a generous cash donation from Mario. There was no honeymoon.

When Mario was twelve years old, he had a life-changing experience in Italy that affected him for the rest of his life. He had witnessed gruesome murders in an alley in downtown Naples. They were the result from Mafia battles. His father told him not to be afraid of the dead bodies because they were only statues, but the horrific experience permanently traumatized him. Even in adulthood, he remained afraid of statutes, and he had reoccurring nightmares about death and murder.

Thanks to the money that Rosella gave him, combined with profits from the sale of her house, they were able to buy a small grocery store. Mario quickly developed into an ambitious and hardworking businessman. He was friendly and worked hard to provide his customers with what they wanted, but most were unaware of his violent temper or the underhanded techniques that he sometimes used to intimidate and bully others to get the best products for the lowest prices. He let his employees know he was the boss and demanded unquestioned loyalty from them. If anyone questioned his judgment or disobeyed his orders, he fired him.

He was ruthless in business and placed a higher priority on loyalty and profits than hurting others. He was very generous to those who provided him with what he wanted. This approach to deal-making was highly effective for keeping a large, fresh supply of meats on hand. Mario was popular in the Italian community, and his grocery store never experienced a food shortage of any kind. Mario worked long hours every day. The grocery business allowed him to make many friends and acquaintances. He was well informed and skillful at extracting confidential information from others when he wanted to find out about a specific topic.

Rosella was an obedient wife who played a passive role of servant and helper. Very seldom did either spouse take the time to foster a loving understanding of each other's needs. Rosella was unable to conceive children, and this prompted Mario to think about adopting a child. He became intrigued in a tavern one evening when he overheard a very attractive Italian girl complaining how sad it was that her brother was not able to marry the girl he loved, even though his girlfriend had given birth to his baby.

"My parents are poor, and the child support payments they are required to make every month are difficult for them to afford. I hope someone adopts my brother's baby soon," she had explained remorsefully.

Mario liked her mature, shapely figure; beautiful smile with large white teeth; and dimples on her cheeks. He liked her shiny brown hair, brown eyes, and smooth olive skin. He automatically assumed her brother's child would be physically strong and attractive.

"Was the baby a boy or a girl?" Mario inquired.

"We think it was a boy, but we don't know for sure," she replied sadly.

"What does your brother look like?" Mario asked inquisitively.

"He looks like me. Some people think we are twins. He was an excellent athlete. Everyone calls him the Italian stallion because he is strong and masculine. He is a hard worker who never got in trouble. He is a very good-natured guy with lots of friends. We don't know where he is now because he joined the marines and was sent overseas," she responded happily, knowing that someone was finally paying attention to her.

Mario had a forceful personality, and he was accustomed to getting what he wanted. He ordered one of his friends to secretly investigate the situation. His informant complied with his request, and he was able to discreetly point out several other family members at the annual spring Italian festival. The girl's entire family was attractive, strong, and healthy.

Mario was very thorough when conducting research on topics that concerned him. He was a methodical investigator who was rarely caught off guard. He was pleased to learn that both the biological father and maternal grandfather had worked as butchers. Another positive result of the investigation was the age of the child because it had already passed the negative infantile crying and diaper-changing stage. The information he received was positive, and he made up his mind to adopt this specific child.

ROSELLA WOULD ONLY AGREE to adopt if Catholic Social Services acted as the intermediary. Mario tossed a cash-filled envelope onto Father Hennen's desk and explained what he wanted in return. Father Hennen knew immediately which baby Mario was talking about because he had known the mother and father ever since they were in junior high school, and he had counseled the baby's mother after she had become pregnant.

Without hesitation, Father Hennen telephoned CSS and asked to speak with Gertrude Schweinhaus. "I want you to deliver the Rossi baby to Mario and Rosella Romano for adoption as soon as possible. How soon can you do it?" he demanded to know.

The urgency of his request surprised Gertrude. She had explained that it might be too late because the foster parents had already applied to adopt the child he was inquiring about. "The child has been with them for a year, and they have become highly attached. I doubt if they will be willing to release the child without a fight."

Father Hennen was reluctant to upset Mr. Romano or return the envelope containing his contribution, so he repeated his request to Miss Schweinhaus more assertively the second time. "If you want to keep your job at CSS, you will listen carefully to what I say and comply with my request immediately. I have the perfect Catholic couple in mind. How soon can you prepare the legal paperwork and transfer the baby to them for adoption?"

Miss Schweinhaus understood what was at stake and agreed to comply. "Forty-eight hours," she replied submissively, demonstrating respect for his authority.

Miss Schweinhaus tossed the Engelmanns' request-to-adopt form into the wastebasket and filled out a new application on behalf of Mr. and Mrs. Romano, as Father Hennen had directed. A Friday morning meeting was arranged with Mario and Rosella at the courthouse for the exchange of the baby.

Miss Schweinhaus called the Engelmann home, ordered Barbara to inform her parents of her decision, and prepare the child for a quick departure. Her disregard for protocol irritated her older more experienced coworker. "I am opposed to the removal of a one year old child from a stable loving family environment. I am shocked by your decision to wave the required background check on the Romanos, who have no parenting experience, based solely on the orders of Father Hennen. Your decision is against policy and lacks good judgment."

Miss Schweinhaus grew impatient and criticized her coworker for being too sensitive and overly educated."Married couples with high incomes have the means to provide the best homes, medical care, and good educations for their adopted children. The combined income of Mario and Rosella Romano is much higher than the foster parents have. Mr. Romano has been a major financial contributor to the church, and Father Hennen's endorsement carries a great deal of weight with me," she rationalized defensively.

ROSELLA BOUGHT ALL THE necessary baby supplies and clothing on the list that Miss Schweinhaus supplied to her. She was planning to modify the curtains, pictures, furniture, and other decorations in the child's room at her earliest convenience. She purged the living room and kitchen of all expensive, breakable, and sharp objects within three feet of the floor, cleaned and dusted the entire house, and turned up the thermostat to increase the temperature.

In his haste, Mario had assumed the Rossi baby was a boy. He gasped when he saw his new baby dressed in a red snowsuit with pink boots and pink ribbons. He was furious because, in his mind, he had been duped.

"I requested to adopt the Rossi baby boy. This is not the baby I requested. I'll be damned if I am going to let you trick me. I paid to get the baby that I wanted. Get Father Hennen on the telephone immediately," Mario said angrily with his blood pressure rising.

His face was red, and his neck muscles were tense. Judy quivered at the sound of his loud, angry voice. She felt threatened. She was afraid to look at him, and she covered her face with the hood of her snowsuit.

"I assure you this is the child you requested. You never asked me if the child was a boy or girl," Father Hennen apologized for the confusion.

Mario redirected his anger toward himself for his own lack of investigation and verification, something that had seldom happened. He had placed himself in an embarrassing dilemma because he had already informed his employees, family, friends, and neighbors that he was adopting a child. A big weekend celebration had already been planned. Mario wondered if there was any other important information about this child he had missed.

Miss Schweinhaus suggested a compromise, "You can keep the baby for three months. If you aren't satisfied, you can return it." Mario didn't appreciate the comparison with shopping for a new car, but gradually softened to the idea. Knowing that her adopted child was a girl, Rosella had suddenly become more interested in accepting her motherly responsibilities.

Mario had a big nose, oily hair, rimmed glasses, and a dark mustache. Unfortunately, little Judy was traumatized during the exchange and vomited on Mario's shiny shoes. Rosella was wearing a large, bizarre-looking hat. She approached Judy too quickly and directly, which caused her to tremble and cry. Judy stiffened her arms and struggled to free herself from Rosella's tight grasp.

"It is normal for an adopted child to be uncomfortable around new people. It will take several months for her to adjust to her new surroundings. Don't be alarmed if she regresses and is unresponsive or stops talking altogether for a while until she gets used to you," Miss Schweinhaus said with an air of confidence and authority, even though she had limited knowledge and no firsthand experience in these matters.

Rosella ignored her remarks as unnecessarily sensitive. Rosella attempted to convince Mario that it was still a good idea to proceed, "I would prefer to raise a girl. I will take full responsibility for raising the child."

While Mario was making up his mind, Miss Schweinhaus told him about the hostile car chase. "Leave the courthouse through the rear entrance and be cautious and suspicious of strangers. The foster father is very upset and may still be canvassing the neighborhood searching for his child. I hope he won't initiate legal action, but it is possible."

Mario signed the legal papers and departed in a huff with the baby. "You tell the little bastard that this is my child now. If he tries anything, I'll break his kneecaps," Mario said on his way out the door.

His threatening remarks stunned Gertrude, and she regretted she hadn't completed a thorough background check, as her co-worker had reminded her. The foster parents were angry and upset. Judy was unnecessarily traumatized. The gender mix-up had exasperated Mario. At least Father Hennen was delighted with the monetary contribution he had received.

JUDY HID HER FACE because she didn't want to be held or touched. She kicked and fussed when Rosella tried to remove her red snowsuit.

Rosella was surprised to discover a beautiful, lilac-scented floral note card under Judy's pink blouse. She opened the card and read the note.

Dearest Judy, I love you. I miss you, and I will pray for you. In my heart, I will always be thinking of you until we meet again. I will never forget you, Love, Barbara.

Rosella wondered what the note was all about and considered saving it, but changed her mind and quickly disposed of it when she heard Mario approaching.

The majority of packages that arrived in the mail congratulating Mario and Rosella on the arrival of their new baby contained boys' clothing with Green Bay Packer and Milwaukee Brewer sports insignias on them. Mario had many friends, and he kept an accurate record of who was on the gift-giving list. He was only concerned with being remembered and ignored the actual gifts.

Judy's whole world had been irrevocably turned upside down in a single day. She sorely missed William, Priscilla, and her four foster sisters. She was lonely and confused. She had a stomachache and refused to eat. Judy's glum, sullen demeanor and antisocial behavior bewildered Rosella. She wondered if Mario would trade her for a boy before the ninety-day trial period ended.

Detective 8

Dear Mom, Why was I taken away? Where are my sisters and parents? I am afraid. I miss my bed, my soft pink baby blanket, and my stuffed, floppy-eared bunny. I miss our little white dog that was always barking at me and licking my face. I miss my toys, walks in the park with my family, my highchair in the kitchen, and my baby bowl and spoon. I miss the attention I received from my sisters and the routines that took place each day of the week that were my daily rituals.

Love, Judy

RING. RING.
"John H. Bridgewater Detective Agency. How may I help you?"

John, a donut-loving, cigar-smoking, golfaholic retired chief of police, had large, hairy arms and thick neck. He enjoyed playing the role of detective to impress others, but seldom did anything more important than spy on married couples when infidelity was suspected. He advertised himself as an adoption detective because he had found a niche for helping birth parents and adoptees reunite, but he had seldom been successful because most adoption records were sealed.

"My child was kidnapped," William said anxiously. He was eager to find a sympathizer to support his version of the story and blurted out the first thing that came to mind without paying attention to details or the chronology of events. "I chased the social worker all over Milwaukee in my car, but she eluded me. I need you to find out where she took my daughter. You need to get on the case right away," he said urgently.

"Kidnapping? That is a serious offense. Have you called the police? Give me the details." John looked forward to some excitement.

"Gertrude Schweinhaus, a CSS social worker, came into my house without warning and rudely took my daughter away in front of my wife and children without providing any explanation. I am worried about the severe emotional trauma this might cause my foster child. I am eager to get her back. Can you help me?"

Detective Bridgewater agreed to investigate the situation and called CSS to make an appointment. Bookkeeper Kathy Fingleton, a young divorcee, responded that she doubted Miss Schweinhaus would discuss the case with John because she had a cantankerous personality, but she was intrigued with his detective credentials and agreed to meet with him after five o'clock. Kathy explained she was responsible for the financial records in her office, but was unwilling to disclose the names of any of the clients or do anything illegal or unethical.

Her open blouse and ample bosom distracted John. His eyes wandered inquisitively toward her white thighs as she swiveled her chair to face him.

"Our files are proprietary. A court order is required to disclose this information, but, if William Engelmann has authorized you to be his legal representative, I can show you his file. You can't remove any items, but you are welcome to take notes," Kathy explained with a flirty smile and slow wink.

John reviewed the contract William had signed, but it was no help. Another folder contained a record of visitation dates by CSS representatives, medical prescriptions, receipts, and general correspondence. Four client evaluations, including a recent one by Miss Schweinhaus, provided glowing praise of William and Priscilla as excellent foster parents. John took notes and made a record of each document in the file, including a recommendation by Miss Schweinhaus telling her superiors that William and Priscilla should not be allowed to adopt because there was a shortage of qualified foster parents.

Kathy's Dolce Vita perfume temporarily anesthetized John as she leaned across her desk to hand him a list of married couples requesting adoption.

"Where does Gertrude Schweinhaus live?" John played the role of macho detective, assuming Gertrude would be assigned adoption cases on her side of town.

"I can't give you her exact address, but I can tell you she lives in Pewaukee." Kathy flirted expressively with a smile showing more than a little interest in the detective.

John scanned the list of names to determine geographic location and ethnicity. Four of the applicants lived on the west side of town. He recalled that William had been miffed because he claimed Miss Schweinhaus had discriminated against him because he was German, whereas Judy was Italian. Gertrude had been hoping to place her with an Italian family. Mario Romano was the only Italian name on the list living in Pewaukee.

Before leaving, he offered to meet Kathy at the Rams Head Tavern later that evening for a gin martini to thank her for her cooperation. She gladly accepted.

JOHN DROVE DIRECTLY TO the residence of Mario Romano to see what he could find. He stopped to speak with an attractive couple walking past the house. "Are you Mario Romano?"

"No. He is the owner of Food Land grocery store on the north side of Milwaukee near Fond du Lac Avenue. I'm Mark Gould and this is my wife, Mary. I build roads and bridges and dig up dinosaur bones. Here's my business card."

"Thanks." John jotted down the name and address. He drove slowly around the block before parking in the rear. He slipped his black leather jacket over his concealed thirty-eight Ruger LCR revolver and strolled confidently into the store. "My name is John Bridgewater. Is Mr. Romano available?"

Skeptical of his intentions the store manager, Jim Yellico, was reluctant to disturb his boss. "He is a very busy man. What is the nature of your visit?"

"It is about his adopted child," John explained truthfully.

He assumed John was a friend of Mr. Romano coming to offer congratulations. Several others had also stopped by recently with cigars and baby gifts.

Mr. Romano's windowless office was plain and undecorated. Black notebooks lined the shelves on the wall behind his gray metal desk. The floor was bare concrete, and the furniture was drab government surplus. Mr. Romano was suspicious and reserved with strangers. He refused to meet with solicitors.

"I am investigating the disappearance of a child." John was accustomed to bullying others to extract information from them, and he had perfected his techniques during his twenty years on the police force.

Mario confirmed, "Yes, I have a new baby girl."

"The foster family wants their baby back. They have a prior legal claim to adopt her and hope you will amicably see their point. They applied to adopt Judy six months ago and believe an aggrieved error in the spirit of the law has been made. They are hoping you will voluntarily return the child to them and accept another one in its place."

Mr. Romano had heard enough. He exploded in a fit of rage. He jumped out of his chair and jammed it into the bookshelf behind him. He resented John's intrusion into his private office, and he was furious with the message John had delivered. His face turned red as he clenched his fists. He shouted in a booming, intimidating voice, "There is no chance I will concede anything. I will not make any deals or exchange this child for another one. Get out immediately, or I'll throw you out. Tell those ungrateful sons of bitches that the girl is mine. If you or anyone else is foolish enough to ever call me again, you will seriously regret it. You tell the foster father to go piss up a rope."

John was highly intimidated and feared Mario might even pull a gun out of his desk and shoot him in the head. His heart rate was elevated, and his muscles were tense. His knees were weak and shaky. He put both hands in the air and slowly backed out the office door. He hurried down the aisle, trying not to accidentally knock any cans off the shelves. He cowardly drove away. In his mind, this case was closed. Mr. Romano was a powerful character in the Italian community who was used to getting what he wanted, and John wasn't about to lose his life to an angry, irrational person. This case was not for him.

A BLACK CHRYSLER SEDAN with narrow, blackened windows pulled into the Engelmann driveway. Two dark-haired, Italian men dressed in navy blue pinstriped suits and sunglasses got out of the car. One of the men knocked firmly on the Engelmann's front door while the other one cased the neighborhood. William was expecting Detective Bridgewater. Instead, two suspicious-looking men were standing on his front porch. William opened the front door, but kept the screen door locked.

One of the men kept his hand in his jacket pocket as if to intimidate William by making him think that he was holding a revolver. The other spoke deliberately with a measured cadence in an intimidating voice punctuated with an Italian accent.

"Forget about the foster child. You are never going to see her again.

This decision is final. Your life will be very miserable if you ever attempt to contact this child again."

With that said, the two hoodlums backed away and left. One hour later, John drove up the driveway and slid out of his car. William answered the door and looked pale and faint. His hands were shaking as he poured out his feelings.

"You should have been here an hour ago to protect me from two thugs. I was afraid for my life. I thought things like this only happened in movies. How can I expect to get my foster child back under these circumstances?"

"I can't tell you why Gertrude Schweinhaus gave your child to Mr. Romano, but I can sympathize with you because he was unreasonably hostile to me. I was terrified. I actually wondered if he were going to shoot me." John expressed the same fears that William had experienced.

"I'm sorry for what happened to you. There is nothing else I can do. Your only recourse is to hire an attorney and take Miss Schweinhaus and her agency to court, but, if I were you, I would stay away from Mr. Romano," John stated as his excuse for dropping the Engelmann case.

He apologized and abruptly excused himself to meet with a very important female client at the Rams Head Tavern. The sound of the telephone ringing cut their conversation short.

Miss Schweinhaus was finally responding to William's urgent telephone calls. "What are you thinking? Don't you realize you could be fined and put in jail for reckless driving, sending a detective to my office to search my files, and harassing adoptive parents considering legal action against you? I will place a restraining order on you if you persist. And one more thing, I am taking you off the list of available foster parents."

Miss Schweinhaus had never anticipated this much trouble, and now she was blaming William Engelmann for Mario Romano's angry outbursts directed toward her. Click! She hung up.

Three days later, William received a registered letter from the state attorney general reprimanding William for contacting the adopted parents. The letter stated he had no legal status in this adoption matter and warned him that any additional interference with the lives of the adopted parents would result in severe penalties. A second business letter arrived two days later from the board of directors for CSS, stating his services as a foster parent were no longer needed.

William was furious. His family loved Judy. They had cared for her for an entire year, given her love, and provided her with a warm, comfortable home. They were proud of the job they had done as foster parents. Judy was a beautiful baby and source of pride that had captured their hearts.

William conceded the harsh reality that there was nothing more that he could do. The failed adoption fiasco had left William emotionally drained and feeling bitter toward Gertrude Schweinhaus and her agency.

PRISCILLA PRAYED FOR A miracle. She wondered about the adoptive parents and how they would influence Judy. She was certain the unexplained disappearance and unfamiliar surroundings would permanently traumatize her. She was exceedingly worried about lasting negative psychological effects resulting from the sudden change in her life. She loved Judy dearly and hoped she would have a healthy life.

The four girls had baked an angel food cake for Judy's first birthday because she was an angel in their minds. Barbara placed the solitary candle in the middle and lit the flame. They held hands, said a short prayer, took a deep breath, and, through teary eyes, blew out the flickering flame. A lingering vapor of smoke permeated the silence.

Barbara surprised her sisters when she confessed to writing a short message to Judy on one of Priscilla's expensive note cards and secretly tucking it under Judy's blouse before Miss Schweinhaus took her away. She explained she liked the picture on the front of the card because the girl in Sophie Anderson's famous painting, *The Time of the Lilacs*, reminded her of Judy. In her mind, she naïvely believed in fairy tales and hoped her letter would help Judy remember the Engelmanns in her prayers and eventually find her way back to her foster family.

Priscilla prayed that someday, by quirk of fate, her daughters would have the opportunity to be reunited again. Perhaps God would allow them to cross paths on a busy street or provide them with a brief glimpse of each other while riding in a car. She believed in miracles.

THE DISGUSTING MANNER IN which Judy had been forcefully removed from his home left William disillusioned with CSS, government bureaucracies, and the entire state of Wisconsin. The lack of empathy he never received from his brother Carl, an honorary director of Booth Hill Home for Unwed Mothers and popular radio and television personality, was a major source of irritation that caused him to sever family ties with his brother and impulsively accept a job as a stationary engineer in Arizona.

Three months later, he sold his house in Milwaukee and moved his family to Tucson. As the girls were packing their suitcases for the move, they paused to reminisce about their wonderful relationship with Judy.

Mary reminded everyone that she had always been the first to take Judy out of her crib in the morning. "Judy was always wide awake and smiling when I entered her bedroom. She would look at me with her big, brown eyes and a smile on her face. She was always happy to see me and eager to give me a big hug. Thinking about her makes me cry," Mary said forlornly.

Therese thought of herself as Judy's best friend. "I loved to dress her in colorful clothes and bonnets to keep the sun out of her eyes and take her for rides in the stroller."

As the youngest of the four girls, Therese secretly wondered if she had also been adopted, but was afraid to ask because she feared Miss Schweinhaus would take her away, too.

Barbara's nightmares had continued because guilt filled her young mind. She had grieved the hardest over the loss of her baby sister because she blamed herself for not telling her mother Miss Schweinhaus was coming to take Judy away. Barbara vowed never to forget her and planned to carry Judy's baby picture in her wallet every day of her life until they were reunited.

Shirley reminded everyone that, during mealtimes, she had been the one to wash Judy's face, pick up her cup and spoon when it fell on the kitchen floor, and clean up her daily messes.

Priscilla packed all of Judy's keepsakes in a box, including her pink bracelet, baby book, and baby pictures, with the exception of the one that Barbara placed in her wallet. Priscilla wondered if she would ever see her Dearest Judy again. She lovingly kissed the container, held it next to her heart, and said a prayer before placing it in the bottom of a small wooden storage chest.

JUDY WAS NEVER FORGOTTEN. The family honored her when saying grace before meals, and toasted to many happy memories of her on special occasions. Her beloved sisters continued to speculate about how she looked, where she was living, and what she was doing. They agreed that their baby sister Judy had the spirit of an angel and prayed for her good health, well-being, and prosperity. Positive thoughts lingered in their hearts and minds.

Barbara always had the last word. "Good night, Dearest Judy, wherever you are. We love you."

New Surroundings

Dear Mom, The new people put a leather harness on me to keep me from running away. I feel sick to my stomach. I don't feel like eating or doing much of anything. I am afraid of them. I don't like them putting their faces close to mine. I kick and scream when they touch me. If they try to hug me, I throw hissy fits to let them know how I feel about them. Sometimes, I intentionally poop in my pants and keep my head down until they hold their noses and make an ugly expression. They say I look somber. Their house smells unusual, and the food they serve tastes peculiar. The furniture and color schemes are eclectic. My clothes look different and feel scratchy. It is very quiet indoors, and I have no little dog or sisters to play with. My new grandmother looks depressing. She has a wrinkled face with long, white, hairy eyebrows and little, bony fingers. I don't like her staring at me, and it is frustrating to hear her speak in Italian. I think she is saying that my expression is hollow and my mood appears desperate because that is exactly how I feel. I am sad and feeling anxious because I am scared and uncomfortable. I feel nauseous. Love, Judy

ROSELLA ROMANO WAS A prolific oil painter. Strong, pungent smells of paints and turpentine permeated the entire living space. The awful odors burned Judy's eyes and throat. The house was drafty and seemed to be cold and damp near the windows and too hot and dry next to the heater.

Judy had no appetite and refused to accept the unappetizing foods they imposed on her. The lack of adequate nutrition and mental stress weakened her immune system, and she became severely sick shortly after her arrival. Rosella, assuming it was only allergies, was reluctant to take her to the doctor, and her delayed diagnosis of significant early warning signs, including a high temperature, dehydration, and loss of weight, contributed to Judy's physical decline. She eventually developed a fever, resulting in two convulsions and a bad case of pneumonia. Her pediatrician prescribed two antibiotics, penicillin, and a ten-day supply of sulfa drugs. Judy had a severe allergic reaction to the sulfa drugs that caused her eyes to swell shut. The psychological separation from the Engelmann family added to her misery.

Rosella felt awkward and tentative. She was mentally unprepared for the daily routines of taking care of a child. Nuns in the convent never discussed children. The mental patients at the sanitarium where she had worked acted bizarrely and provided no rational benchmarks for judging normal behavior.

The adoption of her child had taken place so quickly that she had no time to prepare for motherhood. Learning how to raise a child was a slow process. Rosella was gradually becoming aware that biological mothers had a huge advantage over adopted mothers because they were together with their baby physically and spiritually for nine months before their child was born. After the birth, they had a natural cognizance of the needs of their babies. Parents with the most experience had an easier time making comparisons in physical stature, learned behavior, and mental progress, and this knowledge was helpful when communicating with their doctors to make informed adjustments in diets, medicines, or implementing homespun remedies for special ailments.

Other parents in the neighbor had many stories to tell about their children, but Rosella had no comparable experiences because she had already missed the first year of her daughter's life. She had nothing to share. She observed that good parents communicated using baby talk, facial expressions, arm gestures, and touching, as well as words, but Rosella was inexperienced and had difficulty using anything other than formal adult language.

Judy locked herself in an introverted shell, and she was in no mood to communicate effectively with words. Her responses were outwardly behavioral, and Rosella had difficulty understanding her gestures for hunger, upset stomach, sickness, bathroom, and tiredness. It was even more difficult interpreting her responses to abstract changes in her environment, including temperature, noise, and smells.

Judy was stoic and standoffish, and her facial expressions were consistently dour. She never smiled because she was unhappy. She pouted, and she was orally unresponsive. She only accepted small amounts of food after she became hungry, and she refused to allow anyone to pick her up.

Mario kept Judy on continuous display in front of his friends and relatives. It was evident to everyone that she was afraid and uncomfortable. Her body language was rigid, and her facial expression was forlorn. She looked out of character standing in the corner, fiercely defending her personal space, which led several neighbors to speculate if she had been kidnapped. Judy glared at a strange man who lightly poked her in the stomach to produce a reaction. When he jumped backward in feigned alarm to elicit a smile, his antics only frightened Judy more, and she continued to watch the crowd anxiously.

Mario's personal psychiatrist, Dr. Michael Brandis, a large pleasant man with an inquisitive nature, presented Judy with an expensive silver baby cup with her name engraved on the side. She grabbed the cup out of his hand and instantly pounded big dents in it by banging it on her high chair and throwing it on the floor. It was the first time since she had come to the Romano home that a quirky, little smile had appeared on her taciturn face.

Rosella was worn out and unhappy because Judy refused to respond to her simple verbal commands, even when she was certain she understood them. She tried unsuccessfully using candy to make Judy respond, but that didn't work either. No matter how hard she tried, Rosella had been unable to break down her sullen disposition or reduce her anxieties. Judy's brooding demeanor was an abrupt contrast to her happy, well-adjusted behavior in the Engelmann home.

A frustrated Rosella left Judy alone to play by herself. When her resistance finally reached a low point, she suggested Mario return Judy to Miss Schweinhaus before the ninety-day trial period was over. She assumed it would be better for all concerned if they traded Judy for a boy, as Mario had originally planned, but Mario was preoccupied with his business and too busy to concern himself with domestic affairs. He spent very little time at home and placed all the blame on Rosella. He demanded she improve her parenting skills.

Judy's personality suddenly improved when Mario bought a new car and took the family on a driving vacation. Judy welcomed the opportunity to be out of the house and away from the smelly oil paints and turpentine. The new sights she observed while looking out the car window moved her. She loved to have the window open and feel the air with her fingers. While on this trip, she attempted to lace her own shoes, and Mario praised her lavishly. She had fewer nightmares, and a slight thawing of her psychological barriers to communication improved her relationship with her parents.

His grocery store was prospering, and Mario bought a quaint stone house on the edge of town with green shutters, flower boxes, and a steeply pitched shake roof. It had a white picket fence and an abundance of shade trees and mature lilac bushes.

Judy gradually increased her interest in food and finally started looking forward to meal times. Eventually, she was willing to share in meal prayers by mumbling along with Rosella. She followed by making the sign of the cross with her hand. Rosella praised Judy for doing an extra good job as she vigorously brushed her teeth with excessive amounts of toothpaste. When she finished, toothpaste foam would be all over her face, stomach, and arms. Each positive step forward made Rosella smile.

Judy was intrigued with the other young girls in the neighborhood, surreptitiously hoping they were her foster sisters, but Rosella was guardedly suspicious of her motive for wanting to play with them. She feared she was trying to reconnect with her foster family.

Mario brought home a small beagle puppy. Judy named it Toby. She bonded with him immediately, and they became inseparable best friends. Toby had an immediate positive effect on her personality because he gave her something to be temporarily passionate about. He was unpredictable and fun. He stepped on her dolls, tracked dirt into her room, jumped on her bed, licked her face, and cleaned up any food she dropped on the floor. He provided random excitement that reduced her social inhibitions and allowed her to respond spontaneously. His unpredictability caused her to smile, and his easy accessibility gave her a warm body to hug. Judy and her girlfriend Grace amused themselves by crawling in and out of his doggy door. Toby enjoyed the excitement, wagged his tail, and eagerly licked their faces.

Toby was a major distraction to her parents and quickly replaced Judy as the object of their scorn. Mario was distraught because Toby left dog hairs all over the carpet and living room furniture. He was furious when the dog chewed a hole in his brown leather slipper. In retaliation, he smacked it with a rolled-up newspaper. Toby yelped and darted into Judy's room for protection. Mario became very upset when

Toby sneaked food off Judy's dinner plate. The dog angered Mario when he developed the habit of barking and running recklessly through the house whenever someone rang the doorbell. Rosella was frustrated when Toby destroyed her flower garden attempting to bury his bone and left his muddy footprints throughout the house. Mario cursed the dog for keeping him awake when Toby intermittently barked at the moon throughout the night.

The final straw came when Mario hurried out of the house to attend an important business meeting. He was wearing a business suit and his most expensive pair of imported Italian shoes when he accidentally stepped in a pile of fresh dog poop in the backyard.

That was the last day Judy saw Toby. She openly mourned the hurtful loss of her beloved dog because he brought her joy, friendship, and spontaneity. She cried uncontrollably and refused to come out of her bedroom for many days. An unsympathetic Mario responded by threatening to make her disappear, too.

Childhood

Dear Mom, My dog Toby disappeared last week, and I don't know where to find him. I am sad because I miss him a great deal. We enjoyed playing together. He slept in my room, and he was my best friend. He made me laugh, and I liked him a lot. It has taken me a long time to adjust to my surroundings and new parents. My mother leaves me alone much of the time to do what I want except when I have to accompany her to church. Father Hennen is the new parish priest at our church, and he is there to greet us every morning before mass. Rosella encourages me to pray before dinner and every night before going to bed. I pray for the birds and the trees, my dog Toby, and you. Love, Judy

"MORE BEER! MORE BEER!" Judy screamed loudly. She happily jumped up and down while raising her glass above her head.

Rosella was embarrassed when the Catholic nuns overheard her little girl yelling for more beer at the annual church picnic. Mario had found it amusing to give her sips of his beer when Rosella wasn't paying attention. The beer made her tipsy and more outgoing. She obviously liked it, and she was obnoxiously begging for more. Judy noticed that it made the adults laugh loudly each time she said the word "beer." The sips of beer Mario gave her turned out to be a significant turning point in her life because the alcohol helped her overcome her shyness and acted as a catalyst that finally encouraged her to start communicating with adults in full, coherent sentences.

Judy had a difficult time making a transition from the mysterious disappearance of her beloved dog Toby. In response to her grieving, Rosella presented her with two attractive dolls to compensate her for the loss. Judy was very pleased with them and named them Barbara and Mary in honor of her foster sisters. Rosella was unaware of the significance of the names Judy assigned to them and automatically assumed she was referring to her cousin Barbara and neighbor Mary.

Prior to this time, Judy had been orally unresponsive to her parents, but she carried on lengthy conversations with her dolls Barbara and Mary behind closed doors. They were her new best friends, and talking with them greatly improved her verbal skills. She arranged tea parties and pushed them in her doll stroller. She hugged them every night before going to sleep. The dolls were therapeutic, and having two of her four surrogate foster sisters gave her a pleasant sense of familiarity and contentment.

Rosella read a very old book by Dr. Benjamin Spock, the first to use psychoanalysis to understand child needs and family dynamics. His liberal ideas about hugging and pampering children were contrary to Rosella's and Mario's upbringing. Her parents had been tough-minded and never spared the rod. Rosella's life on the farm had been entirely regimented, and her experiences in the convent severely restricted ordinary living. Mario had also worked hard all his life, and he had little tolerance for the type of liberal socialism that Dr. Spock promoted. Neither parent held back when it came to spanking their child as the best form of discipline.

MARIO ENTHUSIASTICALLY ANNOUNCED THE grand opening of his new grocery store, and Judy was going to play an important role in the gala event by cutting a large, red ribbon in front of the main entrance. He was convinced that a big celebration would provide first-class publicity, and he knew a cute, little seven-year-old would be a media attention-grabber. The event was well publicized in the newspaper and on the radio. The size of the crowd that showed up greatly exceeded expectations. Hundreds of customers were lined up, waiting for the doors to open.

It was a Hollywood-style opening with searchlights scanning the sky, a large blimp, and spirited music. Free samples of choice products and coffee, door prizes, and temporary low prices were provided.

"Cut the ribbon!" someone yelled from the back of the crowd.

The shoppers flocked closer to get a better look. The crowd cheered when Judy posed for pictures. The photographer captured pictures of her with his oversized camera and bright flash. She wore a red and green tartan skirt with button-on black suspenders and a white blouse with puffy sleeves. Rosella helped her cut the ribbon, and the grocery store was officially opened for business. A large color photograph of the crowd with Judy cutting the ribbon appeared in the newspaper the following day. Headlines described the event as a "Grand Opening Carnival."

Mario was a good financial provider. The family could afford expensive televisions, new cars, vacations, and a large cabin cruiser. They traveled to exotic locations and ate at formal restaurants. Mario took Judy to professional baseball games, where she delighted in wearing her shiny black sports jacket and baseball hat, eating hot dogs, and cheering for the home team.

Every Sunday, Mario and his family had dinner with his parents. Family photographs and pictures of Italy covered the walls. His father Nicholas served homemade red wine in liberal amounts, while his mother, Mirella, served spaghetti and meatballs with generous helpings of homemade tomato sauce topped with fresh Parmesan cheese. Judy quickly learned that the best way to make her grandmother happy was to ask for second helpings of her handmade spaghetti. Warm homemade bread and butter and a tossed lettuce salad seasoned with Italian olive oil and vinegar always accompanied dinner. On special holidays, she added chicken to the platter of meatballs and prepared homemade ravioli as a memorable treat. Romano family dinners were the highlight of the week for Judy and her grandmother and a contrast from her normal uninspiring evenings alone with Rosella. Mirella was kind to Judy. She appreciated looking at her grandmother's pictures and hearing about her life in Italy as a young girl even though her English vocabulary was limited. Mirella's facial expressions were highly animated and expressive, and she used a plethora of unique hand gestures for emphasis.

Mario worked late every evening. He routinely explained to Rosella that he had important business meetings at various clubs and restaurants downtown. On many evenings, he never came home at all.

Mario and Rosella had little in common and only seemed to tolerate each other. Mario spent his free time fishing, boating, and golfing with friends, and he showed little interest in Judy's schoolwork or extracurricular activities. He had nothing to discuss with Rosella and frequently belittled her in public. Rosella was a frequent and easy target for Mario's rage. He had a very short fuse and an explosive temper.

His words were often rude and insulting. If he didn't like what Rosella cooked for dinner, he would throw a temper tantrum and yell obscenities at her. His abusive behavior miserably disturbed Rosella, but she had no other recourse. His offensive treatment hardened her, and she became increasingly resolute and stoic. She internalized her stress and spoke only to her parish priest, Father Hennen, about her marital situation. Because of her troubles, Rosella was frequently in a bad mood and impulsively took out her anger on Judy.

It troubled Judy that she had an irritable, crabby mother and an abusive father. She was mortified knowing that the neighbors could hear her father cussing at her mother. When this happened, she sought refuge in her bedroom.

Judy continued to show evidence of shyness as she grew older, and her emotions became more complex. She preferred to take the backseat in the classroom and follow rather than lead in large groups. Her teacher, Sister Bronwyn Kelch, was friendly and encouraging and a master at drawing the best out of her students. After some special attention, Judy responded positively to her teaching methods and finally started performing well in the classroom.

Her first communion ceremony was a major milestone and special occasion in her life. Rosella had looked forward to this day ever since Judy had been adopted. Mario spared no expense when it came to buying a beautiful, frilly, white dress with a white, lacy veil held in place by a stiff headband decorated with small, pink flowers that matched her collar and ribbon waistband. She wore a wrist corsage and held a jeweled cross of gold with white beads adorning the rosary. She carried a prayer book with both hands as she solemnly walked down the aisle to the altar to receive the sacrament of the Eucharist and accept her role as the Bride of Christ. It was an intense moment of pride for Rosella as she wiped the tears of happiness from her cheeks.

Rosella had inherited typical Northern European facial features of pale skin with naturally wavy, blonde hair. Judy had classic Italian light olive skin and straight, shiny brown hair with dark eyes and dimples on both cheeks. Their dissimilarities in physical appearance were proof they were not biologically related. Partly for that reason, Rosella resolved to tell Judy on her eighth birthday that she was adopted.

Mario referred to Judy as his own daughter because she had attractive Italian features similar to his. He had grown fond of his daughter, and their experiences in public had always been positive. It angered Mario that Rosella wanted to expose the truth by telling Judy about her adoption. He was concerned about other men questioning his manhood and gossiping about him behind his back. It angered him when Rosella reminded him that Judy was not his biological child.

Mario angrily slurred his words after downing his fifth shot of whiskey and tossing the newspaper on the floor. "If you want to disappoint our daughter by telling her that you are not her real mother, leave me out of it. You will have to do it alone."

Self-Awareness 11

Dear Mom, We have a comfortable lifestyle, but I agonize about the long-term stability and unity of my family. I feel insecure because my parents don't get along very well. They quarrel frequently, and Mario is often angry with Rosella and me. He spends very little time at home, and our future together seems very uncertain. I feel extremely threatened that my parents will abandon me if they get divorced. Do you think Rosella and Mario will walk out on me the same way they discarded Toby, my dog and best friend? Love, Judy

JUDY WAS EAGERLY ANTICIPATING a day of celebration. It was her eighth birthday.

"Come sit beside me on the couch. I have something important to tell you," Rosella unexpectedly blurted while nervously extending her hand.

Judy hesitatingly complied. She knew that whatever Rosella had to say must be important, but she was cautiously suspicious of her motive. She was puzzled to know if she had done something wrong. Her senses were heightened in response to Rosella's uncharacteristic manner of speaking, and she interpreted her unusual body language as unnatural and deliberate. Rosella's unusual tone of voice was much too high pitched for this to be an ordinary conversation.

Rosella instructed Judy to sit on the light gray couch with dark green pillows. Judy sat rigidly at attention with her hands folded on her knees. The bristly fabric was scratchy on the back of her legs. The seat cushions were stiff and uncomfortable. The couch was ergonomically designed for adults and unfit for Judy's small stature. Her legs were too short to reach the floor, and she tended to fall backward if she became too relaxed. Judy was normally highly energetic and unaccustomed to sitting attentively.

It was a drizzly, cloudy day outside. The dark living room curtains were only partially open, leaving the air inside muggy and the lighting subdued. Judy was unaccustomed to being treated this way and automatically sensed that something unusual was about to happen. Rosella was not a warm, intimate hugger. Her overbearing physical proximity caused Judy to writhe in her seat.

Rosella cleared her throat before introducing the topic with a very bold statement. "I am not your real mother."

Judy withdrew slightly and fidgeted nervously in her seat while trying to make sense of what she was hearing. Rosella is my mother, so why is she saying this?

"You are special because you were adopted. Your father and I had many children to choose from, but you were the best so we picked you." Rosella's voice cracked slightly as she finally blurted out what had been on her mind. She wasn't sure if her words sounded like she was informing Judy or confessing.

Judy stiffened her back and sat upright. Her mind was alert as she attempted to process the information that had been told to her and comprehend what it meant. She had a concerned look on her face because never before had she felt herself under the spotlight or viewed with so much scrutiny. Her mouth was closed; her lips were pursed tightly together. She had nothing to say. Silence heightened the tension between them.

Rosella glanced at her handwritten notes detailing what she was going to say next. She had solicited the opinion of Father Hennen before selecting the time and place to hold this conversation. She had tried to be as organized and prepared as possible. Her childless sister Myna had also filled her with much unsolicited advice. Myna was her most outspoken critic and advice-giver and notorious for interfering in her affairs.

Rosella had rehearsed what she was going to say in front of the bathroom mirror, and she was confident she was doing the right thing. She hesitated before continuing because she had become aware of her own nervousness. Her attempts to speak deliberately and enunciate every word correctly made her voice sound higher pitched than normal. She paused long enough to control the volume and pace of her sentences, thus making it easier to emphasize specific words and phrases.

Father Hennen had suggested she concentrate on reading Judy's facial expressions and body language to interpret how she was reacting to the knowledge she was adopted. He had warned that it would be difficult for Judy to comprehend the complexities of adoption from an adult perspective and natural for her to feel hurt and rejected.

Rosella had never understood why Judy had always been somber, withdrawn, and introverted because she had been unaware of the circumstances surrounding her first days in an orphanage and tragic loss of her foster family. Judy's continuous suffering had imposed a great strain on Rosella. In response, her patience had often been overtaxed. Her normal reaction had been to walk away and leave Judy alone to play by herself. She had avoided discussions about sensitive topics and failed to offer comfort to her daughter when it was badly needed. Her only solution for awkward situations had been to pray harder and more often.

Rosella tried to project happy feelings toward Judy to create a positive outcome, but Judy had a faraway look in her eyes as though she was preoccupied with the past. Judy squirmed uncomfortably on the couch and folded her arms across her chest as she considered the significance of what it meant to be adopted. She was stoic and reserved, and her facial expression was poker-faced.

Rosella had her own fears, frustrations, and emotions about motherhood. She desperately wanted her child to love her. Rosella was sensitive to the fact that her daughter wasn't her biological child and feared Judy might turn against her when she learned Rosella was not her real mother. She enjoyed possessing a child that she could dominate and manipulate. For that reason, she had seriously considered following Mario's advice by not telling her at all. This conversation was a once-in-a-lifetime opportunity because, after Judy learned the truth, there was no possibility of retracting her statements.

Rosella paused to organize her thoughts before continuing. "You had another mother before you were adopted. She gave birth to you and named you Judy. She played the violin."

Judy did not blink and reacted tentatively to what Rosella told her. She was baffled about why she had been adopted and curious to know if any of her friends had also been adopted. In her mind, adoption had a negative connotation because her dog Toby had been adopted and he had mysteriously disappeared without explanation.

Judy was disappointed knowing that Rosella was not her real

mother, but comforted knowing she had been chosen because she was special. She created a mental image of her birth mother looking exactly like her neighbor, Helen Redford, who was young, attractive, and enjoyable to be around. She politely acknowledged Judy's presence and made her feel welcome in her home. She gave her warm cookies and milk after school, paid attention to what she had to say, and gave her many compliments.

Judy was jolted out of her daydream when Rosella started speaking again. "Your mother was not legally married. You were an accident, and she was forced to give you up for adoption because she was very young and you were illegitimate. The court decided that your father and I could do a better job of raising you than your own mother could. That is why you are our child now," Rosella stated maliciously with the morally corrupt intent of disgracing and demeaning Judy's birth mother to make her seem more worthy.

Her rigid body language was making a strong statement that Judy was uncomfortable and confused. She had no comprehension about what the word "illegitimate" meant, and she was baffled about why she would ever be referred to as an "accident." She understood the basic meaning of adoption, but the underlying ramifications were more mysterious than clear. At that moment, she needed spontaneous love and reassurance. She desperately wanted Rosella to stop talking and hug her, but no hugs were forthcoming.

Rosella abruptly ended the conversation and returned to her normal duties in the kitchen. She felt a sense of relief that the moment she had dreaded for so long was finally over. Perhaps an opportunity for positive bonding could have occurred if Rosella had simply hugged Judy and invited her into the kitchen to help decorate her birthday cake or engage in some other mother-and-daughter activity. Instead, Judy was coldly left alone to clean her bedroom and finish her daily chores.

Judy thought carefully about her family situation with the Romanos. She was reasonably comfortable compared to friends and neighbors. They lived in a decent house in a pleasant neighborhood, but there was something esoteric about being adopted that left her feeling empty. Other children didn't have this issue to deal with, and it was difficult for her to express exactly how she felt about her circumstances to others. In some ways, it was a relief knowing that Rosella was not her real mother, especially when she did something embarrassing in front of her girlfriends.

Rosella had not provided Judy with any specific information or details about her birth mother other than the fact that she was very young and unmarried and played the violin. Listening to classical music on Sunday mornings stirred up thoughts about her birth mother. When she closed her eyes, she visualized an attractive, young woman playing the violin with a symphony orchestra in London or Paris. She smiled, and she was secretly proud of her birth mother because she knew the violin was a difficult instrument to play. She had daydreams and fantasies about her and prayed for a miracle that she would someday be able to view a photograph of her birth mother playing the violin.

Knowing she was adopted moved Judy to develop a new awareness about how she related to her adopted parents. She realized Mario and Rosella were closer in age to her girlfriends' grandparents, but, more than anything, her instincts helped her understand that she and Rosella didn't look alike or share the same way of thinking. Their personalities were different, and they didn't seem as closely bonded as her girlfriends and their mothers.

Her parents' methods of instruction and discipline were heavily weighted with risks and rewards. Rosella wasn't one to spoil the child and spare the rod or patiently mentor Judy into doing the right thing. She believed a crisp smack to the behind with the back of a hairbrush was the best way to correct her behavior. She did not feel obligated to explain why rules were important and made it clear that Judy must follow her instructions or suffer the consequences.

Following what she had been taught in the convent, Rosella drilled Judy into recognizing and avoiding the seven cardinal sins of lust, gluttony, greed, sloth, wrath, envy, and pride, and she had her memorize the seven parallel and opposing holy virtues of chastity, temperance, charity, diligence, patience, kindness, and humility. Judy was browbeaten on a regular basis with Rosella's attempts to impose her ideas that were always implemented in a domineering manner, thus leaving very little leeway for Judy to exercise her own free will, but her authoritative approach to learning only created resentment that caused Judy to rebel.

The topic of adoption rarely resurfaced, but, when it did, Rosella was quick to cruelly discredit her birth mother by saying nasty things about her. This had the opposite effect than she intended because Judy thought she was being uncharitable because her birth mother was not there to defend herself.

After finding out about a marital affair between Mario and her sister Myna, Rosella became enraged and actively vented her resentment by angrily launching an irrational verbal assault against Judy's birth mother. "Your birth mother didn't keep you because she didn't love you. She was selfish. She didn't care anything about you!" she shouted angrily, expressing her own hurt feelings of low self-esteem and rejection.

Judy would never forget that incident. It was incomprehensible why her mother would say such things to her. Rosella's words produced a stinging emotional welt that left a permanent impression on her mind. Her uncharitable comments were like a cold slap in the face that destroyed her confidence. Her mother's spiteful, angry words were powerfully toxic and continued burning into her consciousness long after they had been said.

"Your foster mother didn't love you either. If your foster parents loved you, they would have let you keep your baby blanket and toys!" Rosella shouted directly in Judy's face.

Judy was afraid to ask for an explanation because Rosella was still expelling her frustrations as a jealous wife. In between her angry outbursts directed at her husband, she was blaming some obscure people labeled as foster parents who she blamed for selfishly screwing up Judy by keeping her toys and security blanket.

What toys and baby blanket was she talking about? Her outrage was unrelenting, and she even criticized Father Hennen for some ambiguous reason for being remotely involved in her adoption. Rosella vilified and blamed wretched social worker Gertrude Schweinhaus for mishandling the adoption and giving them a girl instead of a boy.

Judy was merely a child and stood dejectedly off to the side with her eyes lowered with an injured expression on her face. Rosella's angry outburst was hurtful and left her feeling rejected, confused, and unloved. Judy had no idea what she was talking about, and she had to assume that her mother was making up stories to vent her rage. Judy was shocked by her accusations, bewildered by her statements, and quick to realize that her origin was more complicated than she had ever imagined. She was dumbfounded by her mother's desire to build up her own image by harshly discrediting everyone else, but her efforts were a miserable failure because her opinions came across as uncharitable and mean-spirited. The entire episode left Judy wondering if Rosella loved her at all.

She wanted to reach out and give her mother a hug, but it was impossible because Rosella had made it perfectly clear that she was not Judy's real mother. The reality of finally knowing that Rosella perceived Judy as her adopted daughter was devastating. For that reason, an immediate unconditional reconciliation between them was not possible. She was an adoptee, and it was up to her to make the best of her situation one day at a time.

ROSELLA NEVER ATTEMPTED TO smooth over the situation. They each retreated into their favorite corners of the house where Rosella devoted herself to painting dark, ominous landscape scenes and portraits of faces in somber moods. None of her oil paintings was characterized as sunny, bright, or cheerful.

Judy internalized her opinions and feelings and learned how to act independently and look out for her own interests. She became cognizant of her own unique identity and temperament and gradually learned to distinguish herself as an individual. She began to have vivid dreams about her birth mother and fantasies about the mysteries of her biological roots, but she kept her visions private and never shared any of them with Rosella. In the back of her mind, she fantasized that, if she stayed alert to the possibility, she would eventually find her birth mother. In response, she developed the habit of studying the faces of strangers to search for others with features similar to her own.

On a quiet Sunday morning while Beethoven's *Symphony No. 4, Violin Concerto* was playing softly in the background, Judy envisioned a beautiful, young woman with long, brown hair and dark eyes playing the violin in a large orchestra in Vienna, Austria. She leaned back in her chair, closed her eyes, pensively dreamed about her birth mother as a real person, and whispered to herself. "Finding my birth mother would make me the happiest girl in the world."

First Lilac Club

Dear Mom, I am resolved to the fact that I am the adopted daughter of Mario and Rosella Romano. I maintain a positive outlook on life. I am fairly well adjusted, and I have many quality friends. We have a comfortable lifestyle. Our home is in a pleasant neighborhood, and we can afford a few luxuries and vacations, but something still enchants me. I think about you often and wonder what life would be like if you were my mother. I fantasize that the mother of my best girlfriend is you because she is young, attractive, and fun to be with. She understands me, and she is sensitive to my feelings. She makes me smile and helps me get over my shyness by encouraging me to have fun. She is my surrogate mother, and I like to pretend she is you. Love, Judy

"HOMEMADE PIZZA WITH FRESH meats and the best ingredients," a good-looking Italian vendor yelled out to Rosella with a wide grin.

The man had attracted a crowd, and Rosella was pleasantly surprised to see so many customers in Mario's grocery store. Bruno was very persuasive, and Rosella impulsively bought three of his large homemade pizzas.

"Hello, I'm Bruno, and this is my daughter Linda," the outgoing, good-natured man placed the pizzas in Rosella's shopping cart.

The eerie physical similarity of the man and his daughter to Judy made Rosella uneasy and caused her to wonder what the chances were of accidentally encountering a biological relative. On the way home, she mentioned their remarkable similarity to Judy, but immediately wished she hadn't because her observation had inadvertently inspired Judy's self-consciousness about her appearance and encouraged her to compare herself to others. Acting overly friendly with strangers was dangerous behavior that should not be encouraged because it could get Judy into trouble with kidnappers or child molesters.

The pizza man and his daughter escalated Rosella's curiosity about the identity of Judy's real parents, heightened her fears of losing her daughter, and increased her possessiveness. Rosella jealously vowed to never encourage her daughter to compare herself to others because she didn't want Judy thinking about anyone besides her.

JUDY WAS HAPPY AND well adjusted and maturing normally. Her teachers liked her, and she was comfortable speaking to adults. Her behavior was within the natural range of variability for her age, but knowing she was adopted slightly altered her thoughts. Her unnatural separation and inability to bond with her birth mother and the emotional scars caused by the trauma of being ripped away from her foster family on her first birthday had gradually become foggy memories that had been nearly forgotten.

Her life was good. She was fortunate enough to travel to Europe and Mexico with her parents. She had an audience with the Pope at the Vatican, visited the Roman Coliseum in Rome, watched a bull fight in Spain, visited Yellowstone National Park, hiked on Mayan ruins in Mexico, and kissed the Blarney Stone in Ireland. Her father had a yacht and took the family on exotic boating excursions. Christmas was celebrated at beach resorts in Florida. All of these family experiences were unique and interesting. Traveling strengthened the bond with her parents and distracted Judy from thinking about the stigma of being adopted. Her inner thoughts about adoption were subdued and forgotten during enjoyable times like these.

Overall, life in her neighborhood was pleasant. There were many children to play with, and the elementary school was within walking distance. Automobile traffic was minimal, and the majority of homes were new. Every house had lush green grass and a sidewalk leading to the front door. Many had small flower and vegetable gardens. American elm trees provided abundant shade. The mayor of Milwaukee lived half a block away, and a police officer provided twenty-four-hour security.

Judy was observant of how other children in her neighborhood related to their parents and enjoyed making comparisons with hers. She daydreamed what her life might have been like if another family had adopted her, and she naturally gravitated toward adults she assumed were similar to her biological family.

Adoption was a multifaceted topic with many hidden secrets, and Judy didn't fully comprehend the ramifications. She kept her thoughts secret and bottled up inside because it was hurtful knowing her own mother had abandoned her. Thinking about her adoption usually left her feeling fragile and vulnerable, and it was difficult as a child to verbalize her subliminal inner thoughts and feelings.

ON A WARM SPRING afternoon, Judy crawled beneath the overhanging branches of the lilac bushes in her backyard. She watched in awe as a butterfly in unfurling glory, highlighted by an intense ray of diffused sunshine, and slowly dried its large, brightly colored wings. It was the perfect sanctuary and idyllic location for meeting with her girlfriends. She cleared a small space under the lilac bush and rolled five, large stumps into a circle. The air under the lilac bush was warm and fragrant. Rays of sunlight penetrated the branches, creating an ephemeral mosaic of light and dark shapes that danced across their faces. The scent of lilac flowers and rays of sunlight dispersing through the green leaves above them permeated the atmosphere. The buzz of honeybees, incessant chirping of robins, and freshly mowed grass, combined with the ambient smell of lilacs in full bloom, was an ideal setting for privacy.

The shady, compact space provided a secure environment where the girls felt relaxed and comfortable. The proximity of the seating arrangement facilitated intimacy, whispering, and the sharing of secrets. Only then did Judy decide to tell her girlfriends she was adopted. Adoption was a multifarious topic, an idea that young minds easily understood when it came to pets, but human adoption was a mysterious subject about which the other girls had no personal experience.

"Rosella is not my mother. My real mother was too busy to take care of me. That is why I was adopted," Judy quietly revealed. She was curiously wondering how her girlfriends would react.

Surprised by her startling revelation, they stared at her in astonishment with their mouths wide open, uncertain how to respond.

Grace was whimsically optimistic. "You are lucky you were adopted. Your family is wealthy. You take vacations on your father's yacht and can afford to buy many nice things. You should be happy this happened to you," she concluded encouragingly.

Susan S. Morris

Kathy was fidgety and uncomfortable. Uncertain what to say, she had a delayed, subdued reaction. She felt bad for Judy and sympathetically squeezed her hand as a gesture of friendship before expressing her sincerest condolences. "I'm sorry, Judy. I feel sad knowing that you don't know your real mother."

Renee was bewildered and embarrassed. The information Judy had disclosed about herself left her with feelings of uncertainty and doubts about her own family situation. She listened intently to what the others had to say. She was curious to know where Judy's real mother lived, what she was doing, and if Judy expected to meet her sometime.

Diane was the oldest and most mature. The other girls looked to her for advice and reassurance. Her words were reasonable and comforting. "We are all best friends. It is good to share our thoughts with each other. Judy should not feel embarrassed because she was adopted or keep this secret from us. Adoption is not weird or something to feel lucky or sad about, and it is not a reflection on her. It's just another way of making a family. We are all lucky to have nice parents who love and provide for us."

Judy looked up and smiled. She knew her friends still cared about her before she dug a shallow grave in the loose dirt under the lilac bush. The girls had collectively mourned the unexpected disappearance of her dog Toby. When the hole was finally finished, Judy ceremoniously wrapped his doggie tag in Rosella's favorite red silk scarf and reverently laid it in the hole. The girls held hands, closed their eyes tightly, and listened respectfully while Judy read a short poem memorializing her beloved Toby.

"My dog Toby has taken flight, and I miss him with all my might."

The First Lilac Club was an exclusive group of friends who trusted each other with their most embarrassing moments and deepest secrets. Judy choreographed a short ceremony whereby each member promised to keep the location of the club hidden, and protect the privacy of its members. To commemorate its founding, the girls arranged a beautiful bouquet of spring flowers in a wicker basket as a symbol of their unity. A brightly colored butterfly on its first conspicuous, fluttering flight landed softly on the handle, and slowly fanned its wings as a symbol of joy, wonder, and transformation. After they agreed to the ideals of the club, Judy presented each girl with a single lilac flower as a symbol of their sisterhood.

The First Lilac Club was an instant success because it encouraged camaraderie, sisterhood, and bonding between members. The girls became very comfortable sharing secrets with each other. Judy's adoption became a favorite reoccurring topic that alerted Judy to the possibility of becoming an adoption detective when she grew up so she could solve the mystery of her own adoption.

"Time of the Lilacs" was selected as the motto for the club because she was born in April and spring was her favorite time of the year. The girls loved their secret hiding place, and the experience was enhanced even more whenever Judy provided warm cookies and milk. They had great fun gossiping about the boys in the neighborhood, laughing, and telling stories about their parents. Judy listened intently because their remarks were often candid and highly revealing.

Judy persuaded them to make money for the club by picking their neighbors' apples and peaches when they were away on vacation and selling the fruit to other families in the neighborhood to raise money for candy and snacks.

When the girls weren't meeting in their secret clubhouse, they enjoyed exploring the outdoors on bicycles and playing board games and marbles indoors on rainy days. They drank lemonade, ate potato chips, played rock and roll music, and did silly dancing.

Judy created a playhouse in her basement. The girls dressed in hilarious outfits and put on several productions for their parents, including a magic show. One of the plays called for a small boy to be placed in a large wooden hope chest to be used as a coffin. Their parents roared with laughter, cheered loudly, and enjoyed the revelry.

During the summer, she organized sleepovers in her garage. Everyone brought her own bedding and cots. The girls felt mature and grown-up when they were allowed to sleep outside by themselves. They routinely stayed up late telling scary ghost stories and making figures on the wall by shining their flashlights across their hands. Despite the overwhelming smells of gasoline, paint thinner, insecticides, and lawn fertilizer and the presence of spiderwebs inside the garage, the girls fell asleep feeling happy and satisfied with their friendships.

Her girlfriend Diane was one year older and a good role model. Her parents Eleanor and Hans were pleasant to be around. Hans had a large aquarium filled with colorful tropical fish, a tub full of snapping turtles, and a woodstove in his garage to keep himself warm while he tinkered with small projects. He was usually in a good mood because he was often seen sipping red wine or brandy. Hans, an accountant for a large manufacturing company, wore polished black leather shoes and a white shirt with a bow tie. He carried a very large, brown leather briefcase stuffed with papers.

Eleanor was a good cook, and her house frequently smelled like fresh bakery. She was a prolific reader and often seen in the living room reading romance novels while sitting in a comfortable chair with an afghan blanket wrapped around her legs. Every Saturday, she asked Judy and Diane to escort her to the public library to check out additional books. Accompanying her to the library was an experience Judy enjoyed and one she would otherwise not have had.

Whenever Judy overheard Diane's parents talking about going to the ice cream store, outdoor picnics, or swimming at Lannon Quarry, Wisconsin, she intentionally hung around and made a pest of herself until she was asked to join them. They were always relaxed and did many interesting things. They were fun to be around. Hans and Eleanor had a good marital relationship, and Judy enjoyed having them as surrogate parents because she considered them good role models to emulate.

Renee was strikingly attractive, and the men in the neighborhood were often overheard comparing her mother Jane to the movie actress Jayne Mansfield. Jane was very attractive, and she wore sexy clothes. When Renee was twelve years old, her parents had another unplanned baby girl.

Renee always seemed to have the latest of everything, and her house was well decorated and furnished in good taste. Judy enjoyed sitting at their large, elegant dining table made of a dark exotic wood and talking with Renee and her parents. Judy thought they were good people even though she had overheard her father speculating that Marvin spent more money than he earned. Marvin and Jane hosted elaborate parties for the kids. On Halloween, they created a haunted house that required the neighborhood children to crawl in and out of the windows. It was a scary experience that created excitement and fond memories.

Marvin looked like Elvis Presley. He owned his own refrigeration company and parked a large flatbed truck beside his garage. He had long, black hair, and he was as big as a football player. He shuffled around the house in his big, baggy blue jeans held up by an old leather belt that was cracked and faded. The white T-shirts that he wore under his faded navy blue work shirt usually hung out, but not far enough to hide his plumber's butt when he bent over. His brown leather slip-on work boots were dull and scuffed up in sharp contrast to Han's shiny black shoes with tie laces. He was frequently seen swigging from a long neck bottle of beer suspended from his knobby knuckles.

Kathy was quiet and shy, and she preferred to follow along and do whatever the other girls wanted to do. Her parents were quiet, private people who interacted very little with others. Her mother Dorothy was a stay-at-home mother who wore a cooking apron every day and spent the majority of her time preparing meals, reading the Bible, and attending the local Lutheran church. Her house was modest and plain. Some of their family routines and interactions were odd and amusing.

Grace evolved into Judy's best friend. She was a good person with many positive attributes. She was good at verbalizing her feelings. She was witty and possessed an excellent sense of humor. Judy admired her self-confidence, assertiveness, and ability to respond intelligently to her father's constant teasing. Her mother Helen taught her to pray and believe in God. Helen often joined the girls in the kitchen for conversation while she drank a frightening number of vodka screwdrivers that never seemed to affect her. She was a good communicator as well as a good listener. She was observant and sensitive. She had a good sense of humor, and she gave good advice. She never held back when talking about personal problems or intimate adult subjects, and she wasn't afraid to use profanity to make her point. She could discuss almost any topic and make it sound interesting. Judy liked Helen and viewed her as her second mother. She and Archie were an ideal couple and model surrogate parents for Judy.

Archie loved his daughter, and they had a respectful relationship. He was a jokester who enjoyed teasing others. He was a car salesman, and his responses to questions were often indirect or contained double meanings. He was accustomed to bartering, joking, and getting one up on others, and he was very good at it. He was a jack-of-all-trades and could fix almost anything around the house. Judy admired his mechanical abilities and workmanship. He bred dogs, raised pigeons, and raced go-carts. He constructed a swimming pool in his backyard, built an additional room on the back of his house, and restored a classic Thunderbird convertible for his wife Helen. He especially enjoyed teasing Judy because, in his words, she was "jumpy and easily frightened."

"Aaaarrrgh! Get your hand out of my refrigerator!" Archie shouted in a loud voice. He snuck up from behind and grabbed her by the neck.

Judy nearly jumped out of her skin, jerked her hand out of the refrigerator, slammed the heavy door, defensively raised her arms above her head to protect her face, and whirled around to protect herself from her attacker. She was startled and embarrassed. Archie laughed. It was a comical scene that repeated itself nearly every visit. Her reactions were so highly animated and amusing that Archie never stopped teasing her.

Mario and Rosella were the opposite. They were very serious people. They never teased each other. Practical jokes made them furious. They never used sarcasm and seldom laughed aloud because they had a low tolerance for immature behavior. It had been easy for the members of the First Lilac Club to spot differences between their parents, but they all agreed that Judy's parents didn't love each other.

Judy liked her surrogate parents because she admired them and appreciated their advice and encouragement. Collectively, the fun and excitement of being around other families encouraged her to become more aware of positive characteristics associated with loving couples and happy families. Her observations of other parents were in sharp contrast to her own family, where it had become impossible to conceal the humiliation of her parents' obnoxious arguing. Excessive consumption of alcohol contributed to Mario's problems, and Rosella's angry rhetorical outbursts were an explosive combination. Everything that Judy admired about her surrogate parents came crashing back to earth each time she returned home to listen to their verbal insults and marital disputes.

Elizabeth and Michelle lived across the street. Their family owned a player piano, and Judy loved to read the words on the sheet music while the piano performed each melody perfectly. The words to her favorite song "Tell Me of My Mother" by Stephen Collins Foster lingered in her memory.

Oh, tell me of my Mother. Is she roaming the skies? I've been dreaming all about her, and awoke with tearful eyes. She was bending o'er my pillow in a deep and earnest prayer, and her voice was like the breathing of the soft summer air. Is the world so full of pain that she will not come again like a sunbeam on the rain? Oh, tell me of my mother. Does she know I'm here alone? Where have my early friends gone and my dearest memories flown? Oh, tell me of my mother.

The sentimental lyrics brought tears to her eyes. She hugged her pillow, created a vision of the time of the lilacs, and fantasized about her birth mother.

Breaking Away

Dear Mom, My life as a teenager is interesting and carefree, and I have the freedom to do what I want. I love riding in cars, listening to music and dancing, and having fun with my friends. My faith in God and acceptance of traditional values give me confidence and optimism about the future. I have learned to adapt to my parents' way of life. My adoption is less of an emotional issue at this stage of my life than when I was a child. I am gradually evolving into a mature individual and becoming my own person. I enjoy being independent and less reliant on my parents. Love, Judy

MARIO BROKE THE SILENCE at the dinner table. "Now that you are fourteen years old, I have a full-time job for you working in the bakery department of my grocery store. You must be ready to leave the house by seven o'clock sharp. Don't be late," he commanded.

The atmosphere in the car on the way to work was thick as molasses. Mario concentrated on his driving; Judy was apprehensive about making correct change for customers and feeling awkward as the boss' daughter in front of the employees.

The bakery department was busy throughout the day, and all of Judy's customers were friendly people. She wore a cute, black, nylon dress with a white apron and a little, white, lacy crown on her head. The attractive smell of fresh donuts was intoxicating and made her very hungry. Every Saturday morning, the bakery counter was bustling with elderly Italian women waiting in line to buy fresh Italian bread and Danish pastries after Catholic mass.

One of the friendliest individuals arrived every Saturday, accompanied by her mother and two sisters. Nina Rossi enjoyed chitchatting, talking about the weather and current events. Judy liked to wait on her because she smiled and gave big tips. She always bought three loaves of Italian bread and a dozen sweet rolls.

"You look just like my niece Linda. Maybe you are my niece, too," she would say with a wink and a smile and a small wave of her hand in departing.

The following summer, Judy learned to wrap produce and display apples and oranges to make them look appealing to customers. She worked in the meat department wrapping, pricing, and displaying meat until she eventually graduated to the clerical office where she organized accounts payable and filed billing statements.

She stayed actively engaged in a variety of activities outside the home. Her teenage years were pleasant and filled with many interesting experiences. She cultivated many new friendships and participated in a variety of healthy social activities. The opportunities she had working in an adult environment helped her accept responsibility and develop mature habits.

Her home life was not so affable. The atmosphere became more unpleasant as her father and mother drifted further apart. Her desire to be carefree and independent contributed to her parents' worries and added to the turmoil. Judy rebelled when they attempted to block her emancipation and suppress her social activities. She enjoyed spending evenings with friends and repeatedly ignored her curfew at the peril of being grounded.

Mario ended his marital relationship with Rosella in a raging fit of anger. His displeasure with Rosella was perpetrated by picking up his dinner plate, flinging it against the dining room wall, and walking out of the house for the last time. Mashed potatoes and gravy dripped slowly off the wall, mixed with broken pieces of china on the floor, as the sounds of squealing automobile tires resonated in their ears. Rosella was relieved to see him go, but felt like a failure as a wife. She sulked and demanded Judy clean up the mess. Judy was caught in the middle, not knowing what to do or say other than be polite to both of them.

Mario's heated departure contributed to Judy's feelings of disappointment and insecurity and exasperated the depressing emotional burden caused by the separation of her parents. Rosella's relationship with Mario was openly hostile and unlikely to ever be resolved amicably. Judy grieved for the personal loss of her father, but there was no recourse other than to make the best of the situation. She contended with her frustrations by eating fast food, drinking alcohol, attending college dances, going sailing and skiing, and driving recklessly. She experienced a sudden loss of contact with her father and avoided all discussions with her mother about her extracurricular activities. Rosella agonized over the failure of her marriage and lost interest in supervising Judy. The de facto freedom her parents' separation provided motivated Judy to become more responsible as her own person.

Mario was out of sight for good, and Rosella spitefully redirected her own sense of inadequacy and internalized her fears and anger toward Judy. Her comments were often emotionally unjustified, unprovoked, and bitter. Her loss made Rosella short-tempered and deeply disturbed. She reminisced about the past by expressing regrets about the consequences of her infertility and the effects it had on her failed marriage. Judy's defiant behavior infuriated Rosella because she perceived her daughter's constant striving for independence as a lack of respect for her. She pouted and acted lonely when Judy emerged herself in activities outside the home, and she had difficulty disengaging from her motherly powers and subjugation of her only child. Her feeble attempts to exercise control only generated more stress and motivated Judy to spend even more time away from home.

"Your poor attitude and impulsive nature is psychologically and genetically inherited from your biological parents. You are predestined to fail because you are a self-fulfilling prophecy emulating your birth parents' original sins and bad behavior."

Rosella's uncharitable remarks shocked Judy speechless. There was no appropriate way to respond to such mean-spirited, inflammatory invective and verbal abuse. Her unkind words were like rocket missiles inflicting gaping mental wounds and shattering priceless memories. Telling someone she was ugly, fat, or genetically inferior was unforgivable. No amount of apology could ever heal the intangible hurt that Judy experienced. Rosella's vindictive comments were hurtful and permanently affected their relationship because they were further proof that Rosella viewed Judy as someone else's daughter other than her own.

Judy adjusted to her mother's wrath by changing the way she described herself to friends. To avoid the hurt she was feeling, she rejected all inquiries about her childhood. It was too painful and embarrassing to inform others that communication with her father had ended and she was mentally estranged from her adopted mother. It was far easier to ignore her dire family situation by concentrating on her homework and entertaining herself with frivolous distractions.

Judy's busy social schedule and the emotional turmoil produced by her parents' impending divorce distracted her from thinking about her adoption. Her passionate dreams and fantasies of her birth mother declined as she adjusted to the reality of her situation. Thinking of herself as an adoptee further complicated her perception of herself. Her view of reality became more complex and multifaceted than it was for other adolescents because her adoption gave her more cause for shame and lower self-esteem. Her detachment from her parents increased her anxiety due to a missing sense of love and a lack of belonging.

She suffered from an identity crisis as an adoptee because she found herself in limbo, vacillating and torn between her adopted parents and her true cultural and family history, which were a complete mystery. As with many issues in life, the psychological trauma caused by adoption varied based on the circumstances of how it was raised in conversation, the intelligence of the participants, and the innate curiosity and temperament of those involved. Judy was a victim of genealogical bewilderment that kept her in a constant state of confusion and uncertainty because she had no roots, but, to her friends, family histories were a form of bragging. Relatives with unique personalities, characteristics, occupations, or special features were often projected onto newborns or assigned to children and grandchildren as terms of endearment. Regrettably, Judy felt handicapped with her peers because she knew nothing about her true identity. She desperately wanted to be able to tell her friends about her genetic background. Knowledge of her ancestors was void, and her only recourse as an adoptee in the pursuit of finding herself was reading self-help, self-discovery, and self-improvement books written to help the reader find herself.

In her dreams and fantasies, she perceived the idea of being with her birth parents as the rightful natural place where she belonged, but, in reality, she was totally dependent and connected to her adopted parents. During the transitional period between childhood dependency and adolescent autonomy, the desire to find her biological roots resurfaced primarily when relations with her adopted parents were poor. Specific life experiences also intensified her interest in genealogy and heightened her curiosity about her biological link.

Peer pressure was an important influence on character building and her personal development during adolescence. Fortunately, the majority of peer pressure that friends exerted on her was positive. She was fortunate to attend high school where the majority of her class-mates were persons of high integrity and character. Her closest friends were individuals of substance concerned with academics and quality relationships. They were less susceptible to deviations from traditional moral behaviors common to many teenagers. Collectively, they had pride in their school. The class motto, "Hard as nails, tough as bricks," stuck with everyone long after graduation. Judy admired her classmates as fellow competitors and friends. There were dozens of leaders who set good examples by being supportive of the good qualities of others, and their friendships lasted many years.

Following her graduation from Dominican High School in White-fish Bay, she attended Marquette University, University of Wisconsin, and completed her education at Sacred Heart School of Practical Nursing before getting a job as a nurse at St. Mary's Hospital over-looking Lake Michigan.

Shortly after graduation, she met Martin Land in an ice cream store. Martin had arrived in town to play hockey for the Milwaukee Admirals, but, every night after the first date, he chose to go to Judy's house for dinner instead of attending hockey practice and sweating on the rink with the boys. It was love at first sight for both of them. His sports career was over. Judy's friendship and homemade lasagna were more important than pucks and broken teeth.

Their wedding reception at North Hills Country Club was a de-lightful formal affair. Coincidentally, Judy was much too excited to no-tice that the waitress who served her wedding cake was the same little girl she had met in her father's grocery store. She had been selling piz-zas with her father many years ago. Nina Rossi had fondly referred to her as her beloved niece Linda.

Judy suspended her career as a nurse indefinitely to accompany Martin on numerous cross-country business trips to attractive resorts from California to New Hampshire and many states in between. They went beachcombing in Oregon, drove the Blue Ridge Parkway in Vir-ginia, and visited the monuments in Washington DC. They stayed at the historic Hotel Del Coronado in San Diego, Christmas Island Re-sort in New Hampshire, Timberline Lodge on Mount Hood, and ca-sinos on the shore of Lake Tahoe. They saw the giant redwood forests, and they went camping in Yellowstone and Glacier National Parks. The opportunities Judy was provided to travel with her husband the first two years strengthened their marital bond and provided many memorable vacations.

Traveling and career building was enjoyable for both of them. When Martin eventually accepted a job planning alpine skiing events for the Winter Olympic Games, they decided to start a new life in Colorado.

Their decision angered Rosella, and she attempted to instill guilt by blaming Judy for willfully abandoning her mother. "You love your husband more than you love your own mother," she had wailed in exasperation.

Judy came face-to-face with the realization that leaving Milwaukee would significantly diminish her chances of ever finding her birth mother, perhaps forever. Martin held her hand as she cried a small lonely tear of vexation, knowing she was leaving her childhood behind and transitioning into an entirely new life.

PART 2

The Search

Resilience, Perseverance, and Persistence

"The process of conducting an adoption search
requires resilience to conquer adversity, perseverance to
overcome injustice, and persistence to achieve your goal."
–Judith Land

Sense of Urgency

Dear Mom, We have never met, yet you have been part of my life for as long as I can remember. I felt your presence when I was a small girl, and, over time, your spirit has gotten even stronger. I can feel it pulling me toward you. Some evenings, I imagine we are looking at the same full moon and stars in heaven, and I get chills knowing you are out there somewhere waiting to be found. My marriage and a successful business have increased my self-confidence and given me more reasons to be optimistic about my future, but something very important is still missing from my life. It is you. My emotions that were suppressed for so long are slowly bubbling to the surface. An investigation into my biological and genealogical roots interests me more as an adult than it did in my youth because it seems more attainable now. Love, Judy

I DREAMED MY BIOLOGICAL clock was hanging on the wall above my head, ticking loudly with the hands spinning around and around out of control. Hours and days were flying past at an accelerated rate. The longer I stared at it, the faster the hands moved.

I was experiencing a midlife crisis. Nobody lives forever. Time was my enemy. Deep thoughts about my adoption that had plagued my psyche forever were stimulating a sense of urgency. My life was passing quickly, and I couldn't do anything to slow it down. The desire to know where I came from had suddenly become central to my thinking as a result of maturity, increased consciousness, and the ability to reach a higher plain of spiritual and mental awareness. I had prayed for confidence, wisdom, and guidance, and my prayers were finally being answered.

My life was settled and predictable, and I had enough time and confidence to face the unknown. Inner feelings of empowerment were outweighing past insecurities and fears that had previously dominated my personality. I was ready to accept new challenges and find the truth about my past because my fantasy of meeting my birth mother was finally crystallizing into a realistic goal, but, if I did find her, I had no way of knowing how she would react or if we would even like each other. Consequently, a jumbled assortment of dreams and fantasies about what might happen if I decided to continue filled my mind.

I lacked verifiable facts about my birth mother. Before I could get started, I would have to confirm that everything Rosella had told me was true. I had naïvely assumed that I could research public records, find what I was looking for, and telephone my birth mother to complete the process, but ethics had become another issue that clouded my thinking. The moral dilemma of whether I should search for my birth mother and birth father was an idea that had never occurred to me as a child because ethics was a subject that was far too complex to understand when I was young. The large number of variables and potential outcomes made my head spin, and abstract thinking never seemed to lead anywhere so I made up my mind to continue regardless of the consequences. I couldn't imagine why anyone would think it was wrong for an adult to find her ancestral roots. I consciously made up my mind to postpone all philosophical discussions until I had uncovered some concrete evidence that my biological mother was still alive.

My optimism and enthusiasm had been growing for several years, but so was a dark cloud of doubt because it was uncertain how to get started. There was a realistic possibility that I might never find them. I had no idea how to research adoption records or whether it was necessary to solicit the advice and assistance of a lawyer, private investigator, priest, social worker, or adoption agency, but I was too shy to mention it to anyone. I didn't have the finances to pay for assistance.

My origins were a complete mystery to me. The more I thought about my background, the more bewildered I was by my very existence because I had no knowledge or personal history to help me get started. Common names such as Erickson, McHarg, Wallenski, and Schmitt could provide clues about ancestry, and it was easy to guess the historical occupations of families named Miller, Forester, Cook, or Barber, but, in my case, I had nothing to even get started. Perhaps if I had some names to go on, I could visit the Mormon Family History Museum in Salt Lake City to research their history.

The idea of an adoption search was invigorating and created a new energy and purpose in my life. It was an opportunity to embark on a mission to link my current life with my unknown past. It was an exciting mystery to solve and the start of a grand adventure, but the consequences of a failed search had an equal possibility of bringing tears and disappointment or happiness and joy. I assumed a successful search would bring completion to my life. The reward would be an increased sense of personal satisfaction. Conversely, if the outcome were unsuccessful, it had potential to be distressing and sad. I was also aware that a negative outcome could significantly complicate my life. There was a risk of developing a deep psychological hurt that could collaterally affect the lives of my husband, son, and adopted parents.

Rosella's descriptions of my birth parents had been untimely, inappropriate, and, at times, downright evil, but, despite our many disagreements, I still respected her because she was the mother who raised me. I didn't want to hurt her feelings because I appreciated all the positive things she had done for me. I forgave her anger because, now that I was an adult, I understood that her lack of understanding, empathy, and compassion had been partly due to her ignorance of basic human psychology. She had accurately diagnosed my awkward body language and fearful, confused state of mind as classic childhood symptoms of separation syndrome, but she knew little about the depth of my wounds or how to soothe them. Her way of dealing with my psychological trauma had always been to deny personal responsibility for my insecurities and antisocial behavior by placing all of the blame for my undesirable behaviors on my birth parents.

My sad face as a child had been amusing to her. I never forgot how painful it was for her to tease me about my nervousness and shyness in front of her friends. When I became angry and agitated, she unkindly described my little temper tantrums and despondencies as cute. She criticized me for being reclusive and didn't like it when I pushed her away. It made her furious when I talked privately to my dolls Barbara and Mary while refusing to talk to her. Unknowingly, she had never recognized the true identity of my dolls as my surrogate foster sisters. She didn't recognize the severity of emotional damage that had occurred or depth of the psychological trauma separation syndrome had created. She had openly condemned my birth parents for all of my negative personality characteristics and idiosyncrasies, including the lack of bonding with her. It was a convenient and simple excuse for her own insecurities, failures, and lack of abilities as a mother.

As a child, I had not perceived the significance or meanings of her disparaging words, but, now that I was older, I resented hearing her characterize my biological parents in a derogatory manner. I had no idea why my birth mother gave me up for adoption, but, intuitively, it didn't seem right for Rosella to be judging her so harshly. She had been unrelenting in her criticisms, but her insensitive comments were the only way I had of visualizing my birth parents. Her description of my birth mother helped me create a childish vision of a spiritual figure seated in an orchestra whose face was never entirely in focus. I imagined her as someone similar to me in appearance but older.

"Your parents were only seventeen and unmarried when you were conceived. There may have been some diabetes or heart problems in the family, but there is no way of knowing for sure. Your birth mother was five-foot-seven and played the violin. Your birth father was an exceptional football athlete and star basketball player. You should be thinking about me and be grateful for all you have been given instead of them," Rosella had said insensitively.

When I was young, Rosella had made me feel like an outcast because I had a light olive complexion while her skin was pale as milk. Her hair was naturally blonde and wavy. Mine was brown and straight. We both knew that our personalities and temperaments were as dissimilar as our appearances.

Her descriptions of my birth parents often entered my dreams and fantasies. I visualized a strong, handsome boy and an attractive, dark-haired girl with a sweet face holding hands and smiling at each other as they walked home from school. I pictured them as high school sweethearts passionately in love with each other. With this positive mental picture in mind, I was finally emotionally prepared to start my personal journey of discovery, but I was painfully shy when it came to drawing attention to myself in public. I was used to masking my emotions. Asking strangers for help was difficult.

My husband Martin and I talked about my simmering passion to find my birth parents at great length. The intensity of our discussions brought us closer together as a married couple and helped him understand and appreciate me. Our talks encouraged him to learn more about adoption by researching the legal and scientific aspects of the topic to help him understand me psychologically. Working together was enjoyable and more desirable than working alone. Our nightly sessions gave us a shared purpose and common interest. I needed encouragement to get started, and it would have been difficult to execute such a big undertaking without someone I trusted.

I assumed that, if I created a positive atmosphere when he came home from work, he would react positively to my proposal. I poured him a glass of red wine, played soft music, and cooked one of his favorite meals, Sicilian steak with tiramisu for dessert. After dinner, I placed my hand in his and calmly gathered the right words to accurately express myself. He was giving me his undivided attention. I gained my composure and spoke in a sincere, sweet voice. I looked directly into his blue eyes and pleaded for assistance.

"I have a strong desire to find my birth parents. I want to initiate an investigation to find them, but I'm not sure how to get started. I am too bashful to do this on my own, and I would be forever grateful if you would support me. You have management skills and wisdom. You work well with others, and you are good at getting to the bottom of things. I really need your support if I am going to do this," I said demurely with a coy expression. I paused briefly. "You are my pillar of steel, and I need you to lean on for emotional support. Searching for my birth parents is likely to be a very emotional journey for me. I get nervous just thinking about it. I will need you to help me stay focused and boost me up when I fail. We both love a good mystery. Together, we can make a good detective team. You are good at understanding physical evidence, and you're an expert at understanding human psychology." I tried to think of every possible reason why he should support me.

"My enthusiasm for finding my biological roots has been increasing daily, and it has finally reached a significant threshold. I want to take action. It will be a challenging adventure piecing together the puzzle of my birth and adoption. What if I am related to famous people? Perhaps my mother is a concert violinist in New York or Paris." I knew that Martin loved talking about Bob Gregson, world boxing champion; Trysil Knut, the Norwegian skiing champion; and the Cowley Knights Templar in his ancestral background.

I could see that he was intrigued with my enthusiasm and curious about my family tree, so I continued speaking with conviction. "When I was young, I thought it was fashionable to talk about my adoption because it drew attention to me as a unique individual. My adopted parents had convinced me that I was special because they had chosen me. At times, I was even happy knowing I was adopted because it made it easier to dissociate myself from the negative behavior of my adopted parents. Now that I am older, there are practical reasons for wanting to have a genetic link to my birth parents and knowing something about their nationalities. Most doctors find value in medical family histories."

Martin had witnessed firsthand how excited and interested I became whenever someone told me that I reminded them of another person with similar features and expressions. These innocuous incidents fed my curiosity and increased my desire to know something about my genealogy. As an adoptee, it was natural for me to become effusive when someone acknowledged my individuality because I perceived every stranger who looked like me as a potential relative. Each coincidental event roused me to daydream about the potential of contacting one of my birth parents, an aunt, a cousin, or other relative, and I would impulsively follow up with questions such as, "Does the woman who looks like me play the violin?"

Martin remained silent and allowed me to finish speaking. "I acknowledge what you are saying and understand why people want to discover their roots. I take pride in my own ancestry and enjoy knowing this information for cultural and human interest reasons. The process of doing ancestral research has potential to be an interesting journey of self-discovery. Doctors Douglas Yajko and Robert Brokering convinced me that knowledge of family history is very important for medical diagnosis and research. You are an adult and a mother. At your age, I know you aren't looking to replace Rosella. As long as you are discreet and considerate of the privacy of others during your search for information, you are not likely to be a detriment to anyone."

I leaned closer and let him smell my perfume before pleading in my most persuasive, loving voice, "Will you please help me find my birth parents?"

Gateway to Adulthood

Dear Mom, My life has finally transitioned from the carefree, fun experimental years that characterized my teens and twenties. I used to spend much of my time looking for reasons to celebrate and have a good time. Now I sense that I have entered a new passage in my life that has allowed me to pass through a gateway into adulthood. I have finally entered a midlife phase with a much greater sense of urgency to accomplish things. At the top of my list is my desire to find you. I have decided to embark on a quest to find my roots and personal history. If I can't find the information I am looking for, I hope you will at least send me a sign to let me know that you are still alive, and I will do the same for you. Love, Judy

"Yes, honey, I will help you find your birth mother," Martin whispered in my ear with his arms wrapped tightly around me.

He had admitted that, from the very beginning, he had been aware that I had a restless heart, looking to find my natural place in the world. On our first date, I had felt a kindred spirit with him and openly shared my deepest thoughts. I told him I was adopted to see how he would react. I secretly wondered if he would reject me as an unworthy outcast, but he had been warmly understanding and sympathetic. He had responded in an appreciative way, knowing I had been open with him by honestly sharing my personal sentiments.

Martin approached the subject from a mature analytical standpoint the same way he attacked problems at work by preparing a personal mission statement, identifying practical well-defined goals, and assigning responsibilities. "We need to thoroughly research the topic of adoption before getting started. That means going to the library, visiting bookstores, reading periodicals, and doing computer research," he enthusiastically stated with authority.

We found a considerable amount of information from many sources and spent the next six months reading magazines, periodicals, and a handful of books. The combination of my personal experience as an adoptee combined with the new knowledge gained from reading greatly increased our insights and wisdom about all facets of adoption.

I contacted the Census Bureau of Statistics to find out the type of information that was available in official government records, but I was greatly disappointed to learn that only records over fifty years old were public. Their records were on ancient microfilm. The process of looking at them was tedious and required special equipment and the assistance of a clerk. None of the records could be removed. Adoption records throughout the United States were legally sealed and unavailable for public viewing. The process of searching through public census records accomplished nothing.

My initial failures to make any progress made me realize that an adoption search was likely to be a long, tedious, complex process. My adoption secrets were buried so deep and long ago in the federal bureaucracy that it might be a mystery impossible to solve.

While casually scanning the library archives, I ran across an encouraging article by Jean Paton stating that reuniting mothers with their adopted children was a wonderful natural event that should be encouraged. She was one of the first to lobby members of Congress for open adoption records. She mentioned *The Adoption Triangle* by Arthur D. Sorosky, Annette Baran, and Reuben Pannor; *Orphan Voyage* by Ruthena Hill Kittson; and *Twice Born* by Betty Jean Lifton as inspiring personal stories of adoption because they provided a good summary of some of the legal and political issues of their day that prevented most adopted children from finding their biological roots. It was reassuring to know that others shared my feelings about adoption, but it was disappointing to find out that so many laws had been written to protect the rights of the birth mothers at the expense of their abandoned children.

Martin took a different approach. He was analytical and primarily interested in learning about some of the scientific, statistical, legal, political, and social aspects of adoption, but, over time, gradually learned to recognize the emotional and psychological depth of the issue for adoptees like myself and other family members directly involved.

He was particularly captivated by the Minnesota Twin Family Study at the University of Minnesota, which seeks to identify genetic and environmental influences on the development of psychological traits. The value of the research was the ability to estimate the inheritability of certain traits, including academic ability, personality and interests, family and social relationships, mental and physical health, and other physiological measurements. Researchers had also studied the prevalence of psychopathology, substance use, divorce, leadership, and other traits. The relevance of the studies pertained to the importance of heredity as a determining factor in shaping our physical appearance, mental acuteness, preferences, personal characteristics, and personality. Researchers found the similarities between twins raised in separate homes with different parents to be remarkably strong.

The research gave significant weight to the importance of genetics as a key factor in determining physical appearance and attributes, as well as personalities and inherent abilities. Their findings caused him to think in depth about my missing ancestry and provided a positive catalyst to continue reading.

"These studies have amplified my interest in knowing something about your genetic background. I never thought you were a good match with your adopted parents for many reasons, but now I know why. Let's use dogs for an analogy. I think your birth parents were golden retrievers, but you were adopted by German shepherds with genetic attributes and psychopathological characteristics much different from yours. This is why you didn't feel close to your adopted parents. Your real ancestors originated from another part of Europe on a different branch of the family tree. It is obvious that each breed of dog was bred for a unique purpose. From an evolutionary standpoint, this is somewhat true of humans adapting to distinct environments, climates, and food sources," he explained with enthusiasm.

"The Minnesota twin study seems to provide hard evidence of the genetic inheritance of personality traits and abilities, as well as physical attributes, but American society has strongly discouraged us from focusing on genetics as a determinant of human potential to prevent prejudice or profiling. When it comes to studying human potential, the scientific method of learning is generally ignored when it comes to social research and academic learning." He admitted his own naïveté and lack of prior awareness.

"I can see now from the perspective of an adopted child why genetics is such an important determinant. The twin studies prove that genetics provide the blueprint from which individuals develop physically and mentally," he quoted directly from a scientific journal.

The more Martin read about adoption, the more convinced he became that searching for my biological mother was an acceptable thing to do from a scientific standpoint. He was proud of his own family histories from England and Norway and hoped I could also eventually share some of the same enthusiasm about my ancestors.

During the initial phase of my research, I was shy and self-conscious about referring to myself as an adoptee in public. Asking for advice and assistance from others was difficult because I was reluctant to draw attention to myself and unaccustomed to speaking in public. I was prone to panic attacks when placed in the limelight. For that reason, I appealed to Martin to be my spokesperson and emotional guide. He responded positively, and he was a constant source of good advice and moral support. He willingly talked with librarians, bookstore clerks, or others whenever I felt unreasonably nervous or vulnerable.

In the beginning, my feelings of guilt had prevented me from taking action, knowing that my adoptive parents would strongly object, but I remained steadfast in my goals and certain that my decision was the right course of action.

Many of my readings discussed relationships between adoptees and their adopted parents. Others discussed the sentiments of the entire range of people involved with the adoption process, not just the adoptee. This broader perspective taught me empathy and increased my appreciation for the motives and values of others. It was informative to learn that adopted children suffered the same psychological trauma, feelings of detachment and insecurities, and a lack of bonding with their adopted parents. Adoptees worldwide shared a common set of behavioral responses to the conditions that traumatized them. It was identical to my situation as a child.

Adoption had potential to create contentious legal, financial, and inheritance issues that were often difficult to resolve. Poor parenting, ethical concerns, criminality, divorce, and difficulties between adopted and biological siblings were also topics of concern.

The media had highlighted awareness of adoption issues in America for many decades as part of a passionate, unresolved national debate. Open adoption records, public funding of abortion, welfare for single parents, same-sex adoption couples, and adoption of foreign babies were a few of the issues that moved opposing moral, ethical, and religious choices. These debates had raged for years. Many who participated had been openly hostile to opposing points of view. Politicians often stated their opinions during campaigns, and many key issues were left simmering and unresolved when individual states held views contrary to federal laws.

From my perspective as an adoptee, national media attention was biased toward the rights of birth mothers at the expense of their unwanted children. Baby seals clubbed to death by Eskimos attracted more media attention and public response than the killing and disposal of human fetuses.

Maturity increased my awareness of world events, public policies, and adoption issues. I could sense that a new phase called midlife was now beginning. I felt differently and viewed the world with a higher understanding. Motherhood provided me with a new point of view that helped me see the world more realistically. I was no longer someone else's child. I was a mother with a child of my own. My son was now the next generation. Marriage had increased my responsibilities. I was more accountable to others, and more people relied on me. Turning thirty-one years old was a wake-up call that inspired a sudden sense of urgency to get some important things accomplished. My life had evolved and changed as I passed through a gateway into adulthood. I had become wiser and attentive enough to know that my life and future happiness of all adoptees could be greatly influenced by which laws were passed.

Rosella was a volunteer for Birthright International, a charitable organization that provided nonjudgmental support to women distressed by unplanned pregnancy. I viewed her position in a new light with more sympathy and understanding of her personal beliefs. Her kindly advice and voice of experience as the mother of an adoptee herself assuredly calmed the spirit of many crestfallen and disconsolate unwed mothers by convincing them it was far more favorable to raise their child as a single mother or have their child adopted rather than abort the fetus. I was thankful she had a concern for the rights of all unborn children and adoptees like me because, without others like her, I would not exist.

The more my husband and I shared ideas with each other, the more informed we became about legal and moral issues. As a team, we were gradually evolving into social, psychological, and legal specialists. As our knowledge progressively increased, we became more aware of the negative effects of separation syndrome on the psychological well-being of adopted children. Separation from birth parent effects were often broadly distributed and comparable to the proverbial stone thrown into a pond to create an ever-expanding negative circle of influence. Birth parents, adoptive parents, grandparents, foster families, siblings, expanded family members, and even close friends all had potential to be affected. The more predictable the psychological concerns were, the closer they paralleled my experiences.

Differences between natural biological parents and adopted parents seemed to illustrate two separate approaches to parenthood. Biological parents seemed to willingly encourage independence at an earlier age and typically treat separation from their children by age twenty-one as a natural and logical step in life toward independence and maturity. Whereas adopted parents were more reliant and uncomfortable about letting their adopted children leave home because they believed their responsibilities as adopted parents should continue for their entire lifetime. They tended to overcompensate by remaining more closely attached after maturity.

Thinking about my adoption increased my curiosity and appreciation for my adopted parents and the important role they played in my life. I wondered if it were embarrassing for them to be sterile and what their motives were for adopting me. I wondered if my father were the instigator and why they had selected me because it seemed like an exaggerated, mysterious fairy tale when they said they had selected me from among many children at an orphanage. Thinking about my adopted parents reminded me that it was important to always unconditionally honor and love them by avoiding hurting their feelings. The only way I could do this was by keeping my research secret from them.

I was curious to know if they had perceived me as their adopted daughter because Rosella had often remarked about my personality and appearance as being different from her own. When I performed badly, she had blamed my behavior on bad genetics rather than admit a failure of her parenting skills. Our relationship as mother and daughter was not ideal, but I still never stopped respecting and loving her for the many positive things she had done for me. Regardless of what her opinions were of me, I knew it would be painful for her knowing that I wanted to find my birth mother. I resolved to avoid breaking her trust.

Mario had a terrible temper and a short fuse. He visited his psychiatrist Dr. Brandis regularly to deal with his fears and anxieties and help him control his temper, but I wasn't sure it did much good because it was common for him to instantly become extremely angry and agitated at the slightest irritation. Even minor infractions made him angry, and, when they did, he would yell threatening accusations and intimidate the perpetrator. At times, I had lived in fear that he might even become violent toward me.

He would consider my desire to find my biological roots a subversive, heretical activity. His reaction to this idea would be highly predictable. He would become extremely angry and threaten to write me out of his will, as he already had many times in the past. My only choice was to respect his opinions and maintain a positive relationship with him for perpetuity. It was a high priority for me to remain compliant and obedient to his wishes. Despite all of his troubles and angry disposition, he was still my adopted father, and he had been good to me in many ways.

Martin and I had been researching the topic of adoption for over six months, and I still knew absolutely nothing about my origins. All of our research and discussions had encouraged me to think about new ideas driven solely by speculation. Thinking about my adoption was a never-ending complex story and bulky maze of intuitive ideas, dreams, and fantasies. My imagination often went spinning wildly out of control because all I had to go on was intuition. I was living in a vacuum and suffering from an identity crisis because I had no facts or details about any aspects of my true self. I knew nothing about my birth parents, their relationship to each other at the time I was conceived, or even if they were even still alive. My thoughts wandered aimlessly whenever I thought about them and why they didn't keep me. Were they too young to get married or simply not in love? And was it simply fate that Mario and Rosella Romano adopted me?

Writer Jean Paton, founder of Orphan Voyage, had inspired me when I read that she strongly endorsed the idea that it was an inalienable human right of all children to know something about their birth parents. She was confident that reuniting adopted children with their birth mothers was the appropriate thing to do. She had been willing to attack any aspect of the law that kept biological children from finding their roots. She was a great inspiration and catalyst who rekindled a deep sense of optimism and enthusiasm by encouraging me to keep trying.

I continued to actively research every site where I might find records of value to assist me. After reading a handful of library books and visiting the Federal Bureau of the Census in Denver, I wrote to the Milwaukee County Department of Health and Human Services to inquire about the types of records they had available. I checked with the Wisconsin Vital Records Office in Madison, but learned that, by state statute, they didn't accept telephone orders for birth certificates or other vital records and did not under any circumstances provide free searches or verifications. I wrote to the Milwaukee Probate Clerk because they maintained all records regarding estates, trusts, guardianships, protective placements, and other court records for children under eighteen years old. These records also included neglect and termination of parental rights, adoption, ordinance violations, and review hearings. Each agency I called responded by suggesting I contact other state, federal, or county agencies that I knew nothing about. Public record keeping was a very scattered and frustrating affair.

I telephoned the Milwaukee Register of Deeds and found that many documents were available, including copies of birth, death and marriage records, real estate transactions, probate instruments, military discharges, transfer taxes, financing statements, and other important transactions. They explained that their mission was to provide an accurate and secure archive that was accessible to the public for a reasonable cost.

I called the State Board of Health and Human Services Department, but their information was confidential. I was told adoptees were not allowed to see their records. I was left with cold feelings about their honesty and potential for financial and political corruption.

I contacted the county courthouse, but so many separate state and county organizations kept records that I had a hard time distinguishing one from another. Even if I could produce a name to get started, it would take months of research because many of the old files weren't computerized.

I contacted Adoptees' Liberty Movement Association, whose mission was to provide information to adopted adults and birth parents seeking each other when the adopted child exceeded age eighteen. Opposed to sealed records, the organization was actively lobbying for open records at the national level and keeping original, unaltered birth certificates in the public record. They maintained a reunion registry databank of information on adopted persons and birth parents searching for their genetic antecedents.

The disadvantage of putting my name on any public adoptee list was a loss of control of my situation. It could turn into a disaster if my birth mother was mentally insane, a prostitute in terrible health, an alcoholic, drug addict, or convicted criminal who might suddenly show up on my doorstep without warning. I was guardedly reluctant to have my life disrupted unnecessarily. For those reasons, I vowed to be cautious and keep my distance before initiating contact on my terms. My personal life was private, and I didn't want an intermediary, adoption organization, or news outlet looking to sensationalize my situation to approach me.

I wrote letters to every agency to verify their list of potential records, including Saint Joseph Hospital, where I was born, optimistically hoping to obtain a copy of my original birth certificate with my mother's maiden name on it. I devised a clever strategy to expedite my request by falsely claiming a Dr. Bruce Lippman in Glenwood Springs needed a thorough investigation of my family medical history to diagnose and recommend treatment of an unspecified ailment.

The incoherence, passiveness, and lack of empathy from agency employees in response to my telephone calls was very discouraging when considering the large number of public records potentially available, but requests from adoptees were automatically rejected by law and statute.

Despite all of my telephone calls, I still had nothing to show for my efforts. Another uneventful month had passed quietly. I finished typing a dozen letters with additional questions, pessimistically placed them in the outgoing mailbox, and waited to see if anyone were willing to help me.

First Clue

Dear Mom, My adopted mother Rosella is the only person who knows anything about you, but she has shared very little information with me. There are many things I want to know about you. I would like to know what you look like, where you live, and what you are doing today. Are you married? Do you have a family? Did you ever regret your fateful decision not to keep me? Was life difficult for you at the time when I was born? Did you ever grieve for your child or suffer psychological trauma resulting from your decision to allow someone else to raise me? I think about you often and hope life is better for you now. Love, Judy

"THIS IS OUR LAST visit. I'm not going to live much longer," Rosella said softly. A tear was in her eye. She believed her cancer had returned.

Chemotherapy made her nauseated and listless. She was pessimistic about the future and lived with the fear that she was going to die soon. She was lonely and reaching out for sympathy and emotional support.

I assured her that I would be arriving shortly to give her support. I should have hugged her the minute I stepped off the plane from Colorado, but my arms were full of packages and luggage. We had never been in the habit of hugging or physically comforting each other even though she had obvious needs. Living in different states had severely restricted the time we had to spend together. Rosella disliked flying, and, for that reason, she had encouraged me to fly to Wisconsin every year to celebrate her birthday. Closing my retail shop was a financial burden, Michael was enrolled in school and involved with extracurricular activities, and Martin had an esteemed job designing and administering ski areas. It was difficult making more than one or two trips to Milwaukee each year.

As a counselor to unwed mothers at Birthright International, Rosella had many personal stories to tell about adoption. She talked with her clients about her experiences as the parent of an adopted child and the history of *Roe v. Wade*, which had inflamed passions and inspired activism on both sides of the issue. Talking about adoption was something Rosella did every day at work, but a topic she seldom discussed with me.

I wondered if Rosella had any dark secrets about my birth parents that she had intentionally withheld from me. Now that she was feigning death, I was hoping she would confess before it was too late. Knowing she was my only connection to my past increased my anxieties and fueled my curiosity. The knowledge she only had a short time to live encouraged me to initiate a conversation with her about adoption.

"Is there anything you can tell me about my past that you haven't told me before?" I asked inquisitively.

Rosella stared at the floor and paused to think before taking a deep breath and blurting out her confession. "I have intentionally kept some information about your birth parents secret, but, now that I am dying, it is important for me to get this burden off my shoulders. When you were two years old, I saw a wedding announcement and picture in the newspaper that caught my attention because it led me to believe that your birth parents may have married each other. The names of the bride and groom were similar to your birth parents. I have always been intrigued about whether they were the married couple pictured in the wedding announcement. I cut the article out of the newspaper and saved it, but I'm not sure what happened to it," she recalled speculatively.

Hearing this information for the first time was an emotional blockbuster that made my head spin. Perhaps my parents were legally married. I tried desperately to appear calm on the surface, but inside I was dancing and jumping up and down for joy as if I had just won a million dollars. My body language was excited but awkward. I stuttered and stammered, but no words came out because I didn't know what to say. I was physically still while my brain was racing at full speed in neutral. I had just been presented with the greatest gift of knowledge about my birth parents I had ever received.

The information was shocking because it seemed entirely possible. I stood still with my hands on my hips and my mouth wide open. My eyes never blinked as I carefully digested every word.

Contemplating the idea of my birth parents united in marriage gave me warm feelings in my heart when I thought about what the odds were of this happening. My intuition had always led me to believe they did get married because there was no evidence to refute it. The idea that my parents might be married to each other was a huge catalyst that drastically intensified my desire to learn more about them, but I didn't quiz my mother any further about the issue because I didn't want to offend her by appearing excessively eager to find them. I tried to appear calm on the outside while hyperventilating on the inside, knowing a display of too much enthusiasm was inappropriate.

Without prompting, she unexpectedly revealed another tidbit of information. "I vaguely recall that your birth mother's name was Becky, Rebecca, Roberta, Loretta Mayor or Maier, or something like that. Her last name started with the letter M. I don't remember your birth father's name, but I am certain it was Italian," she added matter-of-factly.

Her words stopped me cold, as if I had just suffered a brain freeze. I knew in an instant that my life would never be the same because I finally had a valid clue to begin my adoption search. My mind was racing as I digested the explosive effect of this unexpected information, and I was suddenly eager to renew my adoption search. I desperately wanted to know if Rosella was holding back any more information from me, but considered it impolite to ask any more probing questions.

I felt like spontaneously pumping my fist in the air and dancing to rock and roll music, but concealed my emotions that were tightly bottled up inside of me. I exercised extreme control to remain poker-faced to prevent my exuberant joy from bubbling over in front of Rosella.

During the long flight home to Colorado, I thought long and hard about what I had learned. Rosella's comments had sent an unexpected shock wave through my system. An adrenalin rush generated by an uncontrollable excitement buoyantly made my skin tingle. All of my senses were overstimulated. I had the sensation that I had experienced the most critical turning point of my life. I now had a radical choice to make. I could choose to ignore what Rosella had told me and continue living the way I always had or take an abrupt and uncertain fork in the path of life leading in an unknown direction toward a mysterious future and uncertain fate. In my mind, there was no doubt about which path I would choose.

Social Worker

Dear Mom, There are so many reasons why I want to find you. I am intrigued to know something about your background, medical history, cultural heredity, and family roots. I am curious to know if we look alike or have some of the same habits and personal preferences. I have no bad feelings toward you for what happened to me, but I am curious to know why you didn't keep me. As far as my own life is concerned, I feel responsible and mature. I am over thirty years old, and, as an adult, I am no longer searching for someone to replace my adopted mother. Love, Judy

I SAT IN A recliner in the living room and inserted Martin's ebony letter opener from Africa into the corner of the envelope sent to me from Milwaukee County Court. "Your request is denied. The information you are seeking is confidential. As an adoptee, you cannot view the records you are requesting without a judge's order or legal search warrant. Each specific document must be named in the request to prevent open-ended searches and phishing expeditions. Adoptees have no rights or privileges to access our proprietary database unless one of the two conditions above is met. A fee is required to pay for the cost of the search and reproduction of documents."

Every telephone call and letter to the courts and state agencies in Milwaukee over the past twelve months had been summarily rejected in simple form letters and coldhearted denials, often without explanation. None of the respondents offered any encouragement, sympathy, or helpful advice, and some never responded at all. Each agency made it perfectly clear that I had no personal or special rights as an adoptee and the laws of privacy were strictly enforced to keep it that way. One agency rudely issued a warning highlighting a list of the penalties and fines for those who violate the state's privacy laws.

Thoughts about my birth mother had been shaped by childhood

dreams and fantasies that had remained constant for over three decades. Suddenly, the increased probability of meeting her in person
was stirring my confidence and causing me to be more variable, less
certain, and even frightened at times. My emotions were becoming less
stable and tending to swing erratically from high to low. The frequency
and intensity of these drastic mood swings from unbounded happiness and euphoria to panic and fear was becoming worrisome because
I perceived the opportunity for disappointment and failure equal to the
potential reward.

It was summer, and we had decided to take a rare driving vacation
to Milwaukee to celebrate Rosella's sixty-seventh birthday. I stopped
at a local bakery on our way into town to buy six German chocolate
cupcakes and one white candle. She was in a good mood and happy to
see us, especially her grandson Michael.

I helped her prepare a garden salad with fresh pineapple, beef roast
with baked potatoes, vegetables, and homemade bread. After dinner, I
lit the candle on her cake, and we all sang "Happy Birthday." She was
delighted with the attention and companionship. "How old are you
Grandma? What did you wish for?" Michael inquired to know after
she blew out the flame.

The following day, we attended Sunday mass at Saint Albert
Church with Father Hennen officiating. After the service, we took
Rosella to Mitchell Park Horticultural Conservatory. Rosella loved to
smell the beautiful flowers and view the impressive beds of red tulips
and yellow daffodils. We left the conservatory and took a pleasant drive
through the countryside to view some of the prosperous farms that
characterized the rural Wisconsin landscape. It was a wonderful day
filled with pleasant activities.

Rosella was happy and enjoyed the attention we gave her. She was
starved for companionship and feeling talkative. I listened politely, but
added little to the conversation. Instead, I drifted in and out of consciousness because I was preoccupied with my own thoughts about
how to find my birth mother. I was motivated to think about her when
I was in Milwaukee because this was where she had been living when I
was born, and it was a good place to begin my adoption search.

I was daydreaming about the name of the social worker who had
handled my adoption case over thirty years ago. Rosella had made fun

of her in an amusing anecdote when she had besmirched the woman's name by intentionally mispronouncing it with a loud, coarse-sounding accent to make fun of her German heritage and uncouth personality. Ever since then, I had always wondered if the woman were as gruff and mean-spirited as Rosella had implied. "Do you remember the name of the social worker who handled my adoption?"

"Her name was Gertrude Schweinhaus. She worked for Catholic Social Services. I doubt if she would remember you. She is probably retired by now," Rosella responded matter-of-factly.

I wondered if she were still alive and if she would remember me. Martin and I retired to bed early to discuss what to do about the social worker in the privacy of the bedroom. The idea of interviewing her sent incredible shivers down my spine. I was petrified about the idea of meeting her in person, knowing a meeting would be very awkward because she would be certain to be suspicious of my motives.

Martin summed up his advice to me with an analytical approach to the situation and discussed the alternatives. "If you want to contact the social worker, you need to first develop a plan and prepare a strategy on how to implement it. Meeting her will be a onetime shot. It will be difficult for you to ever get a second appointment once you have had your opportunity in the ring. You need to be thoroughly briefed and rehearsed about what to say and how to say it. You don't want to leave anything to chance. If she is still working, she will only reserve a small amount of time for your appointment. You will need to get to the point quickly and avoid talking about frivolous, unrelated issues that consume your allocated time. You must anticipate and avoid any topics or questions that may provoke or irritate her," Martin counseled in a calm, businesslike manner.

To further illustrate his point, he grabbed a clean sheet of paper and began jotting down a list of questions and a clear strategy that described my goal and some of the tactics I should use. His explanations and terminology were engrained and well rehearsed based on his routine business meetings with lawyers and accountants. He enthusiastically outlined his ideas in vertical columns, surrounded with little notes and diagrams and arrows to help me visualize what he was talking about. He summarized his thoughts by explaining how professional competitors used "psycho-cybernetics" to prepare for chess matches, athletic events, and court cases. I admired his ability to visualize and plan a comprehensive, premeditated approach to complex situations, but, the minute he put down the pencil, I got confused again. What he had said made sense, but I found it difficult to concentrate. Some aspects of his abstract thinking went over my head because they seemed unnecessarily complicated.

Together, we hammered out a written list of well-thought-out questions to ask the social worker and rehearsed how to ask them without causing alarm. I was happy with the plan of action, but afraid I would get confused or even panic if she became unfriendly or uncooperative. When we were finished, I copied each question on a clean sheet of paper, and we reviewed them one at a time. Martin made me rehearse each one aloud.

"Will you please attend the meeting with me?" I pleaded for emotional support.

Martin willingly accepted the challenge. "In order to discover the truth, detectives must practice the elegant art of detection with a perspicacious mind. They must deliberately scrutinize the evidence and contemplate questions that remain unasked. You play the role of naïve adoptee on a social visit. I will supplement and enhance your interrogation technique."

His criticisms of my presentation were sharp, honest, and direct. "Your tone of voice, body language, and facial expressions are very important during the interview. Pretend you are a performer, and pay close attention to details to extract the most information. She will be on guard and distrustful of your motives. To overcome this, you must maintain your composure and avoid saying anything that might cause suspicion. You should remain friendly and upbeat, maintain a complimentary tone, and express a sincere interest in Miss Schweinhaus as a person," he emphasized.

My goal was to walk out of the meeting with more information than I had before the interview. My strategy was to stay focused, stay on pace, remain friendly, lead the discussion in the direction I wanted it to go, and coerce or trick Miss Schweinhaus into divulging confidential information that would help me uncover my past. Martin insisted I rehearse each question with him to avoid allowing the social worker to throw me off guard. I felt good. I felt confident. Never before had I prepared this well for a meeting of any kind. I felt organized and slept very well that night.

It was Martin's strategy to pretend to be well informed about my biological parents to see if I could falsely tease her into accidentally confirming my suppositions. By speaking confidently and stating everything I already knew to be true might trick her into agreeing with what I had said. Even a denial could be used as a solid confirmation of fact. We ranked each question by priority in case we ran out of time. As a final backup, Martin handed me a powerful mini-tape recorder to conceal in my purse.

To reduce my anxiety, I took several deep breaths before telephoning CSS to make an appointment with Miss Schweinhaus.

Her secretary Fanny O'Rear startled me with her unconventional response. "Ya dere, hey! Ya betcha! Believe you me, Schweinhaus has worked in Brew City her whole darn life, hey. Pretty soon she aina gonna be comin' to Friday night fish fries or nothin' anymore. She's leaving Mwah-kee and headin' up nord for good. Aina gonna be the same around her without her, hey. Are you comin' by for her retirement party or what?"

Her strong Milwaukee blue-collar accent and poor grammar surprised me. It had been ten years since I had lived in Mwah-kee, as the locals called it, and I had completely forgotten how much slang the average resident used. I exaggerated when I explained that the purpose of my visit was to casually drop in to thank her for the excellent assistance she had provided my family many years ago. I arranged for a two o'clock appointment on Friday afternoon, exactly one week before her planned retirement party. My timing was impeccable. The hand of fate had blessed me because she would not have had access to her files after retirement. The opportunity to interview her would have been lost forever.

I had crossed an important mental hurdle by taking the first positive step in my adoption search, and I was feeling particularly lucky because Miss Schweinhaus was the only known link to my past. I hoped she could recall something about my case because even the smallest clue might be helpful. My personal interview was going to be the once-in-a-lifetime opportunity, exactly as Martin had predicted.

The more times I practiced reading my questions, the more pessimistic I became because the fear of rejection was dominating my thoughts and making me anxious and ill at ease. Even if Miss Schweinhaus did remember me, she was very unlikely to disclose any new information because my file was proprietary and closed to public scrutiny by law. My feelings were the same as any lost child accidentally separated from her mother in a shopping mall during the holiday rush. My lips were likely to be quivering and hands shaking while speaking through sobs and tears, but, at thirty-one years old, why would anyone believe me if I told her I had lost my birth mother? Yet, at the root of my problem, I really was a small, lonely, misplaced child. I really had lost my birth mother and didn't know where to find her.

Martin was an experienced interviewer and good at profiling people. He seemed to have a natural ability to evaluate others. His description of Miss Schweinhaus brought me back to reality. "Miss Schweinhaus is of German descent based on the spelling and pronunciation of her last name. I visualize a humorous stereotype of an older woman who never married because she could never find a male companion who was good enough for her. Choosing never to marry a man is proof that she is uncompromising and an indicator that she does not negotiate, which contributes to her power and dominance over others. She is the victim of an oppressive mother and family caregiver. Her life has probably been devoid of romantic relationships. She is sexually and emotionally frigid and prone to frumpiness and depression. She is a devout Catholic. A strong conviction to her moral and religious beliefs guides her, and she almost certainly cares deeply about moral virtues. You should expect her to be emotionally cold and distant, domineering, and suspicious of the motive for wanting to meet with her. She will wear gray clothes, avoid smiling, and sit with a stiff, formal posture. She will have strong conservative values on some issues and be a tough negotiator who will follow all privacy rules and regulations exactly as written. Her philosophy will be identical to the goals and objectives of the agency that hired her," he envisioned confidently.

His mental descriptions and prognostication of a strong opponent helped me form a mental image of a strict, inflexible, unsympathetic person. If I were David and she were Goliath, as Martin had led me to believe, I would need to be especially strong and clearheaded and practice standing up for my rights. Visualizing a tough opponent was a very powerful motivating tool. It was exactly what successful athletic coaches did every week to prepare their team. I could see now the value of thorough preparation, as Martin had been preaching to me all along.

Interview

Dear Mom, Today is an important day for me. I am unsettled and nervous because I scheduled a meeting with the social worker who handled my adoption case over thirty years ago. She is the one who matched me with my adopted parents Mario and Rosella Romano and the only person who can tell me something about my past. I hope she will be informative and tell me a few new things about you. I think about you every day and wonder what your life was like when I was born. I am curious to know if you ever met the social worker or know anything about her. Love Judy

"THERE IS NO NEED for you to know anything about your birth mother or her background. Your adoption is a closed book. You are an ungrateful orphan who is showing no respect for your adopted parents. This meeting is over. Get out," she said rudely as she physically shoved me out of her office and slammed the door on my heels.

It was a terrible nightmare. I awoke covered in perspiration. I had been worried and had difficulty sleeping throughout the night. Many unresolved issues about my adoption were spinning around in my head. I had dreamed that Miss Schweinhaus was a mean, domineering woman wearing a gray Nazi uniform. She carried a small leather horse-whip and refused to allow me to speak. She stated emphatically that she would not help me and showed no compassion for my situation. She even threatened to sue me if I continued with my investigation.

I shuddered as I washed my face with cold water to increase my alertness and bring myself back to reality. I was glad it was just a dream. I sat down and completed my notes for the planned two o'clock meeting in downtown Milwaukee. I was nervously looking forward to getting this engagement over because I knew it would be challenging and possibly disappointing. I hoped Miss Schweinhaus wasn't going to be as bad as I had visualized in my dream. To avoid embarrassment and conflict, I was seriously considering changing my plan and simply dropping by to say hello because it would be far less traumatic.

I prayed for personal guidance, strength, understanding, and intelligence. I hoped God would help me find the right answers because the powers propelling me forward were very commanding and spiritual. I was motivated to know the truth by a mysterious yearning to be whole as a human being. My desire to find my birth mother was deep-rooted and strong, just like the birds instinctively compelled to fly south in the winter and turtles that migrated across oceans to lay their eggs. A basic human instinct to assure my survival drove me. The requisite I felt to positively identify myself was bubbling to the surface, like a large pool of magma below an active volcano. Thoughts about my adoption were dominating my subliminal consciousness and stimulating me to develop a rational way of thinking about it.

The best explanation I could find to support my behavior and way of thinking came from psychologist Abraham Maslow's hierarchy of needs ladder. He had explained that, if the majority of a person's basic needs were being met, he would concentrate on a higher level that deals with more esoteric needs. My life was simple and complete, and all of my basis needs were satisfied, thus leaving sufficient time and energy to take a step beyond basic secular life.

As I prayed, I looked into my own soul to look for the reasons why I was so tenaciously motivated to find my birth mother and concluded I possessed an innate desire to achieve self-awareness. It seemed natural to me that all people are born with a biological drive and survival instinct to be with their own kind. I rationalized that, if someone is parched, he is automatically driven to satisfy his thirst the way I was uncontrollably longing for contact with my birth mother.

My daydreams and prayers ended slowly. I felt calm and ready to face reality. I had informed Miss Schweinhaus' secretary that I was casually dropping by to congratulate Miss Schweinhaus on her retirement and express my gratitude for my successful adoption. Somehow, I doubted if she would have accepted my request for an appointment if I had told the truth. My strategy was to give the impression that I already knew many things about my birth parents to see if I could trap Miss Schweinhaus into confirming or denying the facts. I was worried she might attempt to dominate or humiliate me. To make my plan work successfully, I knew I had to conceal my assertiveness to avoid direct confrontation and circumvent any outward signs of weakness or shame by demonstrating confidence, poise, and strength. I planned to remain poker-faced and observe her body language as well as listen to her words.

Martin and I left the house feeling calm and confident in anticipation of arriving early and avoiding getting caught in traffic. I was anxiously awaiting our meeting until nervousness unexpectedly returned, and panic and stage fright besieged me. We arrived at Miss Schweinhaus' office fifteen minutes early. I selected a conservative navy blue dress; Martin wore a dark business suit, white shirt, and blue tie.

Fanny O'Rear was a short blonde who was fifty pounds overweight. A large glass jar filled with candies was sitting on the corner of her desk. Her words instantly broke the tension.

"Hey, welcome. Believe you me, I gotcha down for the two o'clock appointment with Gertrude, hey. How's youz guys doing? Glad-ta meet-cha! How bout dat Mwah-kee Brewers baseball team last night? My wacky husband says ya-gotta drink a shot-a brandy and a brewski every inning to survive those games, hey."

Miss Schweinhaus looked very much like the women I had envisioned in my dreams. Her office was drab without decorations or windows. Her hair was tightly pulled back in a bun and exactly matched the color of her faded gray suit. A robust woman, she was above average in height and without makeup. Her movements were precise and deliberate. She sat very straight and erect in her stiff-backed chair, giving the impression she was accustomed to intimidating others and prepared to defend her personal space.

She ordered us to sit in the two, colorless, metal chairs directly in front of her desk and stared at me with a stern expression on her pale, wrinkled face, as if she were scanning for signs of weakness or guilt. In my imagination, I viewed her as a boxer terrorizing the opponent before a fight. When she slid her chair back and reached down to open the bottom drawer of her gray file cabinet, I stealthily reached into my purse and turned on the digital voice recorder. She familiarized herself with the contents of the folder before turning to address me. When I thought the timing was right, I launched into my carefully rehearsed remarks.

"What a joy it is to finally meet you after all these years. It was by the grace of God and your wisdom and foresight that my life has turned out so positive. Thank you for selecting Mario and Rosella Romano as my adopted parents. They are wonderful people, and they provided me with a very normal, satisfying childhood. I am eternally grateful and content with the way my life has turned out. Congratulations on your worthwhile and memorable career with CSS. I wish you all the best in retirement."

I was thrilled with my own performance. My words had come out even better than I had expected. I continued speaking as quickly as I could to get the small talk behind us as Martin had suggested. I briefed her on my childhood, education, career, marriage, and son Michael. I concluded by telling her about my business and beautiful home in Colorado. My enthusiasm was real, and it showed.

Miss Schweinhaus remained reserved and aloof throughout my initial presentation. I wasn't sure if she were listening when it dawned on me that we had nothing in common. She had no husband or children. She didn't live in a beautiful part of the country surrounded by natural beauty and wildlife. She had never been skiing, fishing, horseback riding, hiking in the wilderness, or rafting on dangerous whitewater rivers.

I decided to quickly wrap up my introductory remarks, but, when I paused to take a breath, Miss Schweinhaus startled me with her powerful authoritative voice. "I remember you very well because your adoption was the most complex situation I ever handled. It was my first attempt. Over the years, no other case was as contentious or had as many extenuating circumstances as yours," she said bluntly as if I had been the cause of her problems.

Without looking down, I nervously pushed the tape recorder closer without drawing any attention to my actions.

"I'm retiring and moving next door to my parents in Manitowoc next week," Gertrude said defensively, as if she were expecting me to challenge her decision.

Her comments provided an excellent opportunity to jump into the conversation. I spoke confidently and gradually transitioned into the subject I wanted to discuss. "That is admirable of you to be willing to care for your elderly parents after you retire. Your receptionist informed me they moved to Wisconsin from Germany when you were young. My family history is a subject that interests me, but I know nothing about it," I replied honestly.

I quickly summarized everything Rosella had shared with me. I spoke affirmatively and consciously adjusted my tone of voice exactly as rehearsed, hoping to convince Miss Schweinhaus that I already knew many things about my birth parents.

"My birth mother's name was Becky (cough) Maier (cough)." I lowered my voice to a muffled whisper and intentionally butchered the pronunciation, interrupted by three loud coughs timed between syllables at precisely the right time. I hoped Miss Schweinhaus would correct me. The tactic worked perfectly.

"Rosella never should have told you your birth mother's maiden name was Rebecca Meyer. I am very disappointed knowing that Rosella breached security. Her name was to remain confidential." She sounded much like Sister Bronwyn bawling me out for chewing gum during class, but I was still frustratingly uncertain if Gertrude had said Maier, Mayor, Mayer, Meyer, Maier, or something else.

"I know that Rebecca played the violin and my father was a good athlete. I know many things about them. I have a good idea of who they were and what they looked like." I irritated her even more.

Miss Schweinhaus was appalled that Rosella had shared so much information with me. Each time I spoke, she glanced in the manila folder to verify the information I had given her. Finally, her patience was exhausted. She defensively gripped the folder tightly with both hands, as if expecting me to jump up and snatch it out of her hands.

I thought how ironic it was that she was sitting across from me within arm's reach, tightly holding the entire history of my life right in front of my face. The small manila folder she was grasping contained everything I wanted to know about my life, yet the information remained unattainable. It wasn't fair that a stranger was allowed to have this valuable information when I was not. The situation made me very cross with Miss Schweinhaus and angry at society. I felt like lashing out and seriously considered jumping out of my chair, ripping it out of her hands, and running out the door. I was becoming more agitated and irritable by the minute, but, like a good performer, I disguised my true feelings. I had taken a risk by coming here, and my strategy was working, so I stifled my emotions and continued speaking.

I made up another lie to see if Gertrude would fall for my ruse. "I know that Rebecca, like most young unmarried women of her time, was isolated from her friends and family before giving birth to me to shield her from public ridicule and maintain her social reputation. She was very lonely then," I stated confidently without any prior knowledge or reason to know if this were true.

"Rebecca was sent to the Booth Hill Home for Unwed Mothers for her own protection," she retorted rhetorically without changing her expression.

Bingo! She had accidentally given me an incredible clue. I was eager to research the name because I had no idea where Booth Hill was located, if it were still in existence, or if it had a current connection to CSS. I deceitfully left her with the impression this was something I already knew.

"Did my birth mother ever contact you to inquire about me, my whereabouts, or the condition of my health after I was born?" I inquired politely. I knew I would be exceedingly disappointed if the answer was no.

Miss Schweinhaus took some time to open another file drawer and sort through a second file. She flipped to the last page and used her finger as a guide. I uncomfortably sat on the edge of my chair and leaned forward, restlessly waiting to hear her response. It was tempting to lean over her shoulder and read the information myself. I nervously tapped my knee with my fingers. Time was passing quickly, and I was eager for the interview to continue.

"Your birth mother never signed our registry or inquired about you after you were born. As far as I am concerned, adoptions are permanent. I discourage reunions from ever happening," she said coldly.

Her unkind response was like a stinging welt from a leather belt on bare skin. Her words hung heavily in the air. I felt like someone had punched me in the stomach. My chest hurt. I felt injured knowing that my birth mother had never inquired about me. Throughout my childhood, I had always clung to the hope that she had missed me because she felt remorse. I was disappointed to learn that she had never inquired about me, but decided to add my own name to the registry book anyway. Gertrude begrudgingly complied, but strongly disapproved of my action. She was more guarded, leery, and skeptical about the purpose of my visit after that.

I suddenly felt emotionally disturbed and desperate about my situation. She held all the aces. They were right in front of me within my grasp. I couldn't stand the humiliation of being an adoptee any longer.

Miss Schweinhaus had determined my fate thirty-one years ago, and she was still controlling my destiny. She sat behind her desk and held my adoption files in her stingy, bony, wrinkled hands with crooked fingers. They were my files and more important to me than anyone else in the world, yet she steadfastly refused to share them with me. Internally, I weighed the advantages of going postal and forcing her to give me what was inherently mine.

Why did society give her the right and exclude me? I was angry with every politician who had ever voted to keep the identity of birth parents secret from their own babies and every coldhearted social worker and bureaucrat who enforced secrecy laws. The idea of intentionally separating defenseless babies from their mother's breast in exchange for a few political votes was a distressingly traumatic event certain to traumatize children too young to object. By the time the abandoned and forgotten children reached the age of reason, it was too late because the psychological damage caused by early separation had already been done.

It was impossible to conceal the identity of birth parents and hide their transgressions from their children without lying. From the adoptees' standpoint, the policy of privacy obscured the truth, and it could never build goodwill or friendships. It was definitely not beneficial to all concerned. Secrecy laws ignored Christian wisdom and humanitarian methods of problem solving. Strangers had severely manipulated my life, and they were still holding my history hostage. How was I going to find my birth mother?

The advice of my husband echoed through my head. "You need to face reality by accepting the fact that life is not fair and make every adjustment possible to create your own happiness."

Fanny unexpectedly stuck her head in the door and interrupted our meeting to remind me that my time had expired. Miss Schweinhaus had nothing more to say to me, and our meeting ended abruptly without any definitive conclusions. The more I thought about the interview and my forced isolation from reality as an adoptee, the more incensed I felt about it. Miss Schweinhaus knew my true biological history, yet she had begrudgingly refused to share it with me. I shut off the tape recorder, shook her hand, and walked out.

I was physically tired but mentally alert that evening. I slept fitfully and woke Martin by inadvertently kicking him in the back while dreaming I was wrestling with Miss Schweinhaus on the floor, trying to gain control of the manila folder containing my adoption records.

In the morning, I had a clearer vision about what it really meant to be banished forever into isolation and pounded into submission as an adoptee. The policies and secrecy laws passed to keep children separated from their true identity were finally becoming clear because they affected me personally. Until today, I had never understood the significance and powers of attorneys entrusted to strangers to make monumental life-changing decisions governing the lives of adopted children.

Miss Schweinhaus had made it clear that she was opposed to adoption reunions, and she had offered no empathy, condolences, remedies, or hope for the future. She never smiled, and she had remained expressionless during our entire conversation. I was acutely aware of the lifelong psychological harm done to infants when bonding opportunities with their birth mothers were denied because they were the same negative symptoms I had displayed as a child. I had sorely missed the opportunity to bond with my birth mother, and I was still projecting the same sorrowful maternal yearnings, as one of Harry Harlow's rhesus monkeys desperately clinging to a rag doll in a laboratory science experiment.

Nobody really cared about me as long as I obeyed the law and stayed out of my birth parents' lives. The idea that it takes a village to raise a child was a myth. It takes commitment, personal responsibility, and initiative, and I was the only individual who could make a difference in my life. If I really wanted to discover my roots, it was up to me and me alone.

Hello, Rebecca

Dear Mom, I think about you daily and intend to continue searching until I find you. My intuition is very strong and leads me to believe that you are somewhere close by. All I have to do is keep looking for clues until my dream comes true. I am beginning to feel like an adoption detective gathering facts, analyzing every angle and alternative, and following every lead to find you. Love, Judy

"I WONDER HOW MANY names starting with the letter M there are in Wisconsin. Why don't we start randomly cold-calling a few of them to see if anyone has a relative named Rebecca?" Martin said, ready to take charge and attack the problem.

It was an intriguing idea. I thumbed through the Milwaukee white pages and estimated the amount of time it would take to call all of the names beginning with M. The task looked insurmountable. During a quick scan, I didn't see anyone named Rebecca, but it was even more confusing than I thought because many of the first names were missing. Only the first initials were given.

"What should I say to the person who answers? I would be afraid to call a stranger and startle them by asking if we were related. They would be highly suspicious of my motives. I would be too nervous to tell them I was adopted. I couldn't do it. Besides, I only know Rebecca's maiden name. If she is married, she would have a new last name starting with a different letter," I replied, hopelessly skeptical.

"Yes, that is true, but what if you got lucky and found a close relative such as a sister or brother, aunt or uncle, or even a remote cousin or grandparent? Don't you think it's worth trying? If you are serious about being an adoption detective, you need to take the initiative," he countered with a disciplined sense of realism.

Our time in Milwaukee was quickly running out. We only had a few more days of vacation left. I carried the telephone book into the bedroom when Rosella wasn't looking and thumbed through the white pages before turning out the light. I was restless and couldn't sleep until I made a resolution to start making telephone calls first thing tomorrow morning while Rosella was attending mass.

The first name Rebecca was a very small clue, but enough to get started. I opened the telephone directory and turned to the first page. I perused each column from top to bottom carefully scanning each first and last name, hoping something would catch my attention. I closed my eyes tightly and tried to use my extrasensory powers to see if intuition or luck could provide a helpful surname, but nothing came to mind. It was a slow, tedious process that made my eyes throb. There were too many pages to count. Over five million people lived in the state of Wisconsin. I set the telephone book aside, closed my eyes, and let them rest. My eyes were tired from squinting, and my neck muscles were stiff from leaning over to read the fine print.

My recollection of Rebecca's maiden name was too vague to remember. I wrote down every conceivable combination of letters I could think of and compiled a short list of potential names and numbers that most closely matched my crude attempts at phonetic spelling. I was eager to begin, but my strong feelings of guilt were like a heavy anchor holding me back. I didn't feel good about keeping secrets from Rosella or hurting her feelings. Martin agreed that it wasn't necessary to tell her because we might never find her. Rebecca could be deceased or an undesirable character that I wouldn't want to meet.

"You need to make your local calls while we are in Wisconsin, or you will be charged a long-distance rate. You better start right away because this process may take a very long time because hundreds of names start with the letter M." He snapped me back to attention with a sudden sense of urgency.

His words startled me like a flash of light. I was horrified. I couldn't do it. It was impossible. There was no way I could call a complete stranger and ask if she were my birth mother.

"I have no idea what I would say if she answered the telephone without a formal introduction. Besides, I might give her a heart attack. I can't do it. Would you please make the first call for me and show me how?" I brushed my hair back and pleaded demurely while snuggling up close to remind him of my feminine charm.

Martin agreed to make the first call after Rosella slammed the door behind her. He was aware of the shy side of my personality and familiar with my panic attacks. He thumbed through my list and searched for his first victim. The calling process began.

"Good morning. Is Rebecca there?" he inquired.

"You have the wrong number," the caller said immediately and hung up the receiver.

He scratched the first name off the top of my list. Undeterred, Martin rapidly dialed several more numbers to inquire if any of the respondents had a relative named Rebecca.

"Hello, sir. I am doing family genealogical research, and I was hoping you could tell me if you have a relative named Rebecca who is about fifty years old?"

"No, but I have a cousin named Becky who lives in Oshkosh, Wisconsin, who recently turned forty," he replied in a friendly voice.

His tactic had worked like a charm. The man had cheerfully answered his questions, and he was curious to learn more. He was openly candid and helpful, and he even joked about a black sheep in the family he hoped Martin would intentionally leave off his family tree.

"Thank you very much. You have been very helpful." Martin scribbled the name and age of the woman in the margin.

I was having a difficult time containing my emotions. I was overly excited, exceedingly nervous, and far too out of control, possibly more so than I had ever been at any point in my life. What we were doing seemed like a shot in the dark. What if I really did track down my birth mother and discover who she was? What would I do then? I would be much too afraid to have a discussion with her.

In less than three hours, Martin had called most of the names on my list, but was beginning to question the process I was following. We could randomly continue by indiscriminately calling the names I had placed on my priority list based exclusively on intuition and hunches of whether I liked their names or methodically start on the first page of the telephone book, as Martin had originally suggested and gradually work toward the last.

The calling continued. I listened carefully by eavesdropping on the other line. Restricting my breathing to avoid making noise or causing suspicion was difficult. Each time someone answered, Martin repeated the same story until the conversations became routine. Nobody else had a relative named Becky or Rebecca.

My emotions took a dive. The lack of success left me disheartened and pessimistic. What were the chances of succeeding this way? We had located someone named Becky, but she was far too young. Maybe we were wasting our time because her maiden name was wrong.

The minute we saw Rosella's car returning, Martin hid his list of names and notes, turned on the television, and plunked down in a La-Z-Boy recliner while I vigorously vacuumed the living room carpet. I calmly greeted Rosella as she entered the house through the back door. I lazily stretched my arms above my head, pretending I had nothing to do.

"Welcome home. Can I carry in your groceries for you?" I nonchalantly artificially produced a big yawn.

We were expected at my friend Maggie Lowery's house for lunch, but I quietly implored Martin to stay home to continue the calling process while I was gone. Maggie was an exquisite host with an elegant dining room. The menu included broiled sweet spicy salmon with pineapple on roughly chopped cilantro laced rice, and a classic comfort chocolate cake dessert steeped in nostalgic sweetness with coconut-pecan frosting. For that reason, Erik wasn't very happy about staying home alone, but dejectedly agreed to do so.

The process of calling went fairly quickly. The majority of people were stay-at-home mothers and retired old men. About one in four didn't answer. Martin placed a check mark next to each name he called and crossed out the name if someone answered. He continued the process without interruption for one hundred names. None of them was rude or hung up on him. He was bored and hungry. He poured himself a Coca-Cola and ripped off a chunk of Gouda cheese and large piece of Italian bread before making the next call.

A male voice responded positively. "You must be referring to my sister. She is fifty years old and lives on a farm near Madison. She attended public schools in Milwaukee. She is a country girl who seldom comes to the city because she lives on a dairy farm. She and her husband stay home to milk the cows every day. They sell cheese and packaged honey at the co-op store. I would be glad to help you in any way that I can because I think doing a genealogical research is a creditable objective. I would get her telephone number for you, but I fell at the factory and broke my hip. It is painful for me to get out of my recliner," he said apologetically.

Martin made notes in a small notebook and hid it in his suitcase before returning all the pencils and telephone book to the desk drawer where he had found them. He leaned back in an easy chair and elevated his feet. He was innocently reading a newspaper article about the Green Bay Packers when Michael burst through the back door, followed by Rosella and me. It was evident from Martin's quirky smile and twinkle in his eye that something interesting had happened while I was gone. I turned the television up loud, motioned for Martin to come into the bedroom, and demanded to know what happened.

"Oh my gosh! You found her? Do you really think she is the right one?" I excitedly commanded him to tell me.

"I postponed calling her because I wanted you to be here when I made the call," Martin explained with a somber, controlled expression.

I was excited but panicky. My knees were weak, and my heart was racing. I felt jumpy and nervous. My left eye started twitching. My hands were shaking, and my palms were damp.

Rosella had one more errand to run before dinner. She needed to pick up some of her things at the dry cleaner and quietly excused herself. It was a short trip of less than five miles, and Michael had agreed to keep her company in exchange for the promise of an ice cream cone. The minute I heard the car leave the driveway, I insisted that Martin call the operator to get Rebecca's number.

He carefully repeated the number before hanging up and dialing. After the fourth ring, someone answered. I held my breath as I slowly picked up the telephone in the living room to eavesdrop. I unexpectedly panicked and started to cough when I overheard Martin ask to speak to Rebecca. Impulsively, I pushed the receiver into my stomach to avoid making an annoying distraction and violently started choking on my own saliva when a woman with a pleasant voice answered the telephone.

"Hello, this is Becky," the woman responded politely without any hint of suspicion.

It was she at last. Martin had found my birth mother. I listened intently to every word. I liked the tone of her voice, but she spoke softly, and my own heavy breathing was interfering with my hearing. I envisioned an attractive individual with brown hair standing over her kitchen sink. She was looking out the window at a picturesque pastoral scene with a large white barn, dairy cows in a green pasture, big trees, lilac bushes, and endless rows of corn. I created a mental image of how I thought her house was decorated and dreamed about what she looked like and what she was wearing.

Visualizing my birth mother living on a dairy farm was an exotic new lifestyle and unexpected image of a rural landscape that I had never imagined. I had no experience milking cows, picking corn, or riding tractors and wondered if we had anything in common. I was slowly drifting away from the conversation into my own fantasy. I slapped my cheek to wake up. I was ecstatic. I had finally found my birth mother. It was unbelievable. I had a sudden urge to interrupt the conversation, blurt out my name, and tell her I was her long-lost daughter Judy Ann, but I was catatonically frozen in an awkward position, unable to move my arms or speak coherently. My mouth was wide open, and my eyes were dilated. My heart was beating rapidly. My chest was heaving, and I was taking short, frequent breaths.

Rebecca listened passively to Martin making his pitch as he deceitfully explained that he was doing genealogy research. She was friendly and cooperative and reassured by the fact that he had already talked to her brother.

"I am trying to locate Rebecca Maier. I believe she is about fifty years old and related to my wife Judy. According to my records, she attended high school in Milwaukee about thirty years ago."

Rebecca confirmed she had graduated from high school in Milwaukee thirty years ago. She had been married for twenty-eight years and had three children. She had inherited a large dairy farm near Madison. She was content with her life on the farm and responded positively to all of his questions. Martin continued speaking slowly and calmly to avoid any display of emotion.

I was so excited that I nearly knocked the floor lamp over when I jumped up and pumped my fist into the air. I turned around in a complete circle dancing for joy. I had finally hit the jackpot. I had found my birth mother.

Assuming the mention of my birth date was a logical question to jog her memory, Martin asked if April 28 had any significance to her. She hesitated and then paused for a long time without saying anything. The silence and suspense of waiting for her to answer made me aware of how fast my heart was beating. Did his question strike a raw nerve? It was hard to tell. She was being awfully coy. I wondered if she were in shock. I was hoping she wouldn't panic and hang up the receiver. She must be terrified and feeling intensely guilty. What if she had married someone other than my birth father? My presence would be a total disruption in her life. No wonder she didn't want to confess. My presence was a bombshell certain to ruin a happy marriage.

Martin remained calm. Rebecca seemed like a pleasant person, but their conversation had come to a complete halt and didn't seem to be going anywhere. Martin was hoping not to offend her, give her reasons to panic, or end the conversation. After a lengthy deliberation, he finally asked the big question.

He paused for a long time before continuing cautiously and politely. His tone was sincere and somber. "Thank you for talking with me. You sound like a very nice person. I have something very important to ask you. My wife is an adoptee searching for her birth mother. Please don't hang up on me. We are very amenable people and don't want to cause problems. We can be very discreet about this. If this is an unpleasant topic for you to discuss, I will understand. If you would rather not share this conversation with your husband or family, I will respect your wishes. I hope you can view life from my wife's perspective as an adoptee and understand why it is important for her to find her birth mother. She would very much like to know if you are because, without this information, her life is an incomplete void. Can you help my wife solve the mystery of her birth and adoption?" he said in a humble, respectful, polite tone of voice.

He knew it was best if she had time to think clearly and without fear before responding. He tried to soothe her emotions, avoid forcing her to respond too quickly, or force her into a defensive posture. He wanted her to feel relaxed and assure her that it was okay to reveal her secret, but, when he was certain that she was neither going to answer his question nor hang up the telephone, he finally asked her directly.

"Did you give birth to a baby girl named Judy on the twenty-eighth day of April thirty years ago and subsequently give up that baby for adoption? I can assure you that, whatever you decide to tell me, I will be as discreet as you wish and not reveal this secret to anyone other than my wife … if that is what you desire."

There was a long pause. There was nothing but silence. I could hear myself breathing and my chest heaving and hoped she couldn't hear me eavesdropping in the background. Rebecca said nothing. She neither confessed nor refuted the accusation. She was holding back, and her silence was perplexing. I didn't know what to think. I had never expected a blank response of this sort. My head had been filled with pleasant visions of a hardworking woman standing in her farmhouse kitchen. Now it was as if the lights had gone out. I lost my mental image and visual focus. I had expected her to admit right away that she was my birth mother, but I was beginning to think she never would. I had dreamed that my birth mother would be in high spirits and joyfully respond to my identity, but her lack of excitement bewildered me. Why was she leaving so much doubt in my mind? She must need more time to weigh the consequences before confessing.

"I know this must be an awkward moment for you and shocking to receive a request of this magnitude after all these years. You can take your time responding if you like. I don't want to put too much pressure on you. My wife is a refined person of good character with a bright disposition. She would like to connect with you without causing any harm to you or your family. She was hoping the feeling would be mutual. If you prefer, I can call you later after you have had a chance to think about how to respond," Martin said genteelly in a near whisper.

"I'm sorry," were her final words.

I pressed the telephone to my ear. There was much hesitation in her voice, as if she had more to say. She sounded sad and deep in thought. There was another long pause. She was stoic and neutral. Neither Martin nor Rebecca said anything. Conversation fizzled. Was the risk of revealing her secret too great and too difficult for her to bear? Was the shame and guilt too difficult to overcome? How would her husband and children react if they discovered her secret? If exposed, would her current life be altered forever? If she remained silent, would I ever learn the secrets of my genealogy and family heritage, or would I endlessly wander the wilderness of uncertainty my entire life? I had never dreamed that my birth mother would deny my presence after I had revealed myself. Her vague response was enigmatic. Maybe she had a sister or cousin with a similar name who had given a baby up for adoption and was reluctant to divulge her secrets to a stranger. That was the only plausible explanation that made sense to me.

"Thank you for being so patient with me. I hope I didn't put too much pressure on you or cause you too much excitement. I will call you again soon. Good-bye." Martin slowly placed the telephone receiver back on the hook with a blank look on his face.

Rebecca's response was devoid of any emotion and left me with an unsolvable conundrum. I collapsed in a heap on the couch. Hearing my mother's voice for the first time but not being able to connect with her was depressing. I hugged Martin when he strolled into the room. I was sad and emotionally drained and looking for reassurance. I didn't know what else to do. It would have been much better if she had denied everything or said she didn't want to meet me. I never expected my search to end with such a completely hollow feeling and strangely nebulous outcome. I was glad my husband loved me. I longed for a hug because I needed reassurance. I felt like a cold, wet, orphaned puppy.

The whole situation sent me into an emotional funk. I was confused and didn't have a good feeling about what had happened. I had no idea what to say. Martin and I had used our vacation days wasting time making telephone calls to strangers when we could have been enjoying ourselves, relaxing, and reconnecting with old friends.

My new vision of Rebecca living on an isolated dairy farm in rural Wisconsin with dirty fingernails without jewelry or sparkle didn't fit within the constraints of my childhood dreams or fantasies. My niche had been the city. As a child, I was surrounded with the hustle and bustle of urban life filled with variety and entertainment, shopping, entertainment, restaurants, and many friends. I had always visualized my birth mother as a musically talented, well-dressed sophisticate. She had traveled to international cities to play her music. I wondered if I would ever unlock the mysterious secrets she was hiding from me.

Conundrum 20

Dear Mom, I never expected to find you living on a dairy farm near Madison, Wisconsin. In my childhood dreams and fantasies, I have always perceived you as a city person. Your unresponsiveness is a conundrum. I am baffled why you didn't simply accept or deny the question. If you are my birth mother, I would like to meet with you in person sometime. Perhaps, after you have had some time to reflect on the situation, you will be more receptive to my request. It would mean a lot to me if you would give me an honest answer to end this curious state of limbo and ambiguity. I value your privacy and promise to honor any requests you make to be discreet about our connection to avoid spoiling your reputation. Love, Judy

"WHY WAS REBECCA SO elusive when a simple denial would have ended the conversation? Was she afraid to own up to the truth because it would ruin her reputation?" I mumbled in a confused state of bewilderment.

I had to assume Rebecca had cried herself to sleep on many occasions. It would have been very traumatic and heart-wrenching to abandon her child without any assurance that strangers would properly raise the child. Was she insensitive and callous because her memory of discarding me thirty years ago was so old that she had completely forgotten about me? Was I more sensitive and delicate because I was an adoptee and not clever or experienced enough to know the answers to these questions? My thoughts kept returning to the same starting point. I had to believe that Rebecca was my birth mother because she had never denied it. The entire episode disheartened and perplexed me.

Martin's voice awakened me from my semiconscious state. "Are you awake? I can't sleep. I think the woman I called is your birth mother. I should call her again. Everything seems to match up. She has the right name and age, and she graduated from high school in Milwaukee. It would be logical for a farm girl from the Madison area to be sent to the city to have her baby. She probably had relatives in Milwaukee at the time. We know she has a brother living there because I talked to him. Her parents would have arranged for her to stay with a trusted aunt, grandparent, or friend of the family during the later stages of pregnancy. It is logical to assume she would want to leave her hometown in Madison during the pregnancy."

He rubbed his chin and yawned. Neither one of us had stopped thinking about Rebecca ever since she hung up the telephone.

"I assume she is keeping your existence secret from her husband. Perhaps she never told him before they were married. You can imagine how much chaos there would be if she had to explain it to him now. Perhaps, after she has had more time to reflect on the situation, she will confess. Confidentiality is probably the major issue and the key reason why she decided to remain noncommittal."

He rubbed his eyes and scratched his scalp. "She probably stayed at Booth Hill because her parents didn't live in Milwaukee and she needed a place to stay. It would have been a good place to evade detection by classmates to avoid spoiling her reputation, especially if her parents didn't approve of the father. All the pieces seem to fit together, but you should call her next time."

"Are you kidding? I would panic and lose my ability to speak. I would gasp for air and spoil the moment. I can't do it by myself. Will you please find out the truth for me?" I placed my head on his shoulder.

He always gave in and helped me when my requests were sincere. He was concerned about my happiness and psychological welfare, and he didn't want to spoil my chances for a successful reunion with my birth mother.

"Talking to your birth mother makes me nervous, too. I tried to be gentle, tactful, and tolerant of her feelings during our first conversation. There isn't anything else I can say to help her decide. It is not my nature to coerce, intimidate, or threaten others. I don't want to push her too hard or force her hand before she is ready. She knows what you want. A simple yes or no would suffice, but she refuses to qualify her response, leaving us with no idea what she is thinking. I'm usually good at reading between the lines, but this person completely baffles me. Her lack of cooperation leaves me cold because it is impossible to know what she is thinking. She probably needs to come to terms very slowly and cautiously with the idea of meeting you in person."

He paused a moment to reflect on what he was going to say. "I think it is imperative to do this the right way. We have some alternatives. We could call her again on the telephone, send her a letter, or meet with her in person to see if she will change her mind. We could drive past her farm, do a stakeout on the house with binoculars, and see what she looks like. After all, if she looks like you, that would be a big step in the right direction. We could drive past her farm and pretend to have a flat tire. I could walk up to her house, knock on the door to get some assistance, and ask to use the telephone. That way, we could get a close-up view without attracting too much attention."

I couldn't imagine myself participating in a daring escapade this dramatic. His idea sounded implausible and more like a melodramatic scene from an old black-and-white movie. Pretending to have a flat tire in front of her house was hokey and unreliable because she might not be home. What if severe thunderstorms occurred that day? Besides, I still wasn't absolutely convinced the woman was my birth mother, and my emotions were still swinging wildly between feelings of strength, boldness, action, and confidence, countered by negative feelings of procrastination, shyness, fear, lack of confidence, and panic.

Nothing in life seemed more important to me than finding the truth about my background. I was in a quandary about the entire situation and fluctuating between advancing and retreating. One minute, I felt like taking action and calling her myself. Then I would get cold feet, withdraw, and end up feeling sorry for myself. I was tired of my own state of uncertainty.

"If we do decide to call her again, we need to do it when her husband isn't home so she can speak openly. Can you imagine some isolated and sheltered farm girl passing herself off as an innocent virgin and then having to explain your presence to her husband thirty years later? She may be torn between confessing and wanting to meet you and keeping her secret private because it would be disastrous for her marriage. Living on a farm means she has many reasons to stay home, and she is probably not very worldly. Her simple life would make it easy for her to keep her secrets hidden from others."

The more Martin talked, the more rational and believable her situation seemed, but I wasn't willing to back off my quest to find the truth.

If she never confessed, I would never know my fate or true identity, and that didn't seem like an acceptable conclusion to my adoption story.

"Maybe you should call Rebecca when I'm not there. If you had bad news to report, you could shelter me from any information that might be unpleasant, difficult to face, or distressing." I displayed my sensitive nature.

Martin had thought the same thing. It had occurred to him that I could be the product of rape or incest because those were rational and plausible reasons why Rebecca had remained neutral and noncommittal. If one of those scenarios were true, it would be logical for her to be wary and guarded and not want to confess that I was her daughter. Assuming he found out something catastrophic, Martin would then be capable of breaking the news to me gently. I was glad he cared enough to support me and help me through this difficult and mystifying situation.

A better plan would be to wait and call Rebecca from the privacy of our own home after she had more time to reflect on the last conversation. There were fewer distractions in Colorado, which would give me more time to think and get my emotions under control. If Rebecca did admit that I was her daughter, I needed to be prepared to deal with the consequence of my reality.

It was a long, boring drive home. I spent much of my time daydreaming about Rebecca and wondering what it would be like to raise pigs, cows, and chickens and grow vegetables in my own garden.

It felt good to be home in my own comfort zone again. I didn't ask for advice or assistance. I simply handed Martin the telephone, and he made the call to Wisconsin. I held my breath. Rebecca answered the telephone. She was polite and cordial and gave no indication that she was going to hang up. Martin asked for her sympathy and pleaded his case.

"I'm sorry I can't help you," she said sincerely in a quiet but somber tone of voice.

Maybe she had another clandestine secret in her background or something to hide about my adoption, or perhaps the time wasn't conducive for holding a private conversation. What other reasons were there for being so noncommittal? If she weren't my birth mother, why in the world would she leave me suspended in limbo, without hope or faith, wandering about aimlessly in search of my real identity? Did she give a different child up for adoption other than me? Did she assume Martin was the parent of a child she had adopted? I had so many scenarios to consider that my head was spinning because I saw no plausible explanation for her odd behavior or lack of a rejoinder.

The conversation was over. Martin distressingly hung up the receiver. He was disappointed and befuddled. "Rebecca seems like a decent person. She was talkative and appeared to have empathy for you, albeit guarded and noncommittal. She may be the mother of other adopted children, and that is what concerns her. I just don't know. She was apologetic for not answering me when I asked her outright, but she must be enthralled with another very deep secret that prevents her from confessing."

I grudgingly acknowledged his good intentions and gracious efforts, but the complete lack of any definitive results left me in a shambles. I felt reduced to rubble and despondent.

Rosella and Me

Dear Mom, My life is changing for the better. I feel wiser, more mature, and more responsible than I did in my twenties. I feel better about myself. My perspectives about world events and life continue to grow and mature. I finally feel like a member of the adult generation. My adopted mother Rosella appears visibly older. Her health is getting worse, and it is difficult for her to take care of her house and yard. She is pessimistic about the future and constantly on the alert for a reoccurrence of her cancer. The experience of finding you has given me insight and empathy for you. Even though I'm preoccupied with the care of my adopted mother, I still think about you and wonder if you will eventually reveal yourself to me. Love, Judy

The phone rang, and I picked it up.

"Hi, Judy. I booked an airline ticket to Aspen for your birthday. I thought I should do this one more time while I still can," Rosella said optimistically. She sounded more upbeat and energetic than she had in the last five years.

"That's wonderful. Your health must be improving."

On the day of her visit, I left for the airport one hour early due to inclement weather. Michael had a slight temperature, obliging Martin to stay home to babysit. Rosella was a sixty-nine-year-old cancer survivor who had been predicting a short life for many years. Her doomsday attitude made the future sound pessimistic and depressing and left me feeling unstable and insecure. Despite our many differences, I still relied on her and wanted her to be with me for a long time.

She got off the plane in an irritable mood, complaining about the bumpiness of the flight and angrily demanding to know why Martin and Michael hadn't made the effort to greet her at the airport. She was unhappy and argumentative. Within minutes of her arrival, she brought up a plethora of trivial negative complaints. It was difficult to

avoid getting caught up in her gloomy way of thinking about the mea-
ger assistance provided by airport employees, high cost of flying, lousy
airport food, rude people, dirty bathrooms, and dreadfully snarled traffic.

When she stopped talking about flying, she reverted to talking
about social problems. She watched the news every day, and she was
preoccupied with the usual media coverage of murder, rape, welfare,
homelessness, racial strife, disease, and natural disasters. When it
came to politics and religion, she had the bad habit of telling others how to think. If someone expressed an opinion contrary to her
own, she would callously criticize the person. She constantly challenged me to agree with her. Many of our discussions ended up as
a never-ending cycle of disagreements. Solutions and compromises
could never be achieved because she was more likely to lash out at
me with feelings of self-pity and accuse me of mistreating her than
acknowledge contrarian points of view. Our discussions always ended in a no-win situation because her final argument would be that I
didn't love her or show her enough gratitude. Staying positive was
difficult to do, but I had vowed I wouldn't let her bad attitudes spoil
our visit this time. Instead, I was looking forward to having normal
mother-and-daughter conversations and the opportunity to spend
some quality time together.

Rosella complained that traveling made her tired, and she fell
asleep with her head leaning against the headrest on the way home
from the airport.

I reflected on some of the reasons for our differences. Our energy
levels and methods of communicating were not the same. We had different views about religion, entertainment, business, family, health, and
hobbies. I liked small talk, companionship, and meeting new people. I
was more physical, energetic, happy, extroverted, and emotionally expressive. I was more impulsive and quicker to react to criticism.

She was the opposite: cautious, slow, deliberate, and calculating.
She used sarcasm, and she had a sly sense of humor. She was uncomfortable around strangers and even her own brothers and sisters. She
was reserved, quietly introverted, and pouty. She expected me to be
compliant and obedient, and she kept her emotions bottled up inside
of her like a pressure cooker until the lid would finally blow off and she
would verbally lash out at me. Rosella's education was limited to the

eighth grade, and this was the basis for her limited vocabulary and lack of communication skills.

There were glaring differences in our emotional needs, personal interests, methods of dealing with people, and outlooks on life. We didn't share the same concerns or treat daily issues with the same relevance, and we didn't look alike because we weren't biologically related.

When I was young, it was never clear if she loved me because she had unreasonably enjoyed dominating me. To survive, I had ignored her personal attacks and accepted a passive childhood condition. I had never outgrown those feelings. It was often difficult to relax or feel normal in her presence. Unfortunately, I was not good at concealing my emotions. My facial expressions and body language usually reflected my inner feelings. The harder she pressed me, the more likely I was to show my true feelings. Better communication skills and exercising more self-control would have enhanced our mother-daughter relationship.

My adoption search had inspired me to read many books about psychology and mother-daughter bonding. It was interesting that most scientists universally described parental bonding as a highly critical factor in child development, and the public seemed to agree. Most studies confirmed that the lack of bonding severely damaged children psychologically. Bonding was a very complex subject that inspired me to think about what it meant to the survival of animal species and how it related to the health and happiness of humans.

It disturbed me a great deal when I read about the experiments of American psychologist Harry Frederick Harlow at the University of Wisconsin. Seeing pictures of little rhesus monkeys clinking to rag dolls that mimicked their biological mothers disturbed me. It stirred up deep feelings of insecurity that I had never known existed.

Harlow was best known for his maternal deprivation and social isolation experiments, which demonstrated the importance of caregiving and companionship in the early stages of primate development. In a series of well-known experiments, he removed baby rhesus monkeys from their mothers and offered them surrogate cloth dolls instead. The baby monkeys ran to their surrogate cloth mothers when feeling threatened. When separated from their cloth mothers, they would freeze in fear, crouch down, or suck their thumbs. Isolation from other monkeys resulted in abnormalities such as blank staring, repetitive physical motions, and self-mutilation. Teams of scientists confirmed that separation of rhesus monkeys from their mothers during the first six months of life produced severe deficits in virtually every aspect of behavior from which they never recovered.

It was easy for me to make comparisons between Harlow's psychological experiments on monkeys and my own life because I had been slow to bond with my adopted parents. I wondered if I shared some of the same insecure feelings of separation and loneliness and if my actions mimicked that of the baby rhesus monkeys separated from their biological mothers after birth. I secretly wondered if my lack of bonding as an infant was the motivating force for wanting to find my birth mother. I wished I had photographs and more knowledge about the earliest months of my life before I was adopted because the first year of my life was still a mystery.

Rosella and I had never fully bonded like most healthy biological mothers and daughters. Natural influences and feelings that inherently unite offspring to their parents seemed to be missing. I had intentionally pooped in my pants to express my displeasure with my new surroundings and resisted all efforts by others to enter my comfort zone. Consequently, I was left alone.

A sudden, loud, humming noise caused by the sound of my right front tire running along the edge of the pavement suddenly shattered my daydream. I swerved and nearly hit a concrete barrier before jerking the car back on the highway again. The sudden change in direction caused Rosella to lurch sideways and open her eyes to see what was happening.

"Wake up. Pay attention to your driving," Rosella stammered loudly.

BRIGHT SUNSHINE AND A clear, deep blue sky the following morning put everyone in a good mood. Martin left early for work, and Michael, who was feeling better, went to school. Rosella and I had breakfast at the Village Smithy restaurant in Carbondale. Tulips were poking their heads up in local gardens. Birds were chirping happily. Life was good.

"Have you ever wanted to find your birth mother?" She looked me straight in the eye.

Her question caught me off guard. I was startled and reluctant to answer because my first reaction was one of guilt, immediately questioning if she were trying to trick me into confessing my secret transgressions for contacting Gertrude Schweinhaus and Rebecca. I was torn between impulsively blurting out an affirmative response and holding my tongue until I could surmise her motive for asking.

"I am curious to know because there has been considerable news coverage lately about adoptees finding their birth mothers. As an adoptee, there are some unique things you are entitled to know," Rosella calmly divulged while quietly sipping her tea.

"Some organizations provide false identities to adoptees to prevent them from locating their biological parents. Fake baptismal certificates are commonly used to intentionally deceive them. Your baptism certificate states you were baptized at Holy Angels Catholic Church in Milwaukee, but that is simply not true. The document is a fake. You should write to Saint Lawrence Catholic Church to request a copy of your original baptismal certificate," she suggested matter-of-factly.

Hearing this information from Rosella was an emotional low point of my adoption search. I was disappointed and shocked because it had never occurred to me that anyone would create false documents to protect birth parents from their children. Adults had bamboozled me into believing that Santa Claus existed, and my reaction was the same now as it had been then. They had deceived and lied to me. The justification and rationalization for this policy was a formal conspiracy to appease birth parents living in the fear of meeting their own children. It was a tidy and convenient solution for everyone except their abandoned children.

I had been severely annoyed with government bureaucracy ever since I interviewed Miss Schweinhaus. I wondered if she were the forger who drafted my false baptismal certificate.

"Sealed adoption records protect birth parents wishing to live a secret lifestyle, unwilling to have their lives disrupted by unwanted children they previously rejected. Public policy may seem cold and un-civilized to you, but that is the law." Rosella expressed her religious convictions and commitment to her conservative points of view.

I tried to appear outwardly calm, but talking about my adoption aroused my passions and got me excited. I smiled because it was easier to rationalize my thoughts and behavior from a secular, detached per-spective than the inner spiritual, existential, and emotional base from which my innermost thoughts derived.

"During my nursing training, I learned that medical history is an important factor when screening for certain diseases, such as heart ailments and diabetes. Most doctors claim heredity is important for diagnosing preexisting medical conditions," I politely stated a scientific fact.

"Most people are curious to know something about their ancestors. Stories of your childhood have always been interesting to me because your experiences living in the country were much different from mine. Learning about relatives can be a source of pride and inspiration if someone in the family is uniquely talented."

Thinking about Rosella growing up on a farm caused me to flash back to my visions of Rebecca milking her cows. I wondered what she was doing at this exact minute and whether she ever thought about me. I still wanted to meet Rebecca and ask why she gave me up for adoption. The more facts I had to confirm that Rebecca was indeed my birth mother, the better, but, out of respect for Rosella's sensitive feelings, I decided not to mention my encounter with her. The excitement was overwhelming but tempered by guilt because Rosella was oblivious to the fact I had already found my birth mother.

"I would definitely like a copy of my original baptismal certificate and any other documents I am entitled to receive," I said affirmatively, fully aware that our conversation was a monumental event, but cautiously stifling my enthusiasm to avoid detection.

I was ecstatic because so many positive thoughts were running through my head. At the same time, I was stunned to learn that my baptismal and birth certificates stashed in the bank vault were counterfeit. I had to assume that the fear of imminent death by cancer motivated Rosella, and she was eager to unburden her most cumbersome secrets before she died.

"Well, if you write for your baptismal certificate, you should be able to find the correct spelling of your birth mother's maiden name."

It was difficult to concentrate on writing a letter in her presence. Only after she agreed to take a nap did I feel comfortable enough to sit down and compose a letter. I was suspiciously skeptical the church would honor my request because most clergy were naturally secretive to protect personal privacy. I carefully placed a stamp on the envelope and inserted it into the mailbox. Unaware of the reality that might follow, I was determined to persevere, regardless of the consequences.

Fun activities filled the remainder of the week. Rosella and I went to lunch at the Hotel Colorado and Hot Springs Pool Lodge, shopped in local tourist stores, attended an art show, and watched Michael play soccer. We took pleasant driving trips to the ski towns of Aspen and Vail, walked through Redstone and Marble, and watched tourists raft down the Colorado River through majestic Glenwood Canyon. We sat in the clubhouse at River Valley Ranch, sipped ice tea, and watched golfers hit their balls over the Crystal River. Rosella was very pleased.

"This was my best vacation in Colorado. We participated in many enjoyable activities. I am glad I had the opportunity to see my grandson before I die. This is the last time we will see each other due to my lingering cancer. Thank you for your generous hospitality."

Rosella abruptly turned her back and walked toward the departure gate with a tear in her eye. I wanted to hug her, but she never gave me a chance.

Names

Dear Mom, I believe we have a deep spiritual connection with each other. My DNA and genetics come from you, and, for that reason, I am curious to know if we share any obvious genetic similarities. My intuition is very strong because I feel positive energy coming from you. In my heart, I feel certain that you are a good person. I have visions about what your life is like and look forward to meeting you in the future. I was surprised to hear that I was issued false birth and baptismal certificates when I was adopted to conceal my real identity. I wrote to the church where I was baptized to obtain my original certificate, hoping it would provide me with the correct spelling of your maiden name. Love, Judy

I DROPPED ROSELLA OFF at the airport and went straight to the bank vault to retrieve my baptismal certificate. I immediately recognized that something was glaringly wrong. Rosella was right. The information was incorrect. This was a forgery because it had been falsely issued a year before I was adopted and fourteen months before my legal name was changed to Judith Ann Romano.

Exposure of the fraud that had been perpetrated on me provided a new challenge, sparked my curiosity, and reignited my enthusiasm for continuing my adoption quest. I was eagerly awaiting a response from the church to see if they were willing to send me an authentic copy of the original certificate.

I was still befuddled to know if the woman in Wisconsin was my birth mother. It had been an incomprehensible conversation with an anticlimactic melodramatic ending that was still unresolved. She had intentionally avoided telling me if she were my birth mother. Her unrevealing responses left many doubts in my mind about what kind of person she was because nothing about her seemed ordinary. Her profile didn't sync with the visual image of the woman I had desperately been aspiring to find for so many years. On some obscure, esoteric level, doubts were surfacing about whether this was the individual I had been telepathically communicating with all of my life.

Rebecca had been pleasant, polite, and cooperative, but she was hiding behind an impenetrable brick wall. I had never expected my adoption search to come to an unfortunate dead end on a dairy farm in Wisconsin.

I had given the voice recording of my conversation with Miss Schweinhaus to local stenographer and realtor, Nancy Carlson to be transcribed. She typed the exact words, precisely as they had been spoken, including the part when I intentionally coughed to disguise my pronunciation of Rebecca's last name. I had been very cautious and even practiced aloud in front of a mirror before the meeting to see if I could trick Miss Schweinhaus into thinking I knew Rebecca's maiden name. My ruse had worked perfectly. I had scored a home run.

Judy: "My birth mother's nickname was Becky (cough) Maier (cough)."

Miss Schweinhaus: "I am surprised that Rosella told you your birth mother's maiden name was Rebecca Meyer. She never should have told you."

I perused the transcript meticulously. It was unusual because the transcriber was uncertain of the correct spelling. Was it Meyer instead of Mayor, Mayer, or Maier? Who was right? I pushed the fast-forward button until I found the exact spot and pressed play. I stopped the recorder, backed it up, and played it again, each time turning the volume up louder. It sounded more like Meyer than Mayor, but the spelling of the last name was still unclear.

Martin and I shared the same thought. If my birth mother's maiden name were Meyer, who in the world was Becky Maier, and why had she chosen to remain so noncommittal? She never denied having a baby or giving one up for adoption. Her vague, undefined responses were frustrating and strangely mystifying.

"What are you thinking?" Martin inquired to know.

"I never aspired to live on a dairy farm. I never wanted to learn how to milk cows or make cheese. I would have very little in common with Rebecca Maier even if she were an exceptionally talented person with a generous spirit and beautiful personality. Perhaps she really is my birth mother, but, unless she calls me back to confess, I think we should resume the calling process and continue searching. I still envision my birth mother as another individual yet to be discovered."

"Oh," was all he mumbled in response.

It was an unseasonably warm, sunny day and a good time to buy flowers for my garden. I stopped at the mailbox before leaving for the landscape nursery. In the middle of the stack of mail was a letter from the church. I was so excited I asked myself if I should open it right away or wait until Martin got home from work. If the news were positive, I would have him next to me to share the joy. I decided to wait and carefully placed the pile of mail on the passenger seat.

Martin arrived home from work, walked in to say hello, and greeted me with a kiss. I held his hands and looked into his eyes.

"I am very nervous. I want you sitting next to me when I open the letter from Saint Lawrence Church."

I inserted the letter opener into the crease and cautiously cut the top of the envelope from one edge to the other, being very careful not to destroy its contents. I deliberately pried open the top of the envelope and peaked inside before unfolding the letter.

Wow! I was ecstatic. I almost hyperventilated. There it was in black and white, just what I had hoped to find. In my hand, I was holding my original baptismal certificate. I could tell immediately that it was authentic. I stared blankly into space in stunned astonishment to absorb the significance of what had been sent to me. It was living proof of my heritage by birth and proved I had an identity before I was adopted. The document stated that my baptism took place May 16. Ironically, today was also the sixteenth day of May, exactly thirty-two years later.

The exciting discovery of my birth overwhelmed me, but I was unsure if I should jump for joy or cry to release the tension. I was overcome by a mountain of pent-up emotions that I had carried with me from childhood through my teenage years and into adulthood. I visualized myself as a vulnerable and dependent two-week-old infant completely reliant on others for survival and the reality of what it meant to be abandoned by one's own parents. What states of mind were my birth parents in when they abdicated their parenthood responsibilities, opted to abandon me, and left me with strangers? Who took care of me the first twelve months of my life?

It was comforting to share this information with my husband. We hugged, and I whimpered a few tears on his shoulder. Times like this would have been difficult without his strong emotional support and understanding. I perused the document carefully and kept repeating my birth mother's maiden name until I had it committed to memory, Rebecca Meyer. M-E-Y-E-R. I finally had what I wanted. My tenacious approach was finally paying off because I now held the best clue to my real identity that I had ever possessed, but there was another unknown. Who in the world were William and Priscilla Engelmann? They were listed as the co-sponsors, but I didn't know anyone by those names. How were we linked and why? They might have been key figures in the beginnings of my life, but who was to know?

It would be interesting to comprehend our relationship, but I didn't want to get distracted or waste time looking in the wrong places. I needed to stay focused on the name Meyer. Unless the names William and Priscilla resurfaced, I would have to consider them a low priority.

The mystery of my birth was slowly unraveling at a snail's pace. Each time I discovered another clue to my identity, it raised more questions and exposed another mystery to solve. I was beginning to feel like a private detective, enthusiastically analyzing clues and searching for the truth.

Aunt Frieda

Dear Mom, Staying focused on my goal of finding you has forced me to deal with emotional setbacks, recognize false leads, and overcome stubborn bureaucracies. My quest to find you has required tremendous courage and tenacity. My journey has been a continuous cycle of euphoric, emotional highs compressed between depressing blues when the future appears bleak and exhausting. The compelling force inside me to succeed is strong, but I am concerned about my mental stability and the consequences to my family resulting from all the time I have devoted to finding you. I intend to use my inner strength and courage to continue the process of discovery, regardless of outcomes, until I know for certain what happened to me. I am afraid, but I have the courage to continue sailing through uncharted waters until this mystery is solved. Love, Judy

A WANING ALPINE GLOW from the dying rays of the sun warmed my cheeks and comforted my soul. I smiled and daydreamed optimistically about the future because I finally had the correct spelling of my birth mother's maiden name in my possession, but my concentration was interrupted when Martin snuck up from behind and gently grabbed my shoulders.

"Your preoccupation with your adoption search has been a distraction to our normal family routines. We missed all the community concerts, formal banquets, private parties, and several golf tournaments, and you are committing less time to our son. This is a reminder to strive to maintain a good balance in your life to stay healthy because, when you are happy, we are all happy."

He was right. His prickly statements were a warning and an awakening of the need to spend more time with my family. He was nudging me to work on providing a better balance in exchange for his support. Our conversation concluded with several compromises and a plan about how to continue, including a promise to make homemade lasagna for dinner tomorrow.

My adoption search had brought us closer as a married couple despite the disruption it had created in our lives. My enthusiasm for finding my roots was contagious, and Martin had become entirely committed to helping me. I couldn't imagine myself moving forward without his assistance and support. We had been a highly motivated detective team, and two heads were undeniably better than one.

We had both agreed there was no harm in making a few additional telephone calls to search for Rebecca Meyer now that I had the correct spelling of her last name. Martin had been hesitant to help me at first, but was now fully engaged and just as interested in the outcome. To avoid mistakes in miscommunication, he had wired our telephone to an external recording device to log each conversation for future transcribing by professional stenographer, Nancy Carlson.

I felt panicky. Listening to Martin inquiring about my lost family made my heart ache. Pleading with strangers for assistance dredged up deep psychological wounds of abandonment and isolation I had never fully learned to overcome. I had a horrible feeling of anticipation that something bad might happen. My face was flush. I felt faint.

It was difficult to constrain my fear. I wondered if the early part of my life was a dark place with evil people that I didn't want to go to. Would my actions generate complications and problems as the result of my unwise interference in something tragic and undisturbed? Perhaps I was engaging in an activity that I shouldn't be doing. Was I a modern Pandora too curious for her own good? About to open a sacred box containing all the evils of humankind? It was dangerous walking on thin ice, standing on the edge of a cliff, and playing in the street, but I was willing to take a leap of faith because the potential reward seemed greater than the risks. The one gift from the gods that never escaped Pandora's box was hope, the one thing I had to sustain me.

I held my breath for six slow rings. I was poised like a track star, tensed and primed to sprint to the bedroom and jump under the blankets for security.

"Hello! This is Frieda Meyer. How may I help you?" the woman said alertly, assuming this must be an important call.

She sounded pleasant but cautious. I stopped breathing and held on to a kitchen chair to keep from fainting.

"Hello, Frieda. We are planning a high school class reunion and need Rebecca Meyer's current address and telephone number. Can you help me? I'm sure she would like to attend," Martin said deceitfully. He was proud of his brilliant ploy.

"Rebecca is my niece. We lived in the same neighborhood when she was growing up, but I haven't gotten around much ever since my husband died. I haven't seen Rebecca for quite a few years, but I think she still lives in Milwaukee. It is late. I will help you tomorrow," she explained as her voice tapered off to a whisper.

I had been so eager to begin the calling process that I had forgotten Milwaukee was in a different time zone. No wonder she was tired.

Martin had a big smile on his face as he watched me perform a spontaneous charade of delight. I was ecstatic. I had finally reached someone who could help. I wanted Frieda to stay on the line, keep talking all night, and ask her to tell me everything she knew about my birth mother. I could hardly think straight and exuberantly sang, "Let's twist again!" I dizzily twirled around the kitchen like a whirling dervish as an expression of joy and celebration.

I was much too excited to act rationally. Martin had to persuade me to come to bed. I lay on my back with my eyes wide open and fantasized about Rebecca. I kept wondering what would happen if Martin openly discussed my adoption with her. I hoped he could gain her confidence to extract some information from her.

I awoke before dawn with positive energy and enthusiasm. My expectations were high. Martin had to leave for work early and decided it was best if he called Aunt Frieda from his office.

He opened the conversation by expressing his concern for her health and the weather in Milwaukee. Posing as an old classmate, he eased into the discussion by optimistically asking about Rebecca's physical appearance, much like an old boyfriend would do after thirty years.

"Well, as you know, she is taller than average. She was always thin and attractive. Even in adulthood, she is a beautiful woman with long, silky, brown hair and deep brown eyes. She has a sweet face and smooth complexion," Aunt Frieda said, recollecting precious memories.

Martin continued pressing without provoking suspicion. "Does Rebecca still play the violin?"

"She was very talented and played in public with the symphonic orchestra. She was very good, but I doubt if she plays anymore. She is too busy with their restaurant business and her family," she replied candidly.

Frieda Meyer confirmed everything Rosella had previously told me about my birth mother. Spellbound, he listened intently. Her physical characteristics of brown hair, smooth skin, white teeth, a nice-looking smile, and dimples were remarkably similar to me. Frieda enjoyed the attention, and she was unsuspecting about his motives for asking so many poignant questions. She was feeling important and eager to assist him. They seemed to have a good rapport. The timing was right.

Martin made a hasty decision to be honest. He spoke softly to emphasize the somber importance and private intimacy of what he was about to say. Frieda listened intently.

"I am not a classmate of Rebecca Meyer. I am not calling about a planned high school class reunion. I believe Rebecca Meyer is my wife's biological mother. My wife was born just before she graduated from high school."

Frieda remained silent. "You are mistaken. You are accusing the wrong person because I lived across the street, and I was very close to Rebecca."

Martin could hear her breathing, but wasn't sure what she was thinking or if she were going to hang up the telephone. He must have provoked her by stirring up old memories.

"Are you sure? Your description of Rebecca sounds exactly like my wife."

"Rebecca stayed home from school for an extended time just before graduation due to a serious kidney infection. She spent an entire month in the hospital, followed by several weeks convalescing at home. It never occurred to me that she might have been pregnant. She was so young. To think that her parents could have concealed this from me is highly doubtful," Frieda said, refuting his allegation. "Thirty years ago, it wasn't a good thing for an unmarried girl to have a baby. People were generally not supportive of behavior that might lead to an unplanned pregnancy. All of us were good practicing Catholics. This would have been a difficult situation for the family and would have spoiled Rebecca's reputation if it were true," she added, stating a historical fact.

"I remember quite vividly the anger her mother expressed toward her boyfriend. She was very upset with him and prohibited Rebecca from dating this boy. If Rebecca were pregnant, this would have explained her mother's formidable reaction and hatred toward him."

Aunt Frieda continued speaking about her relatives for the next forty-five minutes. Martin had stirred her memories and given her a lot to think about.

"Rebecca never dated anyone else, and I am fairly certain he was the one she married. Her mother hardly ever spoke to her on friendly terms after that. It was a real shame because I always liked Rebecca. Call me tomorrow evening and I will give you Rebecca's telephone number" Frieda explained remorsefully.

Martin invited me to join him for lunch at the Hotel Colorado to summarize what he had learned. His consulting business was located across the street in the penthouse of the old Hot Springs Lodge, where he was in the process of working on a new master plan for Sundance ski area in Utah.

I sat upright and fully attentive. It was a glorious day in Colorado. The air was fresh and intoxicating. The sun was warm and intense. The air was clear, and the sky was cobalt blue. I felt surrounded by happiness. It was a wonderful day to be alive.

"Rebecca is married. Her husband's name is Bruno. They are in the restaurant business and have three children still living at home. Her husband is Italian. Sicilian actually. Rebecca's father owned a meat market. He was a butcher but unexpectedly died from a stroke. Her mother also died recently from a heart attack."

The large amount of information he had gleaned from Aunt Frieda in one conversation surprised me.

"Rebecca took violin lessons. Her parents stressed discipline and obedience. They were orthodox Catholics who strictly conformed to the traditions of the church. Her mother wanted Rebecca to get a college degree in fine arts and music, but it never happened," Martin explained between sips of lemonade. "Her parents rejected her pleas to marry her boyfriend because she was too young and they feared his Sicilian roots. Aunt Frieda thought he was a pleasant, attractive, young man deeply in love with Rebecca, but she never received her parents' blessing to get married. Rebecca eventually rebelled. When she was legally old enough, she married him anyway. Her parents' decision to withhold their support had grave consequences because they permanently alienated her. She estranged herself from her parents and all of her relatives after she married. Aunt Frieda never understood why this happened, but it makes sense to her now. It is a very sad story, but a logical explanation for what happened," Martin said sympathetically. Using his napkin, he wiped away a small tear from under my eye to prevent it from dripping down my cheek.

"According to Aunt Frieda, Bruno and Rebecca have owned restaurants, pizza places, nightclubs, taverns, and rental properties. Their popular supper club specialized in Sicilian recipes. The food was famously delicious because the flavors were superb. The entire family worked long hours, including their oldest daughter, Linda. The restaurant was thriving, and the whole family was living well until the new highway alignment closed the exit and ruined their business."

I was fascinated. I had never expected to be given this much information at one time.

"Frieda and I agreed to talk again this evening. She is still searching for Rebecca's telephone number."

He reached into his pocket, pulled out the mini-digital recorder, and slipped it into my purse before leaning over to kiss me. "Here, you can listen to the entire conversation yourself," he said with a wink and a smile.

That evening, at exactly seven o'clock, the telephone rang. Martin answered and, without warning, shoved the telephone in my face. "Here! You be the adoption detective. Take charge of your own destiny. Frieda is a congenial woman. She won't bite your head off. Talk to her."

My expressions of refusal were unpersuasive and blatantly ignored. I was dazed. I felt like clutching. I was exposed and vulnerable and feeling unsure of myself. Martin had me pinned against the wall with his arms and forcefully cradled the telephone next to my ear. It was impossible to escape. I shook my head violently from side to side, but to no avail. It was a very scary moment because I had suddenly forgotten how to talk. The door to my cage had been flung open. I could fly into the unknown world outside, but I frantically clung to my perch instead. I was physically crippled and mentally paralyzed. A thousand thoughts were racing through my mind, yet I couldn't speak.

Now that I had been openly exposed to reality, I wondered if I should be doing this. I felt guilty because I might be violating adoption or privacy laws or causing problems for others highly disapproving of my actions. I had cold feet. Was it really appropriate for me to uncover my past? Was I about to cause problems for others or doing something unethical or immoral? What would this mean to my adopted parents if they found out?

Major doubts about my motives surfaced. What if I contacted Rebecca and decided later that I had been better off without her? It would be emotionally devastating if she rejected me or accused me of stalking her for media publicity, financial assistance, extortion, meddling in her private affairs, or some other unlawful behavior. What if she were in jail or turned out to be an undesirable character?

I had a habit of never diving into cold water. I had always entered slowly one foot at a time. I felt the same way this time. Eventually, I could feel myself relaxing. The tension in my muscles was starting to go away. A reunion with my birth mother could be healing and enlightening and give me closure as an adoptee. The mere possibility was an awesome thought, and my curiosity was finally getting the best of me. I softened slightly, gripped the receiver tightly, and pressed it against my ear. My heart skipped a few extra beats.

"Hello, Frieda. This is Judy."

The enormous weight I was feeling was miraculously lifted. I wasn't frightened anymore. Pent-up words unexpectedly flowed out of my mouth. "Please tell me as much as you can about Rebecca. I am fairly certain she is my biological mother," I summoned humbly.

"Rebecca was a very attractive girl with big brown eyes and long, silky, brown hair when she was young. She had incredibly cute dimples when she smiled. She married an Italian boy named Bruno. They have three beautiful children: Linda, Cindy, and a boy named Tim. They are all good kids who stay out of trouble. Rebecca's mother Bertha had been a problem for Rebecca because she was constantly interfering in her daughter's affairs. She had enough money to pay for her grandchildren's college education, but used her money in a negative way as a bribe to coerce Rebecca into doing things her way. Her mother was a very private person, and she was obviously successful at keeping Rebecca's pregnancy a big secret because we were all told that Rebecca had a highly contagious infection when you were born."

"I feel relaxed and comfortable talking to you."

"If I was an adoptee, I would want to find my real parents." Aunt

Frieda was beginning to believe that I really was Rebecca's child. "There is something I need to tell you because it gives me the chills."

"What is it? Please tell me before you forget," I responded politely.

"I know you are a very special person to me."

"Why do you say that? We have never met." I curiously wondered what she was thinking.

"Your voice sounds so eerily similar to Rebecca that I thought I was talking to her. I was certain we were related when you started speaking," she said tenderly.

Chills shot up my spine. It was a provocative thought and an intriguing comment because I had never been aware of my own voice. It was honest proof of a biological connection between us. The longer we talked, the more eager she was to assist me in any way she could to help me contact Rebecca.

"I am not sure what they are hiding, but it is no secret that Rebecca and her family live a clandestine lifestyle. They have an unlisted telephone number, and that is why it took so long for me to find it for you. Call me back tomorrow evening after you call her to let me know how Rebecca responded."

"Good night, Aunt Frieda, and thank you for being so encouraging. The things you said mean a lot to me, especially the part about our voices sounding similar."

I was surprisingly proud of myself for successfully crossing an enormous emotional chasm, but I was now reeling from the aftereffects of total immersion and the ramifications of what I had done. My knees were shaky, and my muscles were weak. The dream of meeting my birth mother was finally becoming a reality.

Frieda painted a very clear picture of Rebecca. More importantly, she had been sympathetic to my desire to locate my birth mother. She could sense my grief and understood my curiosity as an adoptee. It was the very first time anyone other than Martin had demonstrated empathy for my feelings of separation.

He agreed that life's path had some interesting twists because it was an amazing coincidence and act of fate that Frieda had moved to my parish neighborhood to be closer to her favorite priest, Father Hennen. We were both astounded by the irony of knowing that he had been Rebecca's catechism teacher, as well as my own. It gave us goose bumps knowing that Father Hennen had known all along that I was the daughter of Rebecca Meyer. The idea of six degrees of separation was reality.

I awoke early, ate a good breakfast, and took a shower. I was finally ready to take the plunge and call Rebecca. Martin stayed home to provide emotional support. I wanted to remain calm and act friendly. I took several deep breaths and hugged Martin. I cleared my throat and rehearsed my speech by practicing speaking clearly and concisely into the telephone speaker to be sure that Rebecca understood every word I had to say.

I was emotionally drained and numb. I was feeling terrified and distraught because, in the next few minutes, I planned to make the most important telephone call of my life. I planned to call the woman who gave birth to me thirty years ago. It was an incredible thought. There was no circulation in my hands. My fingers were ice-cold. My heart was beating fast, and I was trembling.

I mechanically dialed the number Aunt Frieda had given me and listened intently for a response. The obnoxious mechanical voice I heard was a cold slap in the face.

"Beep! The number you are calling has been disconnected and is no longer in service."

What had started as a wildly optimistic buildup of high expectations had ended in a crushing, humiliating emotional defeat? My fragile spirit had been shattered into a thousand pieces. My sincere peace offering composed of a bouquet of hope and optimism had wilted and evaporated into thin air. Tears flowed from my eyes, leaving thin, straggly stains on my cheeks.

Private 24 Number

Dear Mom, My adoption search is driven by an act of faith and sustained by courage. An eternal flame inside me ignites my passions and illuminates my path. I chose to lead and walk alone because there is no one to follow or guide me along the way other than God. I must learn to read his signs and steady the compass because I don't know my destination and cannot foretell the direction I am going. There have been many twists and turns and looming challenges to overcome along the way. I can't explain the passion that sustains me, but I am determined to continue moving forward, regardless of the difficulties I meet along the way. Each barrier I cross and obstacle I overcome makes me stronger and more determined than ever to achieve my goal of finding you. Internal impediments and doubts are my greatest challenges and require the most courage to overcome. Love, Judy

"HELLO, AUNT FRIEDA. I was looking forward to calling Rebecca last night, but the number you gave me is not valid," I lamented.

"Why would Rebecca do that?" Aunt Frieda was exasperated because she was certain Rebecca had intentionally deceived her.

"Can you spell Rebecca's married name for me?"

"Sure. R-O-S-S-I."

"Did Rebecca and Bruno attend the same high school?"

"Yes, and, by the way, I read in the newspaper that her class is planning a reunion this summer," she responded affirmatively.

I was thunderstruck by the coincidence, which partially explained why Martin's ploy had worked so well. I carefully jotted down the name of the high school in my notebook and thanked Aunt Frieda profusely for her generous insights and descriptions of Rebecca. Our conversation ended sadly because, unless I obtained an outright confession from Rebecca, it would be difficult to know if she really were my birth mother.

I hated the passive feeling of doing nothing. Action inspired anticipation and spawned hope. Meditation and reflection energized me and inspired my curiosity. Dead ends provided mental challenges that caused me to deliberate novel ways to solve new problems and innovation. Fresh ideas generated new enthusiasm and fueled my dreams.

I was inspired to call the high school to see if anyone remembered Rebecca. Perhaps one of her classmates had some insights into her background. The school was closed for the summer, but, by miraculous coincidence, one of her classmates answered on the first ring.

"Hello. This is Barbara Bianconi. I am in charge of a class reunion planned for this summer and just happen to be in the office this afternoon. If you need to talk to administration you will have to call back next fall."

My good fortune amazed me. "I am calling to find out if Rebecca Meyer will be attending your class reunion. Do you have her current address and telephone number?"

"I am building a website with names and pictures, but Rebecca Meyer is not on the list of classmates planning to attend, but I can give you the number of our former class president, Jim Mais. He is a wealthy lawyer who spends most of his time at Blue Mound golf club," she said cordially.

I wondered if any of her other classmates could recall seeing Rebecca when she was pregnant or knew anything about her baby. I called Jim Mais.

"Hello. I am trying to contact Rebecca Meyer. I was hoping you might have her current number and address. She is married to Bruno Rossi," I stated assertively.

Suspicious and dubious about my motives for wanting to contact Rebecca, he responded by aggressively taking the offensive. "Why do you want this information?"

Nervous and panicky for not wanting to expose my reason for calling increased his distrust. He confirmed that Rebecca was a classmate, but that was as far as he would go.

"My business hours are ten to noon. If you need legal advice, contact me at my office," he retorted tersely and hung up.

His cautiously guarded aggressive response shook me. His stonewalling made me nervous. My emotional vulnerabilities had given him the upper hand and pride in his ability to manipulate me. Martin grabbed the receiver out of my hand and immediately called him back. I liked his take-charge approach. He was accustomed to cutting through red tape, and he wasn't afraid to contact ski area presidents or their lawyers at home or any time of the day as long as the issue was important.

"The woman you just talked to is my wife. She was adopted, and she is currently conducting genealogical research to trace her biological roots. I apologize for the intrusion, but she is asking for your assistance to help her find her birth mother. The information she is requesting is proprietary and confidential, but she is making the request anyway because it is very important to her. Your cooperation would be greatly appreciated."

Jim listened carefully, stifled his resistance, and sympathetically agreed to cooperate. "Your honesty impresses me. I trust your motives. I will provide you with some information as long as no harm is done to anyone." His sudden reversal and the unexpected exposure of the humanitarian side of his personality shocked me.

"Let me give you a little background information. Rebecca and her boyfriend were often seen together in high school. I can still visualize them walking home from school together. They were holding hands, and Bruno carried Rebecca's books, but I can't remember what happened their senior year. Rebecca played the violin, and Bruno was one of the best athletes in school. He was the starting tailback on the football team and a vicious linebacker on defense. He also played on our winning basketball team. Bruno had several older brothers and sisters who also attended our school. Be patient while I check the yearbook," he added politely.

I could hear him flipping pages.

"Rebecca's name and face is shown in some of the group pictures, but her individual senior class photo is missing. My notes from our last class reunion say she is married to Bruno Rossi, who is self-employed and owns a restaurant and tavern. The address of the restaurant is listed, but not the telephone number," he offered politely.

I was flabbergasted to learn that the date of the last class reunion was the same day as my birthday, April 28. I wondered if Rebecca were aware of the significance. I was glad Martin had broken the ice because

Jim was speaking freely and openly willing to help with my adoption search.

"As the class president, I should be doing a better job keeping track of my classmates. Rebecca's telephone number should be easy to obtain from the telephone directory. If you can't find it, call our class historian and valedictorian, Jeanne Burke. Good luck researching your family tree. I hope you find what you are looking for," he said graciously.

"Thank you for your assistance. It was very kind of you."

I immediately called the editor of the class yearbook. "Hello? Is this Jeanne Burke? Jim Mais gave me your telephone number. I am trying to locate Rebecca Meyer."

"Are you a friend or relative?" she inquired politely.

I wanted to be honest and straightforward and explain my reason for calling, but I was afraid of damaging Rebecca's reputation.

"I am doing genealogy research on Rebecca Meyer. Jim Mais referred me to you. Can you help me?" I pleaded softly.

"I think I can help you. We were friends in high school. She was very attractive. She got along with everyone in our class. I was the editor of our yearbook and dedicated several pages to the orchestra. Rebecca was highlighted as an outstanding student and highly talented violinist. She played a solo at the annual winter concert."

"Did Rebecca have a steady boyfriend?"

Jeanne responded without hesitation. "She dated an Italian boy named Bruno Rossi. He was a respectable boy who never got into trouble. He played sports, and he was one of the star players. I used to hope that he would ask me for a date, but he and Rebecca were together all the time, so I gave up on Bruno. I don't think Rebecca dated anyone except Bruno. I am almost positive they married after high school. Would you like me to send you copies of their pictures from our yearbook?"

Filled with excitement, I nearly agreed to fly to Milwaukee to meet with Jeanne Burke without delay. "Thank you for offering. I would love to have copies of all the photos of Rebecca and Bruno that you can send me. It would mean a lot to me. How soon can you send them?" I asked excitedly.

Jeanne was cordial and very polite. I wondered if she was reading my mind. "Rebecca Meyer must be very special to you. I will get everything together and mail copies of the black-and-white photographs from the yearbook to you tomorrow. I would give you her number but it is unpublished. I suggest you call the Milwaukee telephone business office to see if they would release it."

Her positive response triggered an adrenalin surge that gave me the urge to do some hard physical exercise to release my pent-up energy. Talking with Jeanne and Jim had helped me break through my veil of shyness that was always holding me back. I was proud of myself for making a breakthrough and securing the confidence of Rebecca's classmates. The positive experience of asking strangers to help me gave me strength and the courage I needed to continue investigating. The process of discovery had a positive influence on my personality by helping me grow wiser and more confident.

All my life, I had tried to visualize my birth mother, but, thanks to Aunt Frieda and Rebecca's classmates, I now had some very valuable clues also leading to the identity of my birth father. Their comments had stirred my imagination. All positive signs pointed to Bruno Rossi. I had no verifiable facts to prove or disprove it, but circumstantial evidence had greatly increased the probability that he was my birth father.

As a final resort, I called my childhood friend Grace, an executive with the telephone company and fellow First Lilac Club sister. She could tell I was wound up because my voice was bubbling over with enthusiasm.

"Hello, Judy. What can I do for you?" She smiled.

I tried to summarize what had happened as quickly as I could by talking very fast, but that approach only made it more difficult for her to understand me.

"Today is the biggest day of my life. I have been searching intensely for over a year. I finally had a hugely significant breakthrough of monumental proportions, a discovery more valuable than money. I feel like I won the lottery because I think I found my birth mother. Ever since I had confessed to being adopted under the lilac bush, I have always wanted to know who she was and why she gave me up for adoption. I think I have discovered the treasure chest of a lifetime, and I need the key to unlock the secrets of my origin. And the key to the treasure chest is her unpublished telephone number."

My predicament astonished Grace. We had not talked for a long time, and she was staggered to learn that I had been pursuing my genealogy with such gusto.

"Wow. What you are saying is amazing. I share your passion. Like you, I have also been curious about your adoption. You remarked as a child that my parents, Archie and Helen, were your surrogate parents because they were your ideal image of a romantic married couple. I hope your dream comes true."

Grace was a dear friend. She was reassuring and confident. She had a good sense of humor and a happy marriage.

"I will call you back tomorrow with the information you are requesting. I hope you understand that disclosing unpublished telephone numbers is unethical and illegal."

Great Expectations

Dear Mom, I have dreamed of being reunited with you all my life. The closer I come to that reality, the more strong-minded and heroic I become. The experience of looking for you has caused me to look at the world in a more positive light, to be mature and wiser, and to be more aware of everyone around me. Searching for you has challenged me to better understand human nature, including my own, but I am still not certain what motivates me so strongly to find you. My adoption is a complex mystery that preoccupies my thoughts. I have a primal spiritual link with you that has remained open since birth and never healed. My motives to find you are the fulfillment of a childhood dream, as well as a clutching, bonding survival instinct for a dependable, familiar mental and physical connection that was never resolved. It wasn't natural to be passed from one nurse to another when I needed you. You willfully abandoned me as an infant. Yet, even today, I still cling to the hope of reuniting with you. Love, Judy

THE STILLNESS OF THE night air was damp and chilling. I slipped out of bed, tiptoed downstairs, and peeked through the curtain to view the predawn sky. It was littered with thousands of constellations, and even the planets were visible. I caught a glimpse of a meteor streaking across the night sky. Knowing it was a positive sign, I made a wish that the dream of finding my birth mother would come true.

I heated up a mug of hot tea with a twist of lemon and sat down at my desk to gather my thoughts. Today should be a day of action. I had successfully acquired my original baptismal certificate with the authentic name of my birth mother. Now it was time to see if my birth certificate were also a forgery.

I searched through my notes to see if there were any key phrases, questions, or methods of addressing the subject that would be helpful because I wanted each letter of inquiry to appear professionally written and businesslike, as well as comprehensive and factual. I wrote letters to Saint Joseph's Hospital, CSS, and the Salvation Army to see if I could glean any new information about my adoption or obtain copies of additional birth certificates different from the one I already had in my possession.

According to the Department of Health and Social Services, someone could obtain a copy of her original birth certificate for a fee unless she was adopted. Adoption records were unavailable, even under the Freedom of Information Act, and impossible to obtain without a court order. The act of conniving them into thinking my request was routine to avoid privacy laws was the only strategy available. I enclosed a personal check in each letter, hoping they would overlook the fact that I was adopted and send me the information.

The second letter was addressed to the Salvation Army in care of Booth Hill, a home for unwed mothers. I decided to call them to see what I could discover before finishing the letter.

"Hello. This is Ken Stein. How can I help you?"

"Can you verify if I were born at your facility?"

"Booth Hill is permanently closed. I'm the former director. I'm in the process of incinerating all of the remaining records. What was your mother's maiden name?"

"Rebecca Meyer. I am adopted, and I have reason to believe I was born at Booth Hill. I'm trying to learn as much as I can about my background. I want to confirm who my birth mother was and the general circumstances surrounding my birth. Do you have any information or copies of my birth certificate you could send me?" I inquired optimistically.

Background noises made it sound like he was in an empty warehouse with people pushing boxes around on a concrete floor. He seemed like a respectable person. He was friendly and talkative and volunteered to share some information about the organization with me.

"You are lucky you called today because, by tonight, all of the records from this hospital will have been placed in dead storage or incinerated, and this telephone would have been disconnected. You are very fortunate that Rebecca Meyer's file is one of the few remaining. The information is confidential, but I'm feeling exceptionally charitable today. I can't voluntarily disclose any of this information to you, but, if you write me a letter, I would be willing to confirm any of the facts you provide," he said generously.

"Can you give me some background information about your facility?"

"William Booth founded the Salvation Army in 1878. He was a British Methodist minister who started a Christian movement with a quasi-military structure. The original purpose was to teach Christian values to the poorest and most needy individuals, especially alcoholics and the unemployed. It soon became popular worldwide in fifty-eight countries with many different affiliations. William's wife Catherine was instrumental in obtaining contributions from the wealthy and eventually responsible for founding many homes and hospitals for unwed mothers throughout the United States, including this one in Milwaukee, which is affiliated with Martha Washington Hospital."

I thanked him for his thorough and gracious explanation about the origins of Booth Hill and the Salvation Army. Another small miracle had lit my path. Once again, I had miraculously passed through a phenomenally narrow window of opportunity that would have been closed forever within twenty-four hours. The timing of my request and the director's compassionate response was an amazing act of fate that encouraged me to stay intently focused until I had finished writing all three letters in record time. I looked up just in time to benefit from the first warming rays of sunshine that were brightening the morning sky and making drops of dew glisten on the flower pedals in my garden.

A SINGLE, LOUD, OBNOXIOUS ring of the telephone shattered the silence and caused me to bolt from my chair. I feared that Rosella was having a medical emergency.

"Good morning, Judy. I found the unpublished number for the Rebecca you requested."

"You are such a dear, Grace. You are dependable, good-natured, and the best friend I ever had. I admire you and appreciate what you have done for me. I promise to keep the source of this information private because I understand the ethics of the situation and the consequences of your action."

My emotions were bubbling over and difficult to contain. I was torn between heroic euphoria and intrepid, cowardly, pessimistic fail-

ure amid fears that Rebecca would either welcome me back unconditionally with open, loving arms or drown me in a tsunami of hostility
by ultimately slamming the door in my face, thus denying any future
possibilities for a positive reunion in the future. I was not anticipating a compromise. The situation would be black or white, win or vanquished. There were no words to capture the emotions of the child
inside me as I sensed the imminent rising of the curtain to reveal my
golden past. Only in a romantic novel or movie theater could I visualize
myself watching the heroine drop to her knees and clutch her breast as
she made her final pleas for clemency and mercy.

My endeavor had ignited my passions until they had spilled over
and could no longer be controlled. My emotions had become radically
changeable and unpredictable and filled with anxiety. Having been
overstimulated too many times in succession and for far too many
months, I had been experiencing severe emotional trauma nearly daily.
Conflicts between the sensations of winning and losing were an en-
cumbrance that cast a long shadow over my personality. One minute,
my dreams were filled with happiness, sunshine, bouquets of flowers,
blue ribbons, and award-winning gold metals draped around my neck,
followed by thunder and lightning, earthquakes, wildfires, scenes of accidental death, and dismemberment by wild animals. I was no longer
normal. My adoption search had become a heavy emotional burden
that I was eager to remove.

Sharing my thought and emotions with Martin was therapy for
me. He was the sole person aware of my plight, but only God could
provide relief from the pressures that were compressing and suffocating my soul.

I spent the remainder of the day thinking about Rebecca and how
to approach her. Quietly contemplating my mission, I sat in a comfortable, oversized leather chair in the living room and tried to relax. My
task was monumental. I needed to prepare the best speech of my life.
I wanted it to be perfect. I was inwardly focused and oblivious to all
external sounds and distractions. I tuned out the sounds of the kids
playing next door, birds chirping in the tree outside the dining room
window, and automobile traffic on the road outside and daydreamed
about my birth mother.

I longed for the valued emotional support and reinforcement my
husband provided because he had accompanied me on the entire jour-

ney. My adoption search had been an adventure of the mind, as well as reality, and we had mutually shared and addressed these topics as a team. He alone could weigh the consequences, predict the ramifications, and interpret their effects on me. He had understood the value of what I was seeking from the moment I had told him that I was adopted on our very first date. His love for me had never faltered. His daily assurances, motivational speeches, and sympathetic words were very dear to me. It would have been impossible to come this far without his continued moral support, sound advice, guidance, and reassuring encouragement.

Thinking about a potential reunion with my birth mother had dominated my thoughts every waking hour and governed my dreams for a thousand nights. My passion for finding my birth mother was about to climax in an unsustainable emotional crescendo.

The Yearbook

Dear Mom, I am your biological daughter. We share the same flesh and blood, and our genetic blueprint makes us similar. I have more in common with you than anyone else in the universe. For that reason, I hope fate will reunite us so we can rediscover our inherent natural connection as mother and daughter. My life is filled with wonder as I linger in limbo, thinking about the mysterious circumstances surrounding my adoption. It is an enigma why we live in isolation. Seeking an end to the negative torments that plague my soul drives my desire to find you as the only way to calm my spirit. As a lost soul, I look forward to a time when I can end the myriad of doubts and insecurities that dominate my dreams. The many obstacles placed in my path to prevent me from finding you have tested my will, and the act of overcoming them strengthened my faith. Can you sense my presence in the back of your mind, slowly eroding away the barriers that lie between us like the relentless ocean waves that inspire me? Love, Judy

TORMENTED WITH DREAMS OF tornados, hurricanes, mudslides, flying insects, and floods, I slept disturbed in a cold sweat. I had a vision of my birth mother. Her back was turned. I wanted to call out her name to let her know that I was her lost child, but my voice was silent because I was insecure and afraid that she might not like me. Passively waiting for her to turn around and recognize me, the vision evaporated into a spiritual mist, leaving me cold and alone.

I awoke with my eyes tightly closed. I tried intensely to re-create the image of my birth mother in the recesses of my mind, but it disappeared in a burst of consciousness. Why was I dreaming about floods, cliffs, and waves crashing onto the shore in anticipation of meeting my birth mother? Pessimism was dominating my thinking about a journey to an unknown place that might be hostile or unsafe. What were the consequences of dredging up deeply held secrets from long ago? Was my mission about to collapse into a tearful melodramatic folly, a traumatizing devastating emotional tempest from which I might never recover? Was I about to unravel all that was good and comfortable in my life due to my irrepressible quizzical nature? Was I making the wrong choice?

I had enough circumstantial evidence to be relatively certain that Rebecca was my birth mother. Perhaps this was a good stopping point. What was the need anyway? The potential for a catastrophic decline in my mother's reputation resulting from my callous disclosure of her sin had potential to create extreme unhappiness, anger, and retribution against her or even result in divorce. It was irresponsible of me to continue without considering the consequences and risks to all concerned parties before taking further action because fear causes panic. Panic is the source of procrastination and the foundation for inert unhappiness.

A week had passed, and I had done nothing other than create a million excuses for not taking action. I was dragging my feet because I wasn't mentally prepared. I washed clothes, cooked meals, compulsively cleaned, and watched television. I was frightened to face the reality of being rejected again.

The key to my past was in my hand, but I was terrified to open the lock and expose all the secrets inside. It was simply too risky. Why should I change my life? My family loved me. I was healthy and lived in a beautiful location with friends and a good job. Why should I give up my peaceful life of tranquility and certainty for an unknown potentially tumultuous future?

Time was slipping away. Each day after work, Martin asked if I had prepared a list of questions to ask Rebecca. Every evening, I had a new excuse.

ON THE EIGHTH DAY, a large envelope arrived in the mail from Jeanne Burke in Milwaukee. I called Martin to share the good news. He arrived home for lunch just in time to see me open the package containing eight incredible black-and-white pictures of Bruno Rossi and Rebecca Meyer from their high school yearbook. When I saw Bruno in his basketball and football uniforms, I knew immediately that he had to be my birth father. We looked very similar. He had dark eyes, a light olive complexion, and the classic chiseled features of a masculine

Italian male. His facial features were similar to mine. He was muscular, and he had a big smile; dark hair; large, white teeth; and dimples on both cheeks.

There were several pictures of Rebecca playing the violin in the high school orchestra. She had long, brown hair and an attractive profile exactly as I had envisioned her. Seeing their photographs for the first time was an incredible thrill. I was as high as a kite and more jubilant than a lottery winner. My happiness was outside the natural range of variability for human emotions. An unknown part of my life had been serendipitously discovered as easily as a butterfly emerges from the cocoon. Discovery of my roots had awakened me from a deep coma. The mystery of my birth had been solved.

Our physical similarities were much too remarkable to be coincidental. The pictures were so convincing that Martin said they could be used in court as proof of our biological connection. My quest to find my birth parents was not a fantasy any more. Rebecca and Bruno were real people. I had seen their faces.

Viewing these pictures stirred new ideas about relationships. I had a new awareness about how people connect with biological relatives that I had never experienced before. I could not rationally or coherently describe the meaning or positive affect these photographs created. The insight and revelation they provided instantly redefined my self-image and perceptions of my true background. I had grown up as the daughter of Mario and Rosella Romano in name only.

A new sense of identity was gushing out of me. Even though we had never met, I had a strong spiritual sense of union with Rebecca and Bruno. I felt like a born-again Christian, overflowing with joy and happiness. I had prayed for guidance and strength and received salvation. The images in the photographs presented a new perspective and inspired a new enigmatic vision of me. It was a paradoxical revelation that stripped off my cloak of secrecy to expose the real person underneath. In the blink of an eye, I had passed backward through a time warp into silent memories that connected me to my past. Knowing I looked like both of them was a traumatic, mind-altering event.

"I can see the wheels in your mind spinning. Watching someone being transformed by a paradigm shift in thinking is a rare monumental event. The average person never experiences a paradigm in thinking as radical as the one you just experienced. The emotions you are feeling run deep and penetrate the essence of your soul because the evidence is unmistakable and indisputable. These pictures provide incontrovertible evidence that you are related. You are fortunate because someone in heaven is smiling on you," Martin said philosophically. He was trying to find words to describe what he had observed. His voice cracked slightly as a sign of empathy.

Martin was genuinely happy for me because my goal to seek the truth had forced me to become a stronger person, more skilled, and less fearful of others.

"If you believe that what goes around comes around, then you will always commit to being a good person who is kind to others. Perhaps that is why you are being rewarded now. You live a Christian life and have a lot to be thankful for. If virtue is its own reward, then you are receiving an appropriate compensation."

It was a conundrum why I was experiencing such a powerful and overwhelming connection with Bruno and Rebecca because I had never met them. I had a new sense of belonging even though we had no shared memories. Perhaps I had been born with a vacant spot in my heart, and, as the vacuum of emptiness was dramatically filled with hope, it created euphoria. A tremendous exhilaration of ecclesiastic fulfillment and ecstatic feelings of self-discovery overcame me.

I pulled a magnifying lens out of the desk drawer and placed the pictures under the desk lamp to examine them in detail. I held them next to my face and looked in the mirror to observe the remarkable similarities. I held them next to my heart and cried tears of happiness.

The pictures were the catalyst I needed to overcome my fears and enthusiastically jump-start my next task. Feeling a boost in confidence, sense of urgency, and resiliency, I was suddenly inspired. Rebecca had to be my birth mother, but I still needed to extract a confession as undeniable proof.

"You are a wonderful person with good values. I love you very much and believe in you. I want to be there to support you when you call Rebecca. Perhaps a reunion will provide a closure to your life that is currently lacking. You are intelligent. I am sure you can handle whatever God intends for you to do with your life. Have faith, and don't be afraid to ask for spiritual guidance when you are uncertain of your fate. I'm prepared to love you regardless of the outcome. It doesn't matter if your parents are poor or uneducated or speak a different language. You have my blessing to continue your search," Martin said with compassionate reassurance.

His eyes were beginning to tear. Spilling out his emotions, he pulled me close and gave me a tender hug. I kissed him good-bye and watched as the rear wheels of his Porsche squealed and smoked, leaving remnant black streaks on the asphalt as he sped away.

Thinking about calling my birth mother moved my heart to palpitate rapidly and made my mouth go dry. Spasms of fear between bouts of terror left me light-headed and feeling faint.

The Rebuttal

Dear Mom, My simple childhood curiosity has blossomed into a passionate quest that dominated my thoughts. I have chosen to relentlessly pursue my goal of finding you with all my heart. Finding you has become my solitary purpose and primary mission in life. Many obstacles have been placed in my path, but I have learned that, with maturity, they can be overcome with patience and perseverance. The most burdensome and wearisome hindrances to conquer are my own self-generated insecurities. My internal fears absorb vital emotional energy and reduce physical stamina, leading to delays in action and the prevention of progress. My life would be simple if I walked away and abandoned my search, but I would always remain hopelessly adrift. The quest to find my self-identity would be forever stalled. No, I must travel onward because you are the essence of my soul that is broadcasting a powerful signal, growing in strength, and becoming more readable every day. Your beacon is a sign from God, letting me know that my banishment from your arms is about to end. Love, Judy

I TOOK A DEEP breath, did some stretching exercises, and said a small prayer before picking up the telephone receiver and dialing Rebecca's number. I opened my notebook and jotted down the time and date on a blank sheet of paper. I had prepared and memorized my list of questions and tried to create a positive mental image of myself by speaking in front of a mirror. I had combed my hair, washed my face, brushed my teeth, applied some perfume, and put on my favorite sweater. I felt like I was standing on a high diving platform, about to initiate my first dive in front of a worldwide audience. I was afraid and tense. The first step was the hardest and a long way to fall if I faltered.

My knees were weak, and my cheeks were pale. My body was numb, and my legs felt heavy. I had to consciously remind myself to breathe properly. Martin sat across from me at the kitchen table with the look of a concerned parent dropping his child off the first day of school. His facial expressions were supportive and encouraging. My carefully written notes were in front of me, but I was on the verge of a panic attack. I wondered if, when I tried to say hello, any sound would come out of my mouth.

My nervousness reminded me of a grade school experience when I had to stand and read aloud in front of my classmates. When it was sometimes my turn to read, I would have difficulty focusing on the text, and no words would come out. When that happened, I faltered and became even more tense and self-conscious. That was how I was feeling now. I was suddenly jolted from my short daydream when the telephone suddenly stopped ringing.

"Hello," a female voice answered rather abruptly.

"Hello, Rebecca. This is Judith Ann," I said softly.

"Who?" she blurted tersely in response.

I took a deep breath and tried to relax. I had to remember to breathe. I began speaking slowly and deliberately. The clumsy beginning of our conversation didn't faze me, and I got right to the point.

"I have something very important to say to you. Are you sitting down? Is this a good time to talk?" I inquired timidly.

"Who is this?" she demanded to know.

"Well, it's a very long story. I have waited over thirty years for this conversation," I said politely.

"What kind of answer is that?" she demanded to know.

"This is Judith Ann ... supposedly ... I don't know how to say this. Well, ah, I think you might have given birth to me thirty-two years ago. Do you remember me?" I awkwardly fumbled my words.

"No, I don't think I do. I can't recall anything like that. Thirty-two years ago?" The woman's voice cracked as her sentence mysteriously tapered off at the end. I recited my next words deliberately as if I were a child in an elementary school play.

"My adoption is a difficult subject for me to talk about. I thought it would be reassuring for you to know that I had good parents and a happy childhood," I said tentatively. I hoped she would like me.

Her cold rebuke was quick and sharp. "I don't have the slightest idea what you are talking about. This is ridiculous. Who are you?"

Her abrupt denial had unexpectedly caught me off guard. I paused for a moment to take a deep breath, gather my thoughts, and decide what to say next before responding.

"Does April 28 mean anything to you?" I anticipated a weakening and an affirmative response when I mentioned the exact day of my birth.

"There is nothing significant about that date. What is this all about?"

Knowing that my birth mother had rejected me at birth rekindled horrible childhood feelings of rejection. Our conversation was not going as planned.

"I am an adoptee. You are my birth mother. I thought you would be curious to know what happened to your baby."

"How did you obtain this telephone number?" Her emphatic rebuke and lack of warmth surprised me.

Wanting to be thoughtful and respectful, I chose my words carefully before continuing. "I mean no harm to you. I'm not looking to replace my adopted mother with someone else. She will always be my mother. I am grateful for the way she raised me."

"Your scornful accusations are false. It is wrong of you to denigrate me. What you are doing is wrong." Rebecca was categorical in her denials, but I interpreted her negative rebuttals as good omens because she was still paying attention and hadn't hung up. "Where did you get this crazy idea that I was your birth mother? It is ludicrous of you to make that accusation. Someone is playing a joke on you because I don't know what you are talking about."

Our conversation had started with such high expectations. I had looked forward to this opportunity for many years. Now the walls were caving in on me and plunging me into a tar pit of depression. My questions were as hard to ask as they were for Rebecca to answer. Maybe I should have been the one to hang up and end this charade.

"It isn't my intention to pry into your private life. I'm just curious to know if you are my birth mother. This conversation is just between us. You don't have to tell anyone. Did you ever think about me after I was born? Aren't you curious to know what happened to your baby? I can send you a letter telling you what I have been doing all these years," I suggested as a token offer.

"I don't have the slightest interest in what you have to say or what you have to offer. I don't fit into your picture."

I thought this was a good idea to call her, but our conversation had evolved into an emotionally hurtful experience. I had always envisioned a positive reunion with open arms and smiles. I had dreamed about this moment many times. I had assumed my birth mother would be thankful to know that I had prospered under the tutelage of a strong surrogate mother. I thought she would be glad to see that I had ten fingers and toes, shiny, brown hair, and white teeth and I was normal for my age. With a pink linen handkerchief, I wiped away a tear that stained my cheek.

I had never visualized a scenario whereby my birth mother would shut me out of her world and deny my existence. This woman wasn't the pleasant, easygoing, friendly individual I was expecting to find at the end of the rainbow. I was certain she was my biological mother when I dialed her telephone number, but I now had doubts as my optimism and curiosity were swapped with fear and rejection.

"Do you know anyone with a name similar to yours who could be my birth mother? My original baptismal certificate lists the mother of child as Rebecca Meyer."

My persistence was giving me the upper hand. My confidence was slowly returning because I could tell that Rebecca was curiously listening intently to what I had to say, albeit denying knowing anything about me.

"You are confused. Somebody goofed. You don't have anything to go on with me because I don't know what you are talking about. You should be questioning the source of your information. Besides, what you are doing is illegal. You are curious. For what reason? Didn't you have a happy life? Weren't your adopted parents good to you?"

"It was very tough for me to make this telephone call." I tried to extract a little sympathy from her.

"Whoever your birth mother was, she only brought you into this world. She has nothing to do with your life. All you can do is give up this crazy notion and forget about her. It is very foolish on your part to do this search. You are not using the good judgment that your adopted mother tried to teach you. She would be very hurt if she knew what you were doing. I don't see what your birth mother could possibly mean to you now," she stated with finality, hoping to end our discussion.

I was experiencing the same negative feelings I had as a child. In the deep recesses of my mind, there was a serious psychological wound.

The trauma psychologists characterized as childhood separation syndrome had been concealed and camouflaged by a thick layer of mental scar tissue that had remained forever sensitive. The wound was so deep and personal that it was hopeless to share with others. Not until I was married did I finally expose my true self to anyone else. I had always felt like I was missing something important, but not exactly sure what it was, other than a sense of loss and feeling of separation from my birth mother. I was excruciatingly aware of subtle feelings of rejection that caused me to be unsure of my true identity.

I was driven by a strong, primal instinct, like the beloved family dog in a Disney story, lost and abandoned in the forest during a camping excursion in the wilderness. The family cried and bemoaned their loss until the dog miraculously found his way back to a small town in Kansas four months later. The family loved him and welcomed him home. The dog wagged his tail, and everyone lived happily forever after. That is how I had expected my own adoption story to play out.

My mind returned to reality. I tried to explain. "Whenever I see people who look like me, I wonder if I am related to them. I ask questions to see if they have similar interests or hobbies or if they have a relative who plays the violin." I intentionally tried to say something personal to shake Rebecca into confessing. "I would like to know some things about my birth mother: what she looks like, if we have things in common, and what makes her unique and special. I am curious to learn about my family tree and medical history. There are many things I would like to learn."

Rebecca was silent.

"No matter what you say, it makes me feel very good hearing your voice and knowing that you really exist." I hoped to soften her resistance.

Her rhetorical response brutalized me. "Well, you are going to have to go on wondering. I can't help you. I was an adoptee myself, and I never had inquisitive thoughts about my birth parents. I was so happy and full of love for my adopted parents. I would not even give anyone else another thought. You have to know someone, live with her, love her, experience life with her, go through tragedies and problems with her, and be part of her. The person you are looking for only gave birth to you. She probably never ever thought about you after that."

I didn't believe her. "You must have dreamed about me or thought of me when you prayed. Or were you especially lonely some nights?"

"Once someone has gone through a pregnancy as an unwed mother, the whole experience that happened in her youth is finished and final. This experience is a chapter in a young girl's life that is closed forever, something to be forgotten," she added coldly.

Her dismissive response epitomized tough love. It was hurtful, and I almost started to cry. Her explanation about the casual dismissal of her child not bothering her was a psychological cuff to the head and heart that left me reeling. I glanced out the living room window at the sun setting over the steep mountain hillside with red rock outcroppings and mature spruce trees. The mountains were warmly glowing in the sunset, but my heart was overcast with gloom.

"I live in a beautiful part of the country. There are mountains in my backyard vividly lit by a brilliant pink sunset this evening. You should not feel threatened by me on the telephone because I live far away in another state. I'm not planning to disrupt your life. I am your child and only seeking acknowledgement of my missing identity."

"There is no point in going any further with this conversation. If you don't mind, I would rather not," she responded, nervously overreacting.

"I have official documents naming Rebecca Meyer as my birth mother, the same name as yours." I returned to square one.

Wanting her to realize that I was a good person with honorable intentions before hanging up, I was becoming concerned that I had pushed her too far. The more she said, the less believable her rebuttals sounded. She must be denying the truth because she didn't want to have anything to do with me. I felt bad.

"I was hoping for a more positive response from you. I apologize for making you feel so uncomfortable. This conversation makes me uneasy, too," I said apologetically.

"There is no point to all this," she exclaimed insensitively.

Her response was blunt and to the point. I could tell that she was getting ready to hang up.

"I would like to send you a letter. Would it be more private if I mailed it to your place of work to avoid arousing suspicions at home?" I sincerely wanted to know.

She must have felt like I kicked the legs out from under her chair because I could hear her gasp and her heart palpitating. She felt threatened and emphatically hammered her point home.

"If you know where I work, then somebody close to our family is giving you information about me. Now this really has me upset. If you ever send me anything with a return address on it, you will really regret it. I will be anonymous as far as you are concerned. You are still nameless, and that is the way I would like it to stay."

I placed my hand over my chest to calm my anxious heart and replied in my most pious and humble voice, "If I gave you my telephone number, would you ever feel like calling me?"

"No, I would never do that. This foolish search will achieve nothing. Your birth mother has the right to remain silent. Do you want to ruin her life by publishing your story? This is absurd. This whole thing doesn't even concern me. Don't ever dare to try contacting me again," she offensively retaliated in a shrill, threatening tone.

Knowing this might be the only opportunity I would ever have to speak with my birth mother encouraged me to persist and relentlessly refuse to stop talking. When her words knocked me down, I resiliently bounced back up again. Her refusal to acknowledge me as her daughter was cruel, but I just kept moving forward into the firestorm of adversity. I tried to remain tranquil, polite, and nonthreatening. Our conversation was like the contract offer of a lifetime. I would not allow myself to be thrown out until our conversation reached an amicable conclusion. When I ran out of adult logic, I pleaded like a child, begging the babysitter for cookies and milk and the opportunity to stay up late to watch television.

"I guess our conversation will end this way for now. I will mail you a letter and send you some pictures to give you a better idea of who I am," I said indefatigably.

Rebecca was weary and still on the defensive. "Please don't contact me. For your sake, I hope you remain unidentified," she scolded, expressing her disapproval.

Click. Her rebuttal was the emotional climax of my whole life. My entire body was trembling. I had tried to sound optimistic, pleasant, and nonthreatening, but her strong denials were an unequivocal total rebuttal of the overwhelming circumstantial evidence in my possession.

Her voice cracked when I told her my birth date. I distinctly heard her voice rise and then drop abruptly like a musical instrument with a full mute. I had wanted to introduce myself slowly and delicately, but my conscience was recklessly screaming in my ear to blurt everything out all at once.

I had expected Rebecca to burst into tears, show remorse, plead for mercy, and ask for forgiveness. I had never expected her to wholeheartedly reject my pleas and fervently deny the truth. It had taken me two intense years of searching to arrive at this point and gather enough courage to follow through with my intentions. She had soundly rejected me, yet I was somehow very happy because I had overcome my greatest fears. The fiasco was over. There were no fireworks. Our connection had fizzled. I had survived my great leap of faith from the highest airplane, successfully pulled the rip cord, and survived the plunge, but I was shaken, weak-kneed, and exhausted from the fall.

What had I learned? Some of her key responses kept echoing in my mind like an old song repeating itself. Instead of taking her comments at face value, I had tried to read between the lines because she was nervous and behaving cautiously. When I asked outright if I were her child, her response had been very malleable.

She had replied, "No, I don't think so."

It was a pathetic, feebleminded response. Did she really expect me to believe that she couldn't remember having a baby? Her rejoinder was deceptively weak, intentionally presented as a ruse to fool me. An honest person would have been more exact and definitive and would have left no doubts in the mind of others. No sane person could ever forget the trauma of giving birth to another human being before tragically discarding it.

I had to assume she was lying. But what if she were telling the truth? Was I falsely accusing the wrong person again, the same as I had already done once before? It was frustrating dealing with two different women in denial who had been equally challenging, cunningly deceptive, and mysteriously vague.

It was difficult distinguishing facts from emotions. Doubts started slipping into my mind. Her denials had been emphatic, but unconvincing. Her responses to my questions had been unexpected, and her attempts to disguise her nervousness had changed the tone of her voice and made her appear guilty.

Why was she so concerned about her privacy? Was her husband

in the Mafia? She must be hiding from someone other than me. I was intimidated by her scolding taunts to expose my deviant activities to my adopted parents because they were sensitive people. Protecting them from emotional hurt was my greatest weakness and Achilles' heel. Rebecca had sensed my vulnerability and intentionally belabored this issue to make me feel guilty. She was right to do so because I would never pursue my dream of finding my roots if my adoptive parents knew I was conniving behind their backs or doing something illegal or malicious.

I tried to reassure Rebecca that our conversation could remain a secret between the two of us, but she had become even more upset and defensive as our conversation progressed, trying to bully me whenever my self-confidence waned. I hadn't prepared for her denials or full in-your-face rejection. I felt horrible. My bubble had burst. I was sad and despondent.

There could be many valid reasons why she would be protective of her reputation. If her husband were not my birth father and she had never told him she had a baby before they were married, she would be in extreme danger of getting a divorce.

I wondered if she perceived me as a stalker in a dark hat and trench coat, wearing large sunglasses, and parked in a gray car on a side street where I could spy on her. She must be paranoid knowing I had access to her private number and the place where she worked. She must think I knew more about her than I actually did. Now that I broke the ice, she would be certain to be nervously glancing over her shoulder, watching for me.

She had naïvely assumed that someone in her family was knavishly stabbing her in the back by giving me inside information. I wondered what the consequences would be if she falsely accused any one of her family members of giving me her private number. It was a huge risk for her to take that could potentially backfire with terrible consequences. For that reason, it was best if I avoided disclosing Aunt Frieda and her high school classmates Jim Mais and Jeanne Burke as my informants.

Despite overwhelming evidence, the mystery of my birth was still technically unresolved. First, I had found Rebecca Maier living on a dairy farm in Wisconsin and now a Rebecca Meyer living in Milwaukee. I was batting zero for two because neither woman had confessed. I was slowly concluding that the origin of my life was more complex than an unsolved Rubik's Cube.

I tried to view the world from Rebecca's perspective and think like an adoption detective, wondering if I could present any overwhelming evidence to force her to reveal her secret and admit the truth because it was looking increasingly doubtful that she would ever feel remorse and willingly confess. I wondered if I were shrewd enough to uncover facts that could be used to trip her up or cause her to incriminate herself.

I was discouraged, but her verbal assaults and adamant denials weren't going to force me to back down. I was still feeling strong despite the huge setback and monumental emotional letdown I had just experienced.

If Rebecca were not my mother, why did she keep talking to me for such a long time without hanging up? Would a person who valued her privacy disclose the number of years she had been married to a complete stranger? If she had a different maiden name, why didn't she simply reveal it to me?

Initially, she had been edgy because I had stunningly caught her off guard. Instinctively, I felt that time was on my side and she would eventually soften and admit I was her child.

I forgave Rebecca for her terse sarcastic responses, but I wasn't going to voluntarily back down or be defeated by her words or intimidation alone. I surmised that, if she lied about her relationship with her adopted parents, she was probably lying about other things as well. Aunt Frieda had emphatically stated that Rebecca did not get along very well with her parents and disowned them after she was married, and her comments were contrary to what Rebecca had said.

Rebecca's statement about someone giving birth to a baby and never thinking about it made me feel horrible. Her comment was hurtful and crushed my heart because I didn't believe it was possible for a woman to discard an infant without giving it a second glance. She must have cried herself to sleep at night, wondering what happened to her baby. She would have felt shame if her pregnancy disrupted her teenage life and education. I refused to accept her denunciation of me, no matter how strongly she had protested the facts.

She said she never thought about me once. Was her statement of denial a confession? If she were innocent, why didn't she end the conversation and hang up instead of talking to me for an entire hour? Ultimately, I was glad we had a conversation now that I had opened Pandora's box and let out all of our emotions. Her senses would be on maximum alert, and her psychological defenses would be greatly intensified now that I had exposed myself. As long as she remained steadfastly committed to denying the truth and we continued pestering her, one lie would lead to another, and I would eventually trap her into confessing.

She was emphatic about not sending her anything in the mail because her privacy was very important to her. What if her husband weren't my birth father? Could she sue me for invasion of privacy or defamation of character? What kind of mother would sue her biological daughter for trying to find her? I really didn't know my rights as an adoptee or anything about the laws protecting her privacy. Her threats of intimidation and lawsuits made me shudder because the idea was cold and the opposite response I had expected.

Maybe I should retaliate and threaten her by giving her the impression I really was stalking her with the intention of exposing her in public. How would she react then?

My call to Rebecca had been a highly emotional ordeal for both of us. I was a ghost from her past, taunting and haunting her by dredging up unpleasant reminiscences from a time forgotten. She was guilty, and her painful memories of me had spontaneously ignited into a flame too hot to handle.

I sprawled on the floor and listened pensively to the unforgettable words of Paul Simon's song, "Mother and Child Reunion."

No, I would not give you false hope, on this strange and mournful day, but the mother and child reunion is only a motion away, oh little darling of mine.

I had faith in myself, and I wasn't going to voluntarily abandon my eternal quest to find my birth mother. Desperately wanting the pain of emotional suffering to end for both of us, I picked up a pen and paper and composed a letter to Rebecca.

28 Letters

Dear Mom, It wounded me deeply when you denied you were my birth mother. Your lack of warmth and rejection of me as your biological daughter is difficult to concede. Naïvely, I had expected you to be more gracious, honest, and curious to learn what happened to your child. You admonished me for calling your unpublished telephone number, but the fear of rejection all my life has hardened me. Even though your reaction was overwhelmingly unenthusiastic, it was exhilarating to hear your voice in person for the first time. I remain steadfastly committed to meeting you in person. I hope you will eventually overcome your trepidation and welcome me into your life. Love, Judy

REBECCA'S THREATENING WORDS OF rejection echoed in my head. "Don't you dare send me any letters with your return address on them, or you'll be very sorry."

Ultimately, hearing my birth mother's voice for the first time in my life was mystical and unbelievably thrilling. Regardless of her brutal rejection and lack of warmth toward me, coming to the realization that she was a real person greatly increased my desire to meet her. When the dust from our brief exchange had settled, I realized that nothing great was ever achieved by making small plans. Small plans had no magic to stir my blood. Aiming high in hope by making big plans was the more exciting and noble course that magically encouraged my imagination to follow through to completion.

My birth mother's voice was something I had longed to hear all my life. I happily pursued her because I had naïvely expected her to be gracious and forgiving. Foolishly, I had anticipated her spontaneously welcoming me to her bosom unconditionally, but my vision of a happy reunion had collapsed in a veil of tears, leaving me afflicted with her verbal taunts ringing in my ears. Personal threats and the potential to be sued were thorny issues to overcome because, in my heart, I knew the only way to reduce the confusion and pain I had suffered all my life was to find the woman who gave birth to me. I was instinctively motivated to heal the deep psychological hurt inflicted on me by being separated at birth. Without her confession, I was condemned to remain unheralded and anonymous forever.

In hindsight, my approach had been unsophisticated and clumsy. It was immature of me to assume Rebecca would confess her sins to a complete stranger. My assumption that she would voluntarily provide me with a reasonable explanation of the circumstances surrounding my birth without an advance warning was unrealistic. Suddenly emerging from the past like a mirage in the desert, I had scared her half to death. It had been natural for her to feel threatened and perceive me as a potential threat.

Powerful childhood emotions triggered by the psychological effects of separation when uncontrolled were at the root of negative behavior attributed to adoptees worldwide, and I was no exception. All adopted children suffer when they learn their birth mothers rejected them. Separation causes them to become introverted and conceal their true natures by avoiding exposure of their personal pain to others, and I had also learned to keep my feelings hidden under a shroud of secrecy. Intentional suppression of my deep sense of rejection and confusion about being an adoptee were beneficial for helping me lead an outwardly happy and productive life. I pretended to be extroverted to appear functionally normal and outwardly happy in the presence of my peers, but few people were aware of my inhibitions, personal obsessions, and fragility of my internal mental structure.

It was normal for healthy children to know something about their most distinguished ancestors, occupations, and nationalities. Orphans were treated differently, automatically shunned, humiliated, and embarrassed by their lack of awareness of their cultural heritage. Claiming they had no interest in finding their birth parents was a deceptive excuse because, in reality, they had no hope of ever experiencing the joy of ancestral worship. It was unnatural for adopted parents to brainwash their adopted children into thinking it was okay for them to be ignorant about their unique personal history and ancestry because a lack of rootedness destroys confidence and diminishes pride.

Whereas many adoptees only lamented their condition, I faced into the winds of adversity and accepted the challenge. I was a maverick willing to earnestly pursue the opportunity to find my biological parents with gusto, enjoying playing the role of adoption detective, embracing the thrill of researching clues, looking for rainbows, and finding the hidden path leading to the pirate's treasure chest of gold and jewels.

Scientific evidence to support the effects of adoption on children was far too overwhelming and predictive to ignore. Selective mutism, extreme shyness, and other social anxiety disorders were evidence of trauma frequently associated with adoption, especially in children under three years old. Selective mutism can be highly functional for a child by reducing anxiety and protecting the child from perceived challenges of social interaction. Individuals with these characteristics were more likely to exhibit this trait in groups with high performance expectations. This is most evident in schools, which heighten anxiety and cause the protective symptoms to be exacerbated. Adoptees with this anxiety might be highly talkative at home with family and friends, but avoid speaking altogether in classrooms, large groups, and social functions.

Selective mutism was a trait I had exhibited in Rosella's presence as a child. She observed I had talked expressively with my two dolls Barbara and Mary, but I would not talk directly to her. My behavior puzzled her, and she did not understand its perplexity. I wasn't comfortable in her presence, and I had reacted by withdrawing. Staying mute was a classic symptom of child kidnap victims and the easiest way to protect myself from someone I had perceived as a stranger and potential threat to my security.

Adoptees with selective mutism have difficulty verbalizing personal thoughts because they are excessively revealing and painful or of a subconscious nature. Spoken communication is not the best way to understand their social anxieties because it is far easier for them to orally suppress their feelings of personal doubt, insecurity, and anger than to disclose them with body language.

Dramatic personal benefits were derived from the research I performed to understand what it means to be adopted. Reading scientific journals provided new insights and enhanced my awareness of the complex bundle of psychological symptoms associated with adoption. Through personal observation, I had ascertained that many adult adoptees appeared outwardly contented, but the majority suppressed a wide range of complex anxieties not readily evident to others. It was disappointing to realize that many social workers, teachers, counselors, spiritual leaders, and even parents with adopted children had never researched the psychology of adoption in depth, even though much of this information was readily available and well documented in books, scientific journals, and the Internet.

Self-motivational books increased my confidence, resiliency, tenacity, and drive. Reading helped me analyze my own behavior, think abstractly, and understand human behavior from new perspectives.

My disheartening conversation with Rebecca inspired me to think long and hard about my mission and all of its ramifications. I decided to compose my thoughts in writing and share them with Rebecca. The written word was a valuable communication medium. Thoughts and expressions were final, more exact, and less likely to be misinterpreted. I focused intently on the computer screen, and words from the heart miraculously appeared.

Dear Rebecca, I unconditionally forgive you for your transgressions and applaud you for bringing me into this world as a healthy, caring person, but my life will never be complete unless we share the blessings of life. The ultimate goal of our conciliation should be to achieve a quiet inner peace of mind as mother and daughter that will last for infinity. It is not honorable for a mother to say without remorse to her flesh and blood that, by her choosing, she is no longer the mother of her own child. Motherhood is an act of creation and an enduring verity that is everlasting. You launched me into this world, and you are my true spiritual and biological link on this earth for all eternity. The genetic blueprint I inherited from you mimics the physiological and psychological characteristics shared by our matriarchal ancestors for survival over the millennia. Our relationship is much more unique and complex than simply biological. The essence of the life force that sustains and connects us as mother and daughter is esoteric, intuitive, spiritual, and much greater than the sum of its parts. My enduring faith in God lit my path and guided me to you. He gave me wisdom, strength, comfort, and the ability to stay focused during my long journey of discovery. He motivated me and honed my spiritual compass that pointed the

way and inflamed my passions when there was little hope of finding
you. Love, Judy

I paused to enjoy the view out my window. I felt blessed. It was
a beautiful day. There was not a cloud in the bright blue sky, and the
temperature was unseasonably warm. I poured myself a cup of coffee
and sat in the sunshine to observe our beautiful flower beds, newly
mowed grass and flowering shrubs, birds and squirrels, and the steep,
velvety, dark green mountain hillside that sheltered our valley. I lived
in a peaceful alpine setting, but, despite all that was good in my life,
thinking about my adoption was a distraction preventing me from feeling settled.

I had ambushed Rebecca, and her instinct had been denial. Unfortunately, I wasn't able to persuade her that I came in peace. She must
have had delusional visions of me grabbing her by the neck as retribution for abandoning me or hallucinations of a television film crew
forcing open her front door and sticking a microphone in her face. I
had terrorized her into thinking the walls were collapsing around her.
She was trapped because she had no place to hide from her own self-
induced guilt and shame. My surprise telephone call exposing her past
was a nightmare that made her feel lightheaded, faint-hearted, and
terror-stricken. Now she feared that I might unexpectedly show up on
her doorstep and ring her doorbell.

After spending a lifetime suppressing her memories of me, I had
been naïve to assume she would jump up and embrace an urchin she
had legally abandoned. When I composed my first letter to Rebecca,
I had internalized my thoughts, and many of my suppressed beliefs
and opinions had flowed out of my head effortlessly. Writing them on
paper was a form of therapy that helped me understand my own mo-
tivations and beliefs. Regardless of what might happen in the future,
we both shared similar sensitivities and a mutual desire for privacy that
needed to be respected.

Thinking it would help Rebecca understand me better if I mailed
her some information about myself, I composed a second letter de-
scribing my life as a wife, mother, and career person.

Dear Rebecca, I live in a small alpine village surrounded by tower-
ing mountain hillsides. We are blessed with clean air, good schools,

and friendly people. The sun is bright, children are always smiling, and world events seem very far away. My son is a source of pride. He has brown eyes, dark hair, and a smooth complexion. He is physically active and enjoys all forms of outdoor exercise, and he was selected junior model citizen this year. My life is simple and complete. I began my working career as a nurse, but the rigors of taking care of hospital patients on nights and weekends kept me away from my family too often. I am currently a part-time college instructor and owner of a weaving and yarn supply store. I have been happily married for ten years. I enjoy cooking and house-keeping. My husband designs and administers ski areas. We ski at famous resorts every weekend and take glorious hikes in the wilderness during the summer season. Love, Judy

Recording my emotions, feelings, and private inner thoughts was difficult, but beneficial for crystallizing my ideas and enforcing or rejecting basic premises motivating me to move forward and act positively and rationally. It was beneficial to my overall thought process to corroborate with Martin because he challenged me to be realistic, think rationally, write clearly, and express empathy for Rebecca. Taking the time to honestly disclose my deepest obscure feelings, ephemeral abstract emotions, and private intimate beliefs was an all-consuming, exhausting, time-consuming affair.

I was raised as an only child. I had no one to compete with, and I was accustomed to having my own way. I didn't have to share my possessions, and I had no siblings with whom to share my feelings. Marriage was the first opportunity, but, even as an adult, I didn't always understand or acknowledge my emotional weaknesses or emotional impediments to good communication.

My husband provided me with new insights and perspectives into issues that better reflected how others might view them. He was a trained, experienced meeting facilitator and mediator, and he used a variety of techniques to help other executives make important decisions. His strategy of using brainstorming and taking slow, methodical steps to problem solving resulted in a more thorough and comprehensive understanding of most issues. The collaborative process he used called "choosing by advantages" gave me confidence and reduced the chances of me changing my mind in the future.

Without his assistance, my decisions were often made impulsively based on ephemeral emotions I was feeling at the time, which was unfortunate because they were often unstable and varied widely from day to day. Some days, I was energetic, happy, and sure of myself. Other days were the opposite when I was lonely and lacking confidence. My earlier emotion-based, shoot-from-the-hip approach did not produce consistent, accurate, or reliable results. Putting my thoughts on paper was very helpful because the deliberation process required me to think clearly and rationally. And when I was in my lowest emotional states of mind and there was no one there to help me overcome distress or discouragement, I found it therapeutic to direct my accepted wisdom to God.

My first two letters to Rebecca had been extemporaneously written from the heart. Ultimately, I needed to convince her that I was sincere and passionate about my lifelong quest to find her. The purpose of my final letter was a plea for empathy, friendship, and open communication to convince her that my course of action was appropriate.

Dear Rebecca, My faith motivates and sustains me. Inspired by my religious and spiritual nature, my inner confidence, happiness, and buoyant outlook on life have joyously peaked at an all-time high. Deep in my heart, I feel I comprehend you, and, even though we have never met, I sense a meaningful spiritual link and psychological connection with you. We are of the same flesh and blood, and, inevitably, we must telepathically think alike in some unknown mysterious ways. When I meditate, I perceive the existence of an inner eye that reads your thoughts and emotions, even from great distances. The imperceptible primordial spiritual link we share binds us and amplifies my desire to find you. Like a lighthouse on a dark and stormy night, your essence is constantly transmitting a message of hope that illuminates my path. The mysterious vitality that is compelling me to take action is powerful and gaining strength, and my instincts will not let me rest until I have found you. No words can describe the enigmatic, mystifying, passionate psychological potency that motivates me. Its dominance is overwhelmingly spiritually based and all encompassing. Perhaps my sixth sense was amplified to overcompensate for the lack of a physical connection and sound of your voice by projecting and receiving mental signals from afar to replace what I was lacking in direct tactile contact. Maybe some biological and psychological bonding took place in the womb before I was born, and the bonding process imprinted our souls with a marker that is a survival mechanism. For nine months, we shared the same foods. I heard you talking, and the tone and rhythm of your speech was recorded in my small, developing brain. I knew when you were awake and when you were hungry, happy, and tense. We shared everything. I was an extension of you and part of you. I was life longing for itself. When I was a child, I saw myself as a clone of you in some obscure but meaningful way. As the years passed, the frequency and strength of my thoughts about you increased. A realistic sense of mortality and vulnerability that is naturally acquired with age and experience kindled a new appreciation for the shortness of life and made me aware there are limited windows of opportunity in life when a person needs to take action or forever regret her decision and lose the opportunity to accomplish her goals. I have compassion for all mothers separated from their babies at birth who must endure countless anxious days and nights of tormented suffering. These traumatic tribulations haunt the afflicted, especially unwanted children selflessly orphaned, abandoned, and clueless. Separation from the birth mother is the confiscation of the child's soul, a mutual occurrence that rips apart and exposes the heart of the child. Orphans amputated from their mother's breast hide their wounds in the darkest subconscious corners of their primal brains, where they remain hidden, but never healed. As mother and daughter, we have equally suffered from the same cerebral wounds, numbness, and sentiments of penitence. Enduring these injuries and suffering in silence is what we habitually have in common. Ultimately, the crushing emotional pain is so formidable that it can only be shared with God. Love, Judy

I was relieved knowing that my letters were finished. My own depth of passion that had miraculously emerged surprised me. I would not quit of my own accord. If Rebecca chose to ignore my written words, I would entice her with photographs. I included pictures of myself taking first communion, graduation from nursing school, and my wedding day. I included newspaper articles featuring my golfing hole in one, retail yarn store, a favorite grouping of family pictures skiing at Vail and Aspen, and pictures of us boating at Lake Powell.

I carefully placed each letter and photograph under a clear sheet of plastic, and I fastened them into an expensive brown leather binder. My precious masterpiece was complete. I placed it in a sturdy box and drove to the post office without regard to speed limits. I prayed that my peace offering of cherished letters and treasured photographs would soften her heart and entice Rebecca to confess. I cautiously hoped she wouldn't implode in another tactless uncaring fit of insensitivity and ruthlessly plunk my biography in the trash.

Tightly clutching my priceless assemblage while suspiciously eyeing the crowd, I comingled in the long line of customers. I was unusually self-conscientious and irrationally worried that a thief might try to snatch it out of my arms simply because it was exceedingly valuable to me. It was a permanent record of my life, and, once gone, it could not be returned. As I stood in line, I conjectured about how to portray the worth of its invaluable contents to the postal clerk when she inquired to know for insurance purposes.

When I was finished, I lightheartedly skipped out of the post office, visualizing Julie Andrews in *The Sound of Music* running through high alpine meadows blanketed with edelweiss and colorful wildflowers. I spontaneously flung my arms in the air, shouted for joy, and let everyone in shouting distance know what my package contained. I was absolutely jubilant.

FURTIVELY HOPING TO BE the first to catch a glimpse of my birth mother's face, my best friend Grace had delightedly agreed to be my clandestine coconspirator by personally handing my priceless collection of letters and photographs to Rebecca at her place of work.

Confession

Dear Mom, Sometimes, life is full of surprises. I hope my package of letters and photographs gives you a better appreciation for who I am and clarifies my motive for wanting to find you. My thoughts seem a little complex and wordy or even amateurish to you, but I hope you will still take the time to read them carefully. I aspire to the dream that, in the future, you will do the same for me. I hope you will view my existence as a positive opportunity for both of us to resolve the past. Please welcome me into your heart. Love, Judy

THREE UNEVENTFUL WEEKS HAD passed since Grace delivered my package of letters and photographs to Rebecca. The encounter had been anticlimactic because Rebecca was not working that day and Grace had simply dropped the package off with the receptionist. I was extremely disappointed knowing that Grace had nothing to report about Rebecca's physical appearance or anything else of importance.

When the telephone rang, the noise startled me.

"God allowed me a second chance to become a free person. I shouldn't have to suffer again what I suffered when I was a teenager. I don't want my life disrupted or have to make excuses to my three children."

Rebecca had caught me completely off guard. The tone of her voice startled me. She never even said hello. Her words were harsh and cold; her reasons for rejecting me were compelling and irrevocable. I felt numb.

"You were part of my past that I wanted to forget. You already have me lying to friends and family. People are questioning why someone from Colorado is calling me. I have a reputation to maintain, which I thought I had established over the past thirty years of marriage. God in his mercy would not want me to go through what I went through for a second time," she replied callously.

Her emphatic rejection distressed and disturbed me. I needed a helping hand to pull me from the dizzying whirlpool that was spinning me around and making me lightheaded and feeling faint.

My voice trembled. "There is no need to tell others. Our secret can remain private and confidential—"

Rebecca interrupted and interjected her own opinions before I finished speaking. "I don't want this interruption in my life. I don't care where you live or if I ever speak to you again. The Catholic sacrament of confession set me free of the sin that I committed. God forgave me. At this point in my life, I shouldn't have to make excuses for what I did as a teenager. I was given a second chance the day I decided not to go on with a child without a marriage at a young, delicate age," she added rhetorically.

Her acknowledgement of me as her daughter was a major admission that left me feeling remarkably sympathetic toward her.

"You were an accident. I don't have to make apologies or explanations to you, nor do I have to go through my confession again. I have three children, and I don't want to explain how this happened."

The sound of her voice made me happy. I ignored her hostility and tried to project positive feelings. "There is no need to tell your children. I just want some questions answered about my background—"

She interrupted and repeated her earlier demand. "I don't expect you to come and disrupt my life. The only question you need answer, my dear, is that, yes, you were born. We have no diseases other than a little diabetes on the Italian side of the family. any medical history from my side of the family because My birth mother meant nothing to me. Nothing! My were the people who loved me, cared for me, and of my problems with me. My mother went into the told her I was pregnant. I made my mother suffer, and want to feel free from that memory."

I reached out to express my sympathy. "Y guilty. I understand your pain and predicament. Wh the past. Your family loves you. They can understand.

My words had a hollow resonation because new that revealing a truth this significant would be stupefying, her children openmouthed, wide-eyed, and curiously intrigued. Rebecca had a good reason to be worried and distressed because explaining my presence could be [   ] y damaging situation, and she was deathly afraid of [ ]

"We [   ] ho knew nothing about relationships. We were very [   ]

I had [   ] Rebecca into confessing. Her suppressed emotions [   ] d burdensome. "Please continue speaking."

"My n[   ] for my failings and made everything worse by telling n[   ] oad to perdition. The church was my salvation. My Ca[   ] ld me that daily prayer was needed for resolving my emotio[   ] lemma and absolving me of my immoral sin," she professed. "I felt guilty. Your birth bothered me a great deal because I was unmarried. The advice from my priest was that I was too young to accept responsibility. Public opinion is much more liberal now," she rationalized.

My determination was unrelenting as I persisted in my demands for honest answers to my questions. "I appreciate your truthfulness." Her voice became less shrill as her anger subsided.

"My best friend's parents got married when they were seventeen. They are still happily married," I pointed out.

Rebecca automatically rebuked my statement. "I don't care about anybody else. My family would lose respect for me. I don't want this hurt in their lives. It wasn't supposed to happen like this." Rebecca firmly stood her ground.

I was speechless and uncertain what to say next. To avoid a lull in our conversation, I blurted out the first thing that came to mind and unintentionally expressed my thoughts as a question. "Are you sure your family would disrespect you if you told them about me? People are so much more open-minded these days," I replied meekly in my own defense.

"Yes, I am sure. We are still old-fashioned. I raised my children this way, and I'm not going to change my thinking. It might be different if my children had their own homes and families. The state of Wisconsin gave me the right at the time of your birth to sign a legal document to protect me from moments like this. I took the advice and signed away a chapter in my life. That is the end of the story," she responded with finality.

I was unfaltering, ignored her statements, and pressed ahead. "If I come to Milwaukee to see you, would you sit down and have coffee with me? You wouldn't have to explain anything to anybody."

Rebecca's demeanor alternated between panic and rage. I could visualize her facial expression when she scolded me. "No! I don't want you intruding into my life. I would be afraid of what might happen," she said unyieldingly.

I refused to back down even though Rebecca was treating me as her inflatable dummy with a weighted bottom that returned to its upright position regardless of how many times it was struck. Her uncaring rebuttals that kept knocking me down deeply hurt me, but I was resilient and refused to be dissuaded.

"What happened is unfortunate, but I forgive you."

Rebecca admitted I was her child, but it was disconcerting when she didn't show any signs of remorse or empathy for me. Our conversation had definitely not met my expectations. Any prospects for reconciliation between us looked bleak.

"I don't care how you feel. My life now has nothing to do with my life when I was young," she protested.

I had been hoping for a demonstration of love and sympathy but received nothing. "My adoption search has been an emotionally draining arduous journey of discovery. You were responsible for bringing me into this world. I was hoping you would acknowledge my situation from that perspective." I expressed my disappointment.

"I don't care," Rebecca repeated coldly.

Her answer was painful. Her indignation hurt deeply, and it was difficult for me to respond without crying. "You really don't care," I said sadly. I choked over my own words.

I tried to keep my chin up. I didn't want to cry. My confidence had waned. Rebecca had the upper hand, and my defenses were finally weakening. She was emotionally shaken and defensive and unlikely to ever change her mind.

"I never thought of you once. I closed the book very thoroughly," she said, angrily raising her voice and slamming the open palm of her right hand on the table.

Rebecca was angry and vindictive. She really didn't care about me. Her refutation that she had never once thought about me after I was born was painful to hear. I just couldn't accept the premise that it was possible for an unmarried woman to have a baby without remorse.

"As a child, I thought about you in a fairy-tale sort of way. The mystery of my birth was intriguing. Thinking about you was therapeutic because I envisioned a blissful eternal ending. I perceived you as a rare mystical spirit with which I had a bona fide timeless connection. My intuition has always been stalwart. I believed the signal you have been broadcasting for my benefit was strong. My esoteric ideas may seem strange to you, but they were authentic for me," I replied remorsefully.

"You were born and permanently forgotten. I wasn't given any information whatsoever after your birth so I could go on living and try to become a normal teenager again," she said, unfeigned by my attempts to communicate with her from the heart.

I seized on this opportunity as a good time to learn more. "Does Bruno still enjoy sports? I understand he was a star athlete in high school." I tried to change the subject to something pleasant.

Rebecca indignantly treated me like an ignorant outsider who knew nothing about her family. "No, that was something left behind in our high school days. He goes to the Eagles Club twice a week to lift weights, swim, and run around the track," Rebecca answered disdainfully, begrudgingly giving me a limited understanding of her private life. "He is a hard worker and a good provider. That is all that really matters."

I could tell she was proud of her husband. She liked him. He must be a good man.

"Do you still play the violin? I heard you had excellent musical ability."

"Playing the violin doesn't fit into my married life. I don't have time for music," she responded tersely. "Look, we have talked long enough. That is all there is to the story. You need not be curious about me anymore."

"Wait! Does Bruno know I contacted you?"

"He knows, and he will want a good explanation about this expensive long-distance telephone bill. This conversation is over," Rebecca said impatiently.

"My husband is alarmed about my telephone bills, too, but he never complains because he supports me," I said with a slight smile, knowing we finally had something in common.

Rebecca never hesitated. Her rebuttals were spontaneous, and she was quick to refute my assumptions. She seldom acknowledged my point of view. She was authoritative and probably accustomed to regularly disciplining her children.

She spoke rapidly with self-assurance. "I still have to live with what happened and wonder who told you this well-guarded secret. You at least have gotten your story. You have reduced your burden and lifted the pressure of your adoption off your shoulders. You made your connections, but it really wasn't right of you to contact me. Someday, I think God will put that into consideration. This kind of information was supposed to stay protected," Rebecca once again responded wearily.

"The state of Wisconsin gave you a piece of paper to put this legal issue behind you, but God wasn't the one who signed it. Our true biological and spiritual relationship between mother and daughter is still unresolved in our private relationship with God. It will remain that way forever until we meet in person. Only then will everyone be forgiven in his eyes," I said with the highest level of sincerity I could muster.

My point of view was genuine. I was proud of myself for speaking up and refusing to take no for an answer. I felt much better even though Rebecca was scornfully rejecting my peace offers.

"Would you object if I talked to your husband?"

Rebecca was defensive and angry. My question pushed her panic button, and she was fuming. Her response was a scathing rebuttal. "Bruno is concerned and unhappy with the way I am feeling about this whole situation. I was so upset and stressed that my body started hemorrhaging. He is very worried about my health," she dramatized.

I wasn't surprised she had waited three weeks to call me because she had been severely distressed the entire time.

"Why are you so worried? I do not intend to harm you. I already have a mother. I just wanted to meet you because you are my biological mother. I thought you would be happy to know that I survived a difficult childhood with my adopted parents. I'm an adult with a family of my own. I don't need anything from you. I just wanted to share a few positive things about my life with you," I pleaded my case.

Rebecca was distressed. Our conversation was coming to an abrupt end, and I wanted it to conclude on a good note. "You are a thorny problem to me. I don't want to lie and deceive my children. I was given that right when I signed you away. That is the way I want it to stay. It was done legally, and that is the way it should remain."

"It's too bad you feel that way. If your attitude was different, you could fly out to Aspen, Colorado, and we could meet," I said optimistically.

Again, Rebecca's response was convincing. "I don't fly. I wouldn't fly to see you or anyone anywhere."

I kept pushing. "We could drive to a neutral place in Chicago and meet in private. It wouldn't be a big deal. I am your prodigal daughter, Judy," I pleaded.

"Well, this whole issue is a big deal to me. I intend to maintain my life as it was before you contacted me. I want to overcome this inception, as I did many years ago. You never should have contacted me," Rebecca said without hesitating to chastise me.

I tried to reassure her that I was not bitter or angry. "I know I am a major concern to you, but you shouldn't be so troubled. After all, you are my biological mother. I exist, and I am here. I am a good person. You shouldn't fear me. You are very important to me. It would mean a lot to me if we could get to know each other," I said honestly.

"Why do you think you have to meet me? I don't feel the same way. I will never feel any different. I shouldn't have to change my views or attitudes or anything," Rebecca said, tightly holding onto her convictions.

Rebecca did not acknowledge my sensitive feelings or anything I said to her. She was not interested in meeting me or participating in any more private conversations. She refused to acknowledge my presence, and she was unwilling to reveal her secret to anyone. She was simply suggesting I vaporize and disappear into thin air forever.

"You are not my child. The name of my first child is Linda. She is twenty-eight years old. That is the way it is. There is no reason for me to discuss this matter with you. If I have to change my telephone number again, I will," she threatened harshly.

I had to assume that Rebecca had tossed my letters and precious pictures in the trash because we had already talked for an hour. She had never referenced them, asked a single question about my childhood, expressed any interest in my adopted parents, or inquired about my family. She had refused to tell me anything. Yet, little by little, she was involuntarily giving me more information. Despite her intimidating style, I wanted her to keep talking so I could learn more.

"Now that we have talked, do you feel relieved knowing that your first daughter is a wholesome, contented adult?" I tried to win her over.

"I never looked backward. My parents gave me a chance to be reborn, so to speak, and start over. That can't be changed now." She defensively rejected any notion that she had ever thought about me.

Her comments were heart-wrenching, and her ice-cold reception was not what I had anticipated. Her cruel rejection had completely neutralized the joy and excitement of finding my birth mother, and nothing I had said thawed her indifference toward me. She did not intend to apologize for abandoning me or express empathy for the life-altering mental consequences my adoption had caused. All I wanted from her was recognition and reconciliation.

Perhaps, my emotions were dulled as a baby when my birth mother was not there to hold me. Maybe the experience of knowing I was discarded made me tougher and more resilient when dealing with adversity, but I was also more sensitive than other children to feelings of intimacy and relationships.

Despite Rebecca's best attempts to rebuke me, I still wanted to move forward. I needed to recharge my batteries and boost my self-confidence.

I wanted to know more, so I continued by asking her to explain what happened to me in the beginning. "Where was I before I was adopted?" I still hoped Rebecca would provide me with information about circumstances leading to my adoption.

"I don't know when the adoption took place. Nobody told me anything. A priest counseled me, and he helped me overcome my anxieties and conceal my memories," she replied indifferently.

"There are so many things I don't know. The first twelve months of my life are a mystery. Did you abandon me at the hospital or drop me off at an orphanage?" I asked inquisitively.

Rebecca was defensive and aloof and ignored my pleas for friendship and assistance. "I wouldn't know anything about where you were or if you had one or more foster parents. As I said before, the day you were born, you were no longer part of my life. That was the only way I could go on and make a new life. The least connection I had with you, the better beginning I would have. My parents were looking out for me, a young girl who needed a second chance in life. They wanted to take what happened and quickly erase it from my mind. That is why everything stopped immediately. It took me weeks to recover. They never gave me any information about you. I had to live down the disgrace. I had to face friends, family, and schoolmates I had known. I had many hurdles that I had to overcome. Don't forget that I was an adoptee, too.

My relatives scorned me and never admitted I was related to them," Rebecca honestly revealed.

I attempted to express my sympathy. "I am sorry for the difficulties you experienced in early life. Adoption is something we both have in common. I was hoping that, as adoptees, we would share some of the same beliefs and philosophies. Our collective thinking could bring us closer together," I rationalized.

"I hurt my mother by having a baby. She never got over it. My mother's family never accepted Bruno, but we got married anyway and proved we loved each other throughout the years."

I could feel her sufferings and wondered if Rebecca was warm-hearted, but my presence had shaken her so badly that she was not acting herself.

"It was a shame your parents didn't like Bruno. Many people make hasty decisions when they are feeling pressured or panicky, enduring physical pain or torture, or facing imminent disaster." I simultaneously expressed sympathetic understanding and offered condolences.

"I searched for love outside my family, and I found warmth, friendship, and understanding from my young boyfriend, but I was foolish," she rationalized.

"It is a great triumph that you and Bruno are still together after thirty years. You must be a good wife." I demonstrated positive support.

"We had our moments, but we persevered. We are very close. Bruno and I do everything together," Rebecca said truthfully.

Rebecca was more relaxed and finally speaking candidly. For a moment, I thought we were carrying on a normal conversation.

"Listen, this conversation has to end because I have many things to do," Rebecca said as she started to hang up.

"Wait a minute. I need to know about my father." I tried desperately to keep the conversation going.

"Well, call me back tomorrow afternoon, and I will tell you more," Rebecca quietly whispered and abruptly ended the conversation.

My knees were weak; my heart was palpitating. Still reeling from the effects of the ambush and refusing to believe that she never thought about me once, I remained emotionally distressed long after our conversation ended. I had expected a more compassionate understanding from someone who would politely answer my questions. Instead, Rebecca had reprimanded me for invading her privacy and interrupting her life.

We were mutually tormenting each other and not making any progress toward reconciliation. It was difficult pursuing my goal of getting to know her in the face of so much adversity and hostility. Her negative thinking about the intrusion I had made in her life was intimidating. Despite my blistering interference, she had suggested I call her again tomorrow. Her conflicting emotions were confusing me.

I wondered if Bruno would be friendlier and more willing to provide additional insights into the circumstances of my birth and adoption. Rebecca had already admitted talking to him about me, and there was still the possibility that he could not be my birth father. I had to find out the facts.

Realizing this was a critical crossroads in my life, I resolved to follow God's will by praying for the wisdom, strength, and strength of character needed to calm my anxious heart. I asked for a sign, either directing me to accept my unsettled fate as an adoptee or follow my heart to completion by satisfying my curiosity and the insatiable mystical forces channeling me toward new relationships, which would forever alter my life and the lives of others.

Peggy Lee's plainspoken song "Is That All There Is" was playing softly in the background and pointing the way as a clear message of hope, optimism, faith, and joyfulness I had been eager to find. I was to happily accept whatever came along and dismiss adversity and tragedy by breaking out the booze and keep on dancing.

Beautiful Thing

Dear Mom, Thank you for revealing yourself as my biological mother. Despite your harsh responses and lack of sympathy for me, I have only positive thoughts about you. Hearing your voice for the first time provided a strong dose of positive mental therapy after many years of being lost in the wilderness without knowing who I was. I understand my intrusion into your life at this time is untimely because fear and shame dominate your feelings. I respect your reasons for wanting to protect other members of your family by concealing my presence and intend to honor your request for privacy. Love, Judy

M Y HEART RATE WAS elevated due to a strong sense of anticipation. Excitement rushed through my veins as I picked up the receiver and, without hesitating, dialed Rebecca's telephone number.

"Hello," a young man said in a deep, bass baritone, sexy, masculine voice responded. He reminded me of rich, dark chocolate. He made me just melt.

"Hello, is your mom there?" I asked spontaneously without questioning his identity.

"Oh, my goodness," I thought to myself in subdued astonishment. "Am I speaking to Rebecca's son?"

"No, she had to run an errand. She should be back in a half hour," he countered.

I reflected on the exciting implications of my discovery. If Rebecca were his mother, then he was my biological brother. It was a thought I had never visualized. My curiosity peaked.

"Who is this, please?" I inquired.

"This is Tim," he replied honestly in a pleasant-sounding voice.

"This is Judy. Rebecca told me to call her at two o'clock this afternoon."

Tim listened carefully to what I said, paused, and replied in a friendly optimistic voice, "Well, then she should be home soon."

"Okay. Good-bye, Tim," I replied with bubbly exuberance and a gaping smile as wide as a brick.

In my mind, I visualized my brother as a tall, dark, handsome prince. I felt giddy, and my pulse rapidly skipped a beat as I wondered what it would be like to have a real brother.

For the next hour, I waited patiently by the telephone, still feeling ecstatic about the fact that I had actually talked to him. His voice was pleasant. I wondered if he could sense an escalating level of excitement in my intonation and the mysterious desire I had for making a personal connection with him because he seemed to be treating me in a special way and smiling as if he were talking to someone familiar.

I was eager to talk to Rebecca and tired of waiting. At exactly three o'clock, I dialed her telephone number again. It only rang once. Someone snatched up the receiver.

"Hello! Is Rebecca there?" I asked politely.

"Uh-huh!" a strange voice replied.

"May I speak to Rebecca?" I asked a second time.

"Just a minute. I'll get her," the voice replied.

It must have been one of my sisters. The very thought of hearing my sister's voice was exhilarating and stirred a sudden euphoric emotional high. I pictured in my mind's eye a stunningly beautiful girl with a sparkling smile. Everything that happened to me in the past lingered in my imagination. When I was a child I saw an angel hovering over me. She had a kindhearted, sympathetic expression. I imagined her as my friend and made believe she was my sister.

"Hello, this is Rebecca," she said guardedly, disguising her voice to openly prevent others from eavesdropping.

"How are you today?" I inquired pleasantly with an open display of my happy disposition.

Rebecca was slow to respond. She paused to choose her words carefully before answering. "I had a busy day. I'm tired. This telephone call wasn't a good idea. You should break off this connection and not bother this family anymore," she whispered, trying to avoid being overheard.

Our conversation began exactly where the last one ended. She was less emphatic and defensive. She was not as callous and didn't sound as afraid of me as she had the last time. I wondered if she were wearing down or softening her attitude. Maybe she was acting reserved because someone was listening.

I responded quickly before she could hang up the receiver. "Before I take your advice, I want to know what Bruno thinks about me."

Rebecca took a deep breath. "He is very angry that I got so sick after the first telephone call. I bled profusely after I received your letters, and he doesn't want me to be ill again. Don't contact me again. You must go on with your life, just as I must go on with mine. We cannot change the past," Rebecca answered her own questions.

I acknowledged her opinion, but continued to resist taking no for an answer. "Do you mind if I call Bruno?"

Rebecca reverted to her original ways and put up her defenses as her hostility was suddenly revived. "You sound much too eager and overconfident. This is the end of the line," she affirmed explicitly. My aggression had caused her to become angry. "If I ever stumble on the informant in this case, I'll make life miserable for him. He'll be sorry for sharing a very dear and vital secret with you. I can threaten because I was given a legal right to remain private. Why do you think you can just walk into my life? How can you expect a civil reaction from me?" Rebecca sternly forewarned and paused. "Bruno would rather not talk to you. He says he cares about me and nobody else. He feels very strongly about his children. That is another reason why he doesn't want to get involved," she cautioned.

I was persistent. I looked down at my notebook to find a good follow-up question. I refused to let her hang up on me. I ran my finger down my list of potential questions until I came to the word "hospital" and impulsively blurted out another question to fill the silence.

"Tell me about Booth Hill. According to my records, you gave birth to me at Martha Washington Hospital."

"Good God, it doesn't matter," she declared emphatically.

"I would like to know where I was born. It does matter to me. Tell me what the circumstances were like when I was born," I inquired politely.

Rebecca was angry and practically cursing at me. "You weren't hatched out of an egg, my dear. That is all you have to know," she said sarcastically.

Her response stunned me.

"You don't have the training that I thought your mother taught you. You said she was religious. She missed the boat somewhere because you didn't learn a thing from her. You shouldn't be doing this," Rebecca said in a loud, domineering, irate voice.

Her words hurt me deeply, like a fatal stabbing to the heart. It was difficult to continue breathing at a normal pace. My voice cracked as I choked back my tears. I continued speaking anyway. "My mother doesn't know I am doing this," I confessed meekly.

Rebecca sensed my weakness and reprimanded me with her insensitive words. "Oh, she doesn't? It may be enlightening if she did know. How would you like me to divulge to her that you have contacted your birth mother and her family?"

"I wouldn't," I admitted guiltily.

I was feeling threatened and afraid. I knew I was strong enough to withstand Rebecca's unsympathetic reprimands, but her threats about telling my adopted parents what I was doing was a genuine concern that sent a chill down my spine because I definitely didn't want to hurt their feelings. Knowing I was compelled to do real detective work to uncover the secrets of my past was something they wouldn't understand. They would think I was rejecting them as parents.

"I thought this relationship could just be between us," I explained.

Rebecca had the upper hand, and she was aggressively keeping me on the defensive. "You have involved more people than you know. You have intruded into my life and created problems for my family. My children want to know who you are and why you are calling me from another state," she repeated.

"They are my siblings," I countered impulsively.

Rebecca realized what my statement implied and immediately rejected the idea. "That's too bad for you because they are not really your sisters and brother. I gave you up. Do you understand? You are as far from being a part of this family as the world can be today," Rebecca spouted angrily. She was excited and reflexively gagged on her own saliva while attempting to subdue her words to avoid calling attention to herself.

Her meanness bothered me. I tried to defend my position. "I am not trying to cause any problems. I just wanted to talk to you because you are my biological mother," I bemoaned.

"I have lived my life and raised my children, and you don't matter to me. The law protects my privacy. I don't want any intrusions. Just leave me alone," Rebecca repeated for what seemed like the umpteenth time.

"I was hoping to get some information from you about my adoption quietly and discreetly without causing stress to the rest of your family. Instead, you are making it very difficult for me." I refused to go away.

Her threats disheartened me, but I continued to tenaciously cling to hope as long as I could keep her talking because she was my only lifeline to the past. The mysteriously familiar sound of her voice still enthralled me.

Eventually, her rejection left me feeling like a mountain climber hanging over a huge precipice high in the Swiss Alps. My life depended on the climber above me, and I would self-destruct in a split second if the rope broke or I released my grip. The only chance I had of surviving was to hold on to the hand of the other climber and hope she had the will and compassion to pull me up to safety. The loss of my link to Rebecca had been a reoccurring nightmare all my life, and I didn't want to lose her now that I had the audacity of hope. She was the person to whom I was desperately clinging and the only one who could save me. My life depended on her.

"Does it give you satisfaction trying to find out scandalous information about me and my family? It was shameful enough when I was young. Why drum up skeletons from my past? Does this make you happy?" she demanded to know.

It was difficult for me to describe my abstract feelings in words when simple handshakes, smiles, hugs, and acknowledges would have sufficed.

"No, as an adoptee, I have a genuine desire to learn about my biological mother. It is difficult to explain why I have always been so intensively motivated to find you. The emotions that sustain me are very powerful. My instincts lead me to believe that I am doing the right thing," I tried to explain and wondered if Rebecca would ever understand me. "I have seen salmon fighting their way upstream, swimming a thousand miles through dams and locks, fish ladders, waterfalls, and fast currents all the way from the Pacific Ocean to the headwaters of the largest rivers in Idaho. A natural urge and survival mechanism compels them to keep moving forward and motivates them to endure all hardships and obstacles in their path. For me, it is a similar deep and unexplained journey I feel compelled to take. I was born with very strong natural homing instincts and committed to expending the energy and commitment required to find my way home. For that reason, I will not stop until my journey is complete."

Rebecca interrupted my lengthy explanation and rebuked me. "I don't believe you. There is no other reason than sensationalism," she said emphatically in a high-pitched voice.

Unshaken, I continued pressing forward. "I would like to know what you look like. I have talked with people who have described you as a very attractive, brown-haired woman with a smooth complexion and beautiful face. The more I find out about you, the more my curiosity increases."

"Don't you think you know enough about me already?" Rebecca said sarcastically.

"I have a copy of your high school yearbook. Bruno's photo is in the yearbook, and he looks a lot like me, which I find very interesting," I replied politely.

She responded more cautiously this time, "It is interesting that the two of you look alike, but I don't know why it should matter to you now."

"I want to know something about my roots," I said calmly.

"Okay! You have your roots. That's all you need to know." Rebecca tried to cut off our conversation.

I took my time to gather my thoughts before speaking again. I wanted to express myself clearly to help Rebecca understand it was natural for all children, not just adoptees, to identify with their family.

"When I grew up, I felt like a golden retriever being raised by German shepherd parents. It was obvious that my emotions, natural tendencies, and personal characteristics were not the same as my adopted parents. Maybe that is why I have been searching for others more like me my whole life. It is normal for all children to want to learn about their ancestors. All people enjoy making history come alive because it enriches their own lives. It is rewarding for people knowing they are related to monarchs and queens, soldiers, farmers, sailors, priests, or whatever," I explained persuasively.

Rebecca was not saying anything, so I continued. "We all have social and cultural ties to our neighborhoods, friends, teachers, coaches, and the parents who raised us, but that is not the same as our biological roots embedded in our DNA. Biological parents give us our physical identity and our genes that primarily determine our personal characteristics that make each one of us unique."

Rebecca refused to surrender her position. "Your mother has done a good job of hurting you, my dear." She faulted me for my unconventional opinions again.

"My adopted mother Rosella did the best job she knew how. I have no complaints. I don't understand why you closed the book so tightly on me. I should be entitled to learn at least a few small things about my real bloodlines. We are both adults. At this point in our lives, I wish you would be honest and less secretive with me," I said with conviction.

Rebecca was quick to put me down again. She spoke rapidly in a demeaning tone of voice. "Your birth mother and your family tree should mean nothing to you. The people who raised you should mean more to you than bloodlines. Your adopted parents were unable to have children of their own. You are theirs in all sense of the word. It is very sad to think that you have not learned that from them." Rebecca arguably expressed her contrary point of view.

I wondered if Rebecca knew something about my parents. How else would she know that they couldn't conceive children of their own? I wondered if Rebecca's mother had fabricated this information to make Rebecca feel better about giving up her child, or did she know this information to be true?

I tried to defend my actions again. "I am thirty-two years old. I'm not looking for a new mother. I'm not a child anymore. I'm a mature adult and mother myself." I staked out my position.

Rebecca cut me off in the middle of my last sentence. "That's for sure, but you are acting like a child who is not showing her adopted parents the respect and love that is owed to them. That is heartbreaking. I was an adoptee like you. I cared for and loved the people who raised me. They were my parents. They were my roots," Rebecca exclaimed loudly as a way of rationalizing her opinion.

"I heard you didn't attend many of your parents' family functions during your married life. You stuck to Bruno's side of the family. They were Italian, and your family was German. That doesn't sound like you cherished your adopted parents very much. Is that right?"

"You better be sure of your facts, young woman. It sounds like you are talking to someone who is very prejudiced against my family. You better not say anything bad about my adopted family. I was glad I married into a large Italian family, perhaps because my own birth father was Italian. It was natural that I went to more functions on the Italian side of the family because there were many more to attend and their parties were fun and enjoyable. I wasn't comfortable with my adopted relatives and didn't care to be with them partly because they never fully accepted me. Whatever the reasons were is none of your business. Whoever is talking to you better not say too much because he doesn't know the truth," Rebecca replied emphatically in a threatening voice.

I reflected on my commonalities with Rebecca, especially our similar opinions about our adopted parents and family life. Hovering in the back of both of our minds were faint childhood insecurities about being adopted and lingering beliefs that something was missing in our lives. We seemed to share a predisposed ambition to surround ourselves with others similar to us.

"There was never a question about what to do with you. My priest Father Hennen, my parents, and everyone concerned encouraged me to give you to someone else because I was too young to handle the responsibility," she rationalized.

"I understand. I really do. I can't feel the pain or humiliation that you suffered at the time of your pregnancy, but I can understand how difficult it must have been for you because adoption is an irrevocable condition. I am sorry that it happened that way for goodness sake, but I forgive you," I said as honestly and sincerely as possible.

"The unanimous advice given to me was that it was better to start a new life and build from there. It was very difficult and a sacrifice to consent to the adoption. The whole situation was an embarrassment to everyone involved, especially my parents because they had a lot at stake, too," Rebecca explained convincingly.

"Why did you name me Judy?" I tried to remain friendly.

"I have no idea who named you," Rebecca responded coldly.

Her terse response and general lack of interest in me was depressing. I felt blue and sorry for myself. Feeling pathetically forgotten and disconsolate knowing that my own birth mother had no idea who named me, I scribbled a small picture in my own image of a frowning face in my notebook with a little tear dripping from one eye. Her remarks had stirred a reticent regression back to my childhood when I had experienced a lonely, isolated, and gloomy sense of despondency.

I grabbed a handful of Kleenex and wiped away the tears that were welling up in my eyes. "When did you give me up for adoption?"

"Right away. I just went there, and it was over. I was pampered, and everyone supported me. The entire affair was handled skillfully. It was a beautiful thing," Rebecca explained.

Her callous description of the most noteworthy event in my life shocked me speechless. "The loss of a newborn child is an unnatural event that would undeniably traumatize everyone concerned. Why do you portray the heartless passing of your child to strangers for permanent disposal as a beautiful thing? Your depiction of the incident makes the willful disappearance of your child sound like a well-rehearsed and choreographed stage performance, methodically acted out in a daytime soap opera with a large supporting cast of social workers, nurses, priests, and parents. I don't see how you could have reached that conclusion without the positive reinforcement of others to convince you that adoption was the best solution. What were you thinking? Do you think they gave you painkillers and other medicines to dull your sanity?" I asked in candid astonishment.

I had naïvely assumed my birth mother had experienced sincere regrets, high anxieties, and feelings of separation, just like I had, but, apparently, she did not. At this instant, I visualized myself as an orphan shamelessly abandoned by my young mother at a Salvation Army hospital for the poor and destitute, wantonly left in the care of strangers because she didn't want me. The perpetuation of her mythical reputation as an innocent victim had been far more important to her than the health and safety of her newborn child.

My birth and subsequent abandonment was not a beautiful thing. It was a terrible thing. My life was permanently altered for the worse because I had no mother to snuggle with and care for me. The lingering effects of the separation trauma I experienced as an infant were still evident in adulthood. For the first twelve months of my life, when most children were clinging to their mother's breast, I had to rely on the goodwill and generosity of social workers and strangers to provide me with the nurturing needed to sustain life. No single individual consistently loved me, hugged me, fed me, or comforted me in a soothing voice to calm my anxieties.

More likely, a rotating team of ever-changing shift nurses took turns changing my diapers and feeding me. Each caretaker was a stranger who looked and smelled differently and had a different way of holding and feeding me. Daily routines in the hospital would have been established methodically based on limited budgets and personnel and mechanically carried out to satisfy basic efficiencies.

I pictured myself as a helpless orphan lying on my back and waving my arms in the air with my mouth wide open, like a baby robin hoping to receive a juicy worm from its mother. Rebecca had never looked back or regretted her decision. She coldly dispensed with me like an unwanted tumor. I was simply cast aside, abandoned, jettisoned overboard, and disowned forever as a temporary inconvenience. I was no longer feeling reserved or shy about talking to Rebecca. She had been overtly candid with me, and I was feeling the same way toward her.

"Claiming immunity and clinging to your legal right to privacy is meaningless to me. What troubles me the most is your choice of words. I was chastised and brazenly left behind at the hospital, as the innocent child who suffered from the result of your actions. I could never envision my separation from you at birth as a beautiful thing," I argued in disbelief.

"The Salvation Army handled the entire affair. They were very thorough. I didn't have to do anything," Rebecca bluntly replied, coldly defending her position.

My energy and enthusiasm waned as exhaustion crept up on me. Overstimulation of my emotions had been fatiguing. I felt weak and lethargic. Our conversation had drained my spiritual energy and left me feeling moody and sluggish.

"I still want to identify the orphanage where I was a resident for the first eleven months of my life," I impulsively injected.

"Good-bye, and don't call this number anymore." Rebecca hung up abruptly.

Our conversation had ended without warning, perhaps forever. I knew instantly that I would never talk to my birth mother again. She had never wished me happiness or good fortune or asked for forgiveness. It was a sad and disenchanting way to end our brief, once-in-a-lifetime encounter. Our biological relationship as mother and daughter had ended before it could even develop. I would never learn anything about my true heritage or lineage or know anything about any of my ancestors, cultural history, or other members of my birth family. Rebecca and I would never share a hug or smile or meet in person.

I wiped a tear from my cheek and said softly long after Rebecca had hung up on me, "Good-bye, Rebecca, my precious, beautiful mother."

I folded my arms, laid my head down, and closed my eyes. I prayed for Rebecca and daydreamed about how different my life would have been if it had followed its natural course. I was raised as an only child in a quiet family where my father was seldom at home. Living with Bruno and Rebecca and three other children would have allowed many opportunities for enjoyable camaraderie, and the constant activity of being surrounded by a large family would have been exciting. The idea of a brother and two sisters intrigued me a great deal. I wondered if there would ever be a discreet way to spy on them without telling Rebecca.

My existence as a real person had rocked Rebecca to the core by dredging up powerful teenage memories she had tried very hard to forget. Her unwanted pregnancy had toughened her. Her spirit had become calloused, and she had fought back against my advances with all of her might, blaming me for reigniting her terrible feelings of guilt. Perhaps I was to blame for gallantly plodding forward with blinders on, without regard to the potential for calamity or the sensitivity of others. There was some truth to the fact that I had acted nervy and impetuous, and some of my actions were audacious and arrogant, but how else could I have produced the same results?

My relationship with Rebecca was over. There was no possibility of resolving our differences, merging our families, or mutually healing the gaping wound that had split us apart. My search had taken a heavy toll on my personality and psyche and squandered a considerable amount of precious family time. I was tired and resolved to the fact that my search was over, but there was still one thing left in the world that was very important to me. I wanted to envision what Rebecca looked like.

Dear Rebecca, I will forever languish in vacuity until I can realistically visualize your image. Please send me a portrait image of yourself that I can treasure and keep next to my heart for perpetuity. This is all I ask of you. Love, Judy

Doldrums

Dear Mom, I have been in the doldrums ever since our last conversation. It was not my intent to intrude into your life and disturb you or your family. I was only hoping to learn more about my roots and family history. Knowing where I came from is very important because it would help me feel grounded. Admittedly, I was hoping for a more benevolent response from you. I had expected you to be more sympathetic and understanding about my curiosity as an adoptee. I thought you would be pleasant and politely answer some of my questions. Instead, you reprimanded me for my actions and made me feel rejected again. It was upsetting to have you question my motives and disappointing to have you scold me for not being a better daughter to my adoptive parents. I hope that, as time passes, your hostility toward me will diminish. Perhaps you will be less fearful and more benevolent in the future when you realize that I do not intend to harm you or your family. Love, Judy

MY TEMPERAMENT WAS LIKE a summer wildfire raging out of control in a dry pine forest, fueled by erratic currents of air in unpredictable directions, devouring everything in my path. Yesterday, I was joyously buoyant, exultantly floating on cloud nine, radiantly light-hearted, and gleefully walking on air. I had awoken feeling highly energized, optimistic, and eager to accomplish my goals. My euphoric highs were accompanied by wonderful ecstatic feelings of high achievement, happiness, success, well-being, and accomplishment. I was contented, optimistic, and one hundred percent confident that searching for my birth mother was the right thing to do.

Today was a dark and dreary, glum and joyless, woefully dispirited, emotionally low kind of day. Rebecca's description of my adoption as a "beautiful thing" and her rejection of my offer of friendship had left me heartbroken and miserable.

Life was a pendulum. Always struggling to work my way up the mountain before plummeting uncontrollably down the flip side, my emotions were attached to an animated roller coaster dominated by the thrill of exhilaration. The higher I climbed, the more precipitous the free fall descents were on the downside. I was either in heaven or hell, sheer bliss or purgatory, heartbroken or loved, or contented or panicked. Transitions were nonexistent, and the intensity of my emotions, whether high or low, was far outside the natural range of variability for healthy living.

Fortunately, I was blessed with a good family living in an alpine resort with abundant sunshine and beautiful scenery. Happy people surrounded me, and I participated in many pleasant, healthy outdoor activities. I was relatively free of stress other than my own self-inflicted reparations. We owned a jeep and enjoyed camping in the forest. We took our son fishing and watched him play soccer and baseball. Martin and I went on exciting romantic dates to the adjacent resort towns of Vail and Aspen and raced through the mountains on warm, sunny days in our Porsche convertible with our Old English sheepdog, Lazy Daisy Tumbleweed, sticking her head into the wind. Climbing to the summit of Mt. Sopris in the Maroon Bells Wilderness was a major accomplishment. Life was good, and I was thankful my situation promoted self-confidence and happiness.

Most days were exceptionally good, but thinking about my journey was a major distraction that made it difficult to concentrate on normal activities. Fear and anxieties caused me to lose impetus and crumbled my solid foundation. My whole system would shut down, and I would feel psychologically zapped. When that happened, I had no physical energy or stamina, my attention span was reduced, and my mental drive was diminished, leading only to procrastination.

Research and book learning had encouraged me to think deeply about the big picture of abortion and adoption in American society because these topics were part of an endless raging national debate. Opinions varied widely, and public consensus was impossible to attain. Media discussions in the political arena produced a firestorm of angry rhetoric where opposing parties held clashing viewpoints about laws, Supreme Court decisions, funding, and ethics. Religious groups promoted their own sets of rules and moral interpretations. Social organizations actively raised funds to promote public awareness, and political candidates extorted their viewpoints. And as a result of natural disasters, war, and collapsing economies, babies from foreign countries de jour were being indiscriminately imported to the United States from opposite sides of the globe in the name of humanity.

My adoption story had become much more complex and complicated than I had ever anticipated, and other parents and adoptees in my circle of friends expressed fervent opinions about these topics as well. For that reason, I kept my personal thoughts to myself and only discussed my situation with my husband. The more I investigated the topic of adoption, the more multifaceted these issues became and the more things we had to converse about. Our discussions were often intense, but always amicable and thorough.

Occasionally, a friend or neighbor would express an opinion or political viewpoint contrary to mine, but usually because they were unaware of the sensitivity of my situation. Asking for emotional support from others with opposing viewpoints would have been fruitless and left me feeling unnecessarily exposed. I certainly didn't want to debate or argue with friends. Surprisingly, it had become more difficult rather than easier to discuss adoption with others because my case was uniquely personal. I had more at stake than others did because I was an adoptee and I was unaccustomed to facing adversity. I had only been looking for solace and reassurance. Keeping my sentiments secret and emotions concealed from others was easy to do because it was something I had practiced doing ever since I was a young girl. My childhood girlfriends and original members of the First Lilac Club were my only friends who understood the passions that had consumed me as a child.

One of the most important lessons I had discovered during my investigations was that it was most effective to enlighten others about what had already been accomplished and never predict the future. I followed this strategy in all aspects of life and business. If I told people what I had already achieved, they withheld their criticism, but, if I told them what I was planning to do in the future, they often deluged me with unsolicited advice contrary to my own.

Discovering my birth mother had been a thrilling event, but she had ultimately rejected me, and now I was sadly craving a time for quiet, introverted reflection. In the beginning, I had immaturely thought very little about the overriding effects to other concerned individuals or the potential collateral damage to second and third parties. When I was feeling emotionally low, fragile, or vulnerable, the most conscientious and experienced counselors and psychologists might have been able to diagnose the root cause of my condition, but I had concluded that only another orphan could empathize with my youthful nostalgia and childlike tender poignancy.

As the weeks and months passed, the results of my search and its effect on me became more intense. Everything had reached a crescendo when I finally contacted Rebecca directly. The event had produced an extremely emotional high, but her overwhelming rejection and cold rebuttal had carried with it a distressingly near-fatal blow to my ego. I was thrilled to have finally talked with her, but the feelings of unequivocal rejection in the final episode had left me emotionally anesthetized and waging a brutal argument in my own mind about what to do next. Should I abandon my lifelong dream as folly and give up my adoption search for good, or should I aggressively continue moving forward in a bullheaded way?

I was temporarily down, but my feelings of anticipation were slowly building again. It was impossible to suppress them. I had come a long way in two years. It would be a shame to stop with the job halfway finished.

The internal forces that had inflamed my obsession were gradually shifting to thoughts of my birth father. Was he the boy whose picture I closely resembled in the high school yearbook, the same person Rebecca had dated in high school and eventually married?

Confirmation

Dear Mom, Hoping to discern a familiar glance, an accidental touch, or something memorable to make it easier for me to identify you, I grew up looking into the eyes of strangers and wondering if we were related. Scanning my world for your face, your smile, your voice, and your arms and searching for nourishment and protection has preoccupied my thoughts since birth. You were a vital character in my fantasies and daydreams, but, now that I have become acquainted with you as a real person, I feel more separated from you than vanquished. Thinking of you brings me pleasant thoughts, and, now that I know you are alive, I can stop worrying and fantasizing. Although you are unwilling to collaborate with me, I will never completely surrender my lifelong desire to reunite with you or abandon my aspirations to trace my family heritage. I will never rest in peace until my quest is finished. Love, Judy

DRIVING THROUGH MAJESTIC GLENWOOD Canyon in our wine-colored Porsche convertible was a glorious way to celebrate our tenth wedding anniversary. With the top down, we had a perfect view of the deep blue sky. Sunshine highlighted the thousand-foot-high cliffs overhead and illuminated the raging white-water rapids in the Colorado River beside us. The music on the radio was turned up loud. "It's Still Rock and Roll to Me" by Billy Joel had me tapping my feet, twisting my shoulders, and clapping my hands.

It was the first day I could recall that my thoughts were not preoccupied with my adoption search. I felt healthy and greatly enjoyed the prospect of celebrating our positive lifestyle together. It was the same enjoyment I had experienced when we first got married.

Following an exciting round of golf at Vail Country Club, surrounded by gorgeous views of the snowcapped Gore Mountain Range as the scenic backdrop, I relaxed with a double martini at the Sonnenalp. We ordered a fabulous Chateaubriand beef dinner for two, a bottle of Chianti Classico Reserva, and strawberry cheesecake for desert. It was a memorable, agreeable, fun-filled day followed by a romantic evening. Life was good.

The following day, I awoke feeling refreshed and happy. Sunshine poured through my south-facing kitchen window and warmed my heart. I felt exceptionally blessed to be experiencing a genuine Colorado Rocky Mountain high. I poured myself a cup of coffee before walking out to water the flowers, smell the fresh air, and pick up the mail. In the middle of the bundle was a letter from the Salvation Army.

Filled with anticipation, I rushed back into the house and plopped down in a living room chair. Four weeks had passed since I had written the letter to Ken Stein. I tore open the letter and my eyes immediately started jumping all over the page, top to bottom and side-to-side, forcing me to reread each sentence three times to make sure I understood what it said.

The letter provided unequivocal verification that Bruno Rossi and Rebecca Meyer were indeed my birth parents. I finally had the corroborative evidence I had been looking for from an independent intermediary. My self-esteem soared. It was a feeling that only an adoptee could experience, although some million dollar lottery winners and Olympic champions might disagree with me.

I was elated. I wanted to stand up and scream rapturous cheers. I was no longer adrift and disoriented or aimless. I knew who was responsible for my birth. I had written proof in my hand. There was nothing missing—no more bewilderment or confusion. I had legal confirmation of my roots; the mystery of my adoption was solved. I had succeeded as an adoption detective by solving my first and most important case. I was no longer an anonymous unidentified outcast trying to solve a whodunit detective novel.

I imagined myself high on a mountaintop, singing and skipping through fields of wildflowers on a sunny day. I was ecstatically overjoyed knowing my birth parents were both alive and married to each other. I felt like celebrating wildly and excessively. I felt like dancing. Music was therapy for me. I turned on the radio and danced to Diana Ross's old song, "My World Is Empty without You."

In the middle of my euphoria, I realized I was more thankful to

God than I had ever been before. I had expended a huge amount of emotional energy, but I felt blessed. My prayers had come true after all.

I clung possessively to the letter as if it were a highly valuable treasure map because it confirmed the fact that my birth parents were married. Before now, I had predominantly focused on locating my biological mother. Now I was equally enthusiastic about meeting my birth father to hear what he thought about my adoption.

Despite her confession, there had always been the possibility Rebecca was not my birth mother. Just because she gave her baby to an orphanage for adoption the same time I was born didn't automatically qualify me as her child. I had followed the wrong lead to a Wisconsin dairy farm once before, and I certainly didn't want to make that mistake again. I studied the letter and carefully perused every word. My birth father's name was Bruno J. Rossi. My birth mother's maiden name was Rebecca Barbara Meyer, daughter of Ben and Bertha Meyer. The letter contained my parents' nationalities, occupations, and birthdays. It had the name of the hospital, dates of admission and release, and name of the social worker, Gertrude Schweinhaus. It was the exact information I had set out to find two years ago that Gertrude and Rebecca had previously refused to validate.

I wanted to call my birth father right away to share the good news with him before realizing of how awkward it would be if I called him at home. More than likely, Rebecca would be very upset and refuse to let me speak with him.

Rebecca had mentioned that Bruno exercised regularly three times a week at the Eagles Club. I surmised that the receptionist would know him and be able to tell me the best time to reach him. I impulsively made up my mind to call Bruno after I could gather my thoughts and muster enough nerve. I set an artificial deadline of ten days to get organized. A key part of my training process was to practice containing my enthusiasm while creating the illusion of being emotionally mellow. I wanted every word to be thoroughly prepared and rehearsed before speaking because first impressions were critical.

I greeted Martin with a kiss and showed him the papers the minute he arrived home from work.

"This information is incredible. The director, Ken Stein, was a patient and considerate man for giving you this information because these legal records are confidential. He was obviously very sympathetic to your cause. You should be very thankful," he said after carefully reading the letter aloud.

I WAS REHEARSED AND finally ready to call my birth father. My hormone levels had stabilized and were normal again, but my natural instinct was to passively avoid the stress. It took a tremendous amount of self-control, willpower, and inner courage to conquer my shyness.

My shaking hands made it physically difficult to pick up the telephone. I precisely dialed the Eagles Athletic club in Milwaukee one painstaking number at a time. I could feel beads of perspiration on my forehead.

"Eagles Club. This is Cindy Casserly." The receptionist sounded like a sexy jazz club singer with a mellow mezzo soprano voice. I wondered if her clothes were as provocative as her demeanor.

"Is Bruno Rossi there?" I inquired to know.

"Mr. Rossi is not here at this time, but I will give him the message that you called," she said with a hint of jealous female intuition.

My heart was racing. I took a deep breath as if I had just accomplished something physically strenuous. I was proud of myself. I had faced my fears by making my second monumental call of a lifetime.

Twenty minutes later, the telephone rang. I immediately sprang into action. The sound of the telephone was louder and more urgent than usual.

"Hello, I'm returning your call," a man said politely. His voice resonated amiably.

"This is Judy."

"I know. How are you?"

"I am fine. How are you?"

"Oh, I feel okay," he said casually as if we were old friends.

"How do you feel about me calling you?"

He chuckled and responded graciously, "Well, you know how Italians are. Life is about loving and forgiving. I'm Italian. I would love to meet you. You are family."

His openness, congenial invitation, and pleasant deportment astonished me. It was a complete reversal in polarization from what I had expected and previously experienced with Rebecca.

"I have a nephew living in Denver, Judy. His name is Johnny Fazio. You should look him up."

I loved the way Bruno said my name because it made me feel important. He made it sound like we were already family. He seemed like such a fine man.

"Do you ever come to Colorado? I live in the heart of the Rocky Mountains between Vail and Aspen ski resorts. We have the world's largest hot springs pool." I hoped to leave a good first impression by giving him the usual chamber of commerce marketing speech about the many resort amenities our town had to offer.

"I vacationed in Aspen last year. I have some friends who wanted me to help them start a restaurant in Breckenridge."

"Wow. That's a tough business in this economic climate." I was happy to know that he was familiar with this part of Colorado.

"Listen, Judy, I'm flying to Las Vegas next week. I could stop and meet you on my way through. I will call you and let you know my plans in a few days," he explained warmly.

"Oh, that would be great. You seem so different from Rebecca. She got so upset with me. She really rattled my cage," I confided to him.

"I know. She told me about your phone calls. I have to agree with her feelings, you know," he said in loving support of his wife.

"I saw the pictures you sent Rebecca. You are a beautiful person," Bruno revealed tenderly.

His flattering statement touched me because he was connecting with me as a real person and his comment had come from the heart.

"Thank you for the nice compliment. I have a picture of you, too, and I can tell that I have your genes because we look similar," I said with a genuinely affectionate smile.

"Where did you get the picture?" Bruno asked curiously.

"I talked to one of your second-grade classmates. I can't remember her name. She sent me a cute picture of you in the fourth grade," I responded.

"You know, you sound so much like my oldest daughter, Linda. You look like her, too. I think this is remarkable," he said with a friendly chuckle.

"I have other pictures of you. I talked to the editor of your high school yearbook, and she sent me pictures of you in your basketball and football uniforms," I said proudly.

"I am a little heavier now, and my hair is thinner, you know," Bruno said laughingly.

"When I saw you in your basketball uniform, I knew you had to be my father because we look so much alike. You had dark eyes and dark hair when you were young, just like me."

"How is your family?" Bruno asked politely.

"Everyone is fine. I have a six-year-old son. His name is Michael."

"No kidding. That is beautiful. I guess I'm a grandfather. It has been very pleasant talking to you, Judy. I will call you in two weeks on my way to Las Vegas," he promised.

"My husband and I could meet you in Denver if that is easier for you," I offered.

"That would be great. I will look forward to seeing you. Thank you for calling. I'll see you soon. My sisters, your biological aunts, would also love to meet you."

"Good-bye, Bruno." I grinned from ear to ear.

My enormous expectations for an exciting future with my birth father and his Italian side of the family had suddenly skyrocketed through the ceiling. When the lead song "Somewhere Out There" by James Horner from *An American Tale* started playing on the radio, my euphoria turned to hysteria. *Somewhere out there, if love can see us through, then we'll be together somewhere out there, out where dreams come true.*

It was a fabulous day. Everything was coming up roses. I was elated. My disposition was sunny and bright. My life was one hundred percent positive, and my senses were heightened to such a high degree that I could hardly maintain my sanity.

Heart Attack

Dear Mom, Despite your nefarious rejection of me, I think about you often in countless positive ways. I understand your fears and why you would like me to vanish and never contact you again to protect your reputation and family, but I am your daughter, and it is impossible for me to voluntarily disappear. I am a real person. I have feelings similar to yours because I carry your genes. You gave birth to me. I am your long-lost daughter—set adrift but now found—and I will not willingly banish myself from this world simply because you ask me to. Bruno and I are secretly planning a serendipitous father-daughter rendezvous in Denver in two weeks. I wish you would come, too. Perhaps your opinion of me will soften after we meet and he convinces you I am a person of good character. If I ever have the opportunity to meet you, I am willing to abide by your desire for confidentiality and honor any conditions needed to gain your trust. I pray you will eventually understand my aspirations and not continue rejecting me forever. Love, Judy

TRIUMPH AT LAST! WHAT should I wear? Will the weather be cool or warm in Denver? Will we be meeting inside or outside? I started planning immediately. To make a good first impression, I bought two elegant dresses, an expensive jacket, and an extravagant pair of Italian shoes. I highlighted my hair, polished my fingernails, cleaned my teeth, basked in the sun to bring color to my cheeks, and vowed to shed five pounds.

To calm my nervous tension, Martin and I floated serenely in the warm healing waters of the natural hot springs pool after dinner. We talked and wandered aimlessly through the fog. Softly rising, steamy vapors obscured our vision and made it difficult for others to see us or eavesdrop on our conversation. Casual stretching exercises while quietly drifting on our backs at a snail's pace in the buoyant hot water facilitated a slackening of the tension in my muscles and diminished my apprehension. Martin held my hand and let me know that he grasped the significance of how happy it made me knowing I had finally accomplished my goal of finding my birth parents. It calmed me knowing he was there to share this historic moment with me, and I told him how much I appreciated his support because, without his moral guidance and encouragement, circumstances never would have turned out so well.

We talked peacefully about my birth father's planned visit and how it should be arranged. Bruno had been incredibly friendly and genuinely kind to me, which had led me to assume that he was acting independently without Rebecca's blessing or knowledge. He had been openly expressive, legitimately enthusiastic, and candid during our entire conversation. It was highly doubtful he would have acted that way with Rebecca present. It was reassuring knowing he had taken the initiative to call me to arrange for the planned reunion.

Several days passed before I became concerned. I wondered how long Bruno would wait to call me with his agenda and the details of our secret convergence. On the seventh day, doubt and pessimism dominated my thoughts, and my emotional stress level peaked. Martin put his arm around me and tried to persuade me to remain in good spirits and optimistic.

"Bruno said he is coming, and he will. I believe him. Nothing has changed. He is a self-employed businessman with a diversity of financial commitments. His plate is full. He has contracts and clients to satisfy. He has to take care of his highest priorities before he can go on vacation." Martin tried to spark a little positive energy and common sense into my listless brain.

He assured me that everything would be all right. He exuded confidence and projected a bright smile. "Remember that patience is a virtue. Go about your daily routines and take care of your responsibilities. Regardless of how strongly you anticipate the arrival of special events, you can't speed up the calendar. You have to take each day one at a time. Stay calm. Relax. Bruno is busy, and he will arrive when the time is right for him," Martin said reassuringly.

I anguished as another seven days passed slowly. It was impossible to remain focused on my daily routines. I had been happily full of enthusiasm, but my physical stamina and mental eagerness had greatly diminished. Imagining the worst, the air in my psychological balloon quietly leaked out. Rebecca must have become dreadfully angry and threatened and intimidated Bruno into canceling his plans. She persuaded him to change his mind; otherwise, he would have called to say he wasn't coming.

Finally, I couldn't stand it any longer. I was worried. Something had to be wrong. I had to do something. Bruno had promised to call me within a few days, yet two uneventful weeks had passed without any contact or excuses. He had sounded eager to meet me. He was the one who had initiated the meeting in Denver. Why hadn't he called me? I forced Martin to sit down with me and discuss the negative state of affairs.

"I agree with you. Bruno should have called you by now. Obviously, circumstances changed." Martin inadvertently added rocket fuel to my pessimism.

He was no longer pretending to be optimistic or falsely attempting to boost my confidence. The facts of the case were unmistakable. He agreed with me. Something was drastically wrong. The date of our planned reunion had already expired.

Martin's response to my plea for help resulted in a brainstorming exercise to analyze every possible scenario why Bruno hadn't come to Colorado as promised. We discussed each alternative separately and then focused on the ones that made the most sense. We agreed that, if Bruno had been tied up at work, delayed for business reasons, or had other extenuating circumstances, he would have called to explain the delay.

Our first scenario was that Bruno had simply gotten cold feet and changed his mind. Rebecca probably influenced him by putting her foot down or giving him an ultimatum. This alternative seemed like the most compelling argument and cause of his absence.

Another drastic scenario we considered was a tragic car accident involving a family member or employee, but that scenario was too far-fetched and melodramatic to be coincidental. I had been intensively searching for my birth parents for over two years, and the timing of a disastrous event such as this was too bizarre to be coincidental. A benevolent God would never allow a heartbreaking calamity to happen within days of my commemorative reunion with my birth father.

Martin was optimistic by nature and sincerely wanted me to succeed. Normally, his decisions were based on simple logic and facts, but, this time, he was finally giving credence and validity to my intuitive premonitions and beginning to feel the same way.

It was too risky to contact Bruno at home because Rebecca would be furious if she found out what had happened behind her back. Until I had a definitive response from Bruno one way or the other, it was possible that he was still planning to eventually come see me, and I didn't want to spoil my chances. I thought about calling Aunt Frieda, but she didn't have a personal relationship with Rebecca anymore. I considered initiating contact with Bruno's nephew, Johnny Fazio, but he might not know anything about me, so I rejected that idea.

During our telephone conversation, Bruno had mentioned that his sisters were interested in meeting me. This was another possibility, but I didn't want to jinx the situation by involving others or cause anyone to become suspicious of my covert situation and relationship to Bruno. I wasn't interested in involving intermediaries in the crisis because this entire affair was confidential and strictly between my birth father and me. Calling the wrong person might induce gossip or promote slander and destroy the limited number of opportunities for a reunion I had remaining.

It was impossible to repress my pessimism. My high-spirited dreams of a castle in the sky and fairy-tale ending to my charming story had faded into fuzzy images of deceased ancestors in black-and-white photographs. My delusions of success, glory, and colorful friendships with beautiful people had been replaced with cold, lifeless, ghostly caricatures in shades of gray.

I was mentally drained, restless, and emotionally unstable. The sustained two-week emotional high I had experienced had been replaced by a lethargic period of inactivity and lack of enthusiasm. The color in my cheeks washed out, and my energy level declined.

Realizing that, if I were ever going to get to the bottom of the situation, I would have to take action and call Bruno directly. My patience shattered. I impulsively called the Eagles Club. Cindy Casserly had not seen Bruno lately, which was highly unusual, because he had routinely visited the Eagles Club several times a week for as long as anyone could remember.

I wondered if Bruno had gone to Las Vegas and bypassed Denver altogether. Maybe he had intentionally avoided seeing me because Rebecca had talked him out of it.

Bruno had mentioned the name of his sister Annie Fazio as the mother of his nephew in Denver. I dialed the Milwaukee operator and requested her number. There was only one listing.

"Hello, Annie. This is Judy. I talked to your brother Bruno on the telephone two weeks ago. Do you know if he stopped to visit your son in Denver on his way to Las Vegas last week?" I hoped she could clarify the situation.

"Yes, I have a son in Denver. His name is Johnny Fazio. He likes it out there in Denver more than Milwaukee," she replied in a friendly voice.

"I haven't heard from Bruno in several weeks, and I was hoping to find out if there were any problems," I explained earnestly.

There was a long pause. I waited, anticipating what she might say next, but no response was forthcoming. Her silence worried me. Something was wrong.

Annie spoke deliberately in a measured cadence. Her words lingered in the air like the notes of a percussion instrument in a sound-proof room. "Bruno had a severe heart attack. He is in grave condition. He can't come to Colorado to see you now," she said somberly.

There was another long pause. I was in a speechless state of apoplexy and uncertain how to respond. "That is terrible. Bruno is my birth father. I was looking forward to meeting him. That is why he never came to see me," I said solemnly. The energy drained from my spirit.

I felt an immediate bond with her because she was my biological aunt. I hoped she would understand my quandary and give me sympathy.

"I know who you are. Bruno told me, but it is extremely important that he not be disturbed. Rebecca is the only person allowed in his room. He is going to have heart surgery to replace some of his arteries. He may be in the hospital a long time. He is a veteran and a tough guy, but I don't think he will be going anywhere for a long time. We are very worried because you never know about these things. Our family has a history of heart problems, and some have died very young," Annie said, elucidating her fears.

"I am very grateful to you for sharing this information. I am sorry to hear that Bruno's condition is life-threatening."

Eventually, she gave me the answer for which I had been hoping.

"I will write you a letter to let you know how Bruno progresses," she promised.

Our conversation ended on a somber note. The minute she hung up, I thought of a dozen important questions I should have asked her, like when it happened, the name of the hospital, and whether he had suffered permanent damage to his heart or brain.

I was miserable. My mind was numb. The timing was unfortunate and depressing and very bad luck. If Bruno died or ended up with permanent heart or brain damage, I could never forgive myself. My first reaction was to call Bruno directly to express my concern and give him my sympathy, but telephone calls were against doctor's orders. I blamed myself as the cause of his heart attack because I was the major contributor to his stress. Rebecca would never forgive me.

Why did this happen at such a critical moment on the eve of our father-daughter reunion? My window of opportunity had expired. It was too late. There would never be another chance to meet him. I had come so close, but failed.

Realizing his heart attack was my fault, I placed my hands over my eyes and bawled. My chest heaved. I cried big crocodile tears. Nobody was there to comfort me. I had given Bruno so much nervous tension that I had nearly killed my own birth father without ever having the opportunity to meet him in person.

Poor Rebecca, she would never speak to me again. She had demanded I leave her alone, but I had ignored her plea, and now look what happened. She had informed me that my first telephone call caused her severe stress and hemorrhaging, and now Bruno was living proof that stress caused his heart attack.

Nobody in the family would ever want to talk to me again. I had barged into their lives and left a contrail of hypertension, ruin, and destruction. I would be forever condemned as an outside troublemaker and cast aside as their lowest priority, an inconsequential being in the overall picture of things. Bruno's health and recovery would be the only thing on their minds from now until eternity.

I had ignored the parable of letting sleeping dogs lie. Now I would have to pay the consequences by being forever banished and excommunicated from my own biological family. Awareness of the result of my actions rekindled the internal suffocating feelings of helplessness and isolation I had experienced as a small child after being told my birth parents had abandoned me.

I was alone and feeling dreadfully sorry for myself. I was in a complete funk. I had sunk to the lowest point in my life. I was spiritually demoralized and desperately in need of a guardian angel to guide me through this gloomy period.

I had allowed my adoption search to dominate my life and consume my fate. My journey to find them had taken a massive expenditure of energy, expense, and precious time away from my family when I could have been hiking, skiing, and raising my son Michael without having to deal with so many emotional problems. My husband would have benefited from additional support in his career.

Martin arrived home from work and found me sitting on the couch wrapped in a blanket while hugging a pillow. I felt like sucking my thumb and swigging down a shot of tequila, but avoided the humiliation. At no other time in my life had I ever needed so much comfort. A couple tears dripped down my cheeks, and my lips quivered as I explained what had happened.

"I caused Bruno to have a heart attack. Now I will never have a chance to meet him," I explained soberly.

Martin tenderly placed his arm around me. "I suggest you take the time to pray quietly because the power of prayer combined with psycho-cybernetics and positive thinking provides comfort and self-healing and restores life. You are very strong and deserve a good life full of joy and happiness, not one dominated by abandonment, loneliness, and tragedies. There were never any guarantees your story would have a happy ending. Life is not a fairy tale where wishes always come true. You accomplished your objective. The results could have been much worse. You must not tarry in the past. Live life optimistically going forward. Count your blessings, think positive thoughts, and focus on the things over which you have control."

Several days later when I was at the lowest point of my life, a letter arrived from Annie Fazio, giving me the name of the hospital with a suggestion I send Bruno a personal note in a couple weeks after he had a chance to recuperate from his surgery. She suggested I contact her son Johnny because we were biological first cousins.

Her personal handwritten letter was a special gift from a compassionate heart that cheered my soul. Her warm message of love and friendship acknowledged my existence and created an obvious sense of belonging with the Rossi family. Her kindhearted, compassionate message brought a wee smile to my face and benevolently made the sun shine brighter. Annie was a beautiful person with a heart of gold. Her message of hope was a ray of sunshine. I was fond of her immediately.

Enclosed with her letter were a hand-crocheted dishcloth and some cherished photographs of the family. I treasured them as a priceless gift from heaven with enormous sentimental value. Her package was a thousand times greater than all the cold census data, gravesites, faded photographs, interviews, and impersonal government records on dusty shelves I had previously pursued.

According to Aunt Annie, her recollection of the events surrounding my birth was still vivid in her memory. She had never forgotten about Bruno's adopted daughter, and she was very happy knowing that, after all these years, I had finally found the Rossi family. Her letter had provided me what I had been seeking all along, complete and honest acceptance as a member of her family. I remained still and interminably focused on the most poignant sentence in her letter.

"You are our blood. Welcome home."

Cousin Johnny

Dear Mom, Please help Bruno live a long life so I can meet him someday. I pray continuously that he will have a full recovery from his heart attack. I am sorry for the stress I caused him and offer my apologies to both of you. I know my presence presents a dilemma for you, and this is not the time for me to be interfering in your affairs, but, regardless of how much you want me to stay out of your life, I still cling to the hope that you will reconsider when Bruno recovers. No obstacle seems too difficult to deter me from accomplishing my goal of meeting you in person. I don't think I will ever be happy or feel completely whole until we have had a genuine reconciliation as mother and daughter. Love, Judy

A N EMERGING CONCERN ABOUT the character of the Rossi family was suddenly stirring my imagination and making my stomach acids churn. Annie's statement, "You are our blood," raised my suspicions and left me with a queasy feeling because her quote was identical to famous lines in several Mafia movies, including *The Godfather* and *Prizzi's Honor*.

I had recklessly charged forward without any prior investigation into the character of the people I was hoping to meet. I had already been uneasy knowing that a few friends of my adopted father had unsavory reputations. One had been gunned down in the street outside his restaurant; another was standing on his front porch. Shortly after that, one of his grocery stores had been sprayed with machine gun bullets, and another was mysteriously burned to the ground following a heated argument with the building contractor and insurance company. Seeing him afraid to leave the house had left me aware of shadowy figures and taught me to be more observant and leery of the moral and ethical character of all people. Living in Colorado and isolated from these negative influences gave me comfort knowing I was purposefully raising my son without any awareness of such happenings.

I wondered if I were getting myself into a situation I would later regret. Rebecca had been adamant about protecting her privacy. Perhaps her family really did have secrets to hide. Bruno was in the restaurant and tavern business, which might automatically put him in contact with seedy customers. And who were his friends in Colorado and connections in Las Vegas? And why was he going there and for what purpose?

Conjecturing about the situation gave me cold feet because I was worried about accidentally getting involved with strangers of disreputable character, even if they were blood relatives. I didn't want to naïvely and unnecessarily take risks by putting myself in an untenable situation I might later regret.

My connection with Aunt Annie had been tremendously positive. For that reason, I was willing to take chances. Her sentiments were extremely important because she was the first to authenticate my presence and provide the accreditation I had been searching for all my life. Her positive response was what I had expected from Rebecca when she said she had never stopped thinking about me ever since I was born. Aunt Annie's comment that I was her blood was a sentimental thought I treasured more than a fortune in gold because it was the decisive culmination of my lifelong quest to find my biological roots that I had been so eagerly yearning to discover.

I called Aunt Annie to thank her for welcoming me into her heart, but her brother's heart attack had shaken her terribly, and her response was subdued. She had no nothing to report because Rebecca was not allowing anyone into his hospital room.

My cousin Johnny Fazio was aware of the situation, and Annie continued to express her desire for me to meet him. I wondered if I were lucky, if my life had been blessed, or if I were simply the recipient of a continuous amount of serendipitous good fortune when Martin came home from work flashing two Denver Bronco football tickets in his hand.

"Look what Jim Noenig, president of Telluride, gave me. Two tickets on the forty-yard line to see the Denver Broncos play the Green Bay Packers. Pack your bags for an overnight. Monday morning, I have a meeting with a New York company planning to buy Vail Resorts,"

Martin said happily with an enormous grin. "Give your cousin Johnny a call to see if he can meet us after the game," Martin said gleefully.

I impulsively consented because I had never met a biological relative, and there was a good possibility of gaining some insight into the personalities of Bruno and Rebecca and their family.

"Hello," a robust voice responded on the other end of the line. "Who is this?"

"This is your cousin Judy in Glenwood Springs. My birth father Bruno told me about you before he had his heart attack," I explained.

"You really surprised him. Your dad is a great guy and my favorite uncle. He definitely wants to meet you. How is he doing? Have you heard from him since he had his heart attack?" Johnny inquired politely.

"No, Rebecca is guarding his room at the hospital and screening all of his calls. I'm not on her list of invited guests and probably never will be," I admitted candidly. "My husband and I have tickets to the Denver Broncos football game on Sunday afternoon. Can you meet us after the game?"

"I plan to be at the game, too. I played professional football myself. I was a fullback for the Philadelphia Eagles. Sure, let's plan on getting together for dinner," Johnny countered encouragingly.

"Meet me by the fountain by the main entrance after the game." I happily looked forward to my first meeting with a blood relative.

I could tell that Johnny was a no-bullshit kind of guy. He sounded masculine and strong, and my first impression was rather intimidating.

Before I made the call, I had been mellow and blue knowing that my actions had such dire consequences and the situation had been further complicated because I was entirely in the dark about his recovery. But now I was suddenly radiantly invigorated knowing I was going to meet my cousin.

I had mentioned where we would be sitting during the game, but had innocently neglected to tell Johnny how to recognize me. The game was exciting and undecided until the final minute. None of the fans left the stadium until the game was over. As we got up to leave, Martin grabbed my arm and held me back. The crowd surged around us and nearly pushed us over.

"Look at that guy on the other side of the stadium. He is cutting diagonally across the flow of traffic and coming directly toward us. Could that be your cousin?" Martin asked inquisitively.

The man bulling his way through the tightly packed throng was a broad-shouldered, rough-looking, handsome man with thick muscles and a dark, menacing mustache. He forced others out of his way as he moved through the stadium crowd until we met face-to-face.

"Hello, Judy. I am your cousin, Johnny Fazio, Aunt Annie's son." He leaned over to give me a warm Italian hug.

I could see Martin winch as Johnny nearly crushed the bones in his right hand with a hearty handshake. Johnny had a pleasant smile. He was hospitable and acting as the welcoming ambassador for all of my long-lost Italian relatives in Milwaukee.

"How did you recognize me? I forgot to tell you what I would be wearing. I was worried we might not be able to find each other in a stadium full of people," I remarked.

"It was easy. You look just like your mother, my Aunt Rebecca. Once I recognized your face, I was certain you were my cousin." He had a big smile.

We arrived at our car just in time to chase a drunk away who had broken into our Porsche. Martin acted out his anger by accelerating aggressively to relieve some of his tension. The rear tires smoked and squealed loudly before gripping the pavement and launching the car forward like a rocket. Martin smiled and winked as he always did when he was showing off.

We met Johnny and his girlfriend at a restaurant where we talked enthusiastically for several hours. He told me many interesting things about my birth parents and the history of the Rossi family originally from Palermo, Sicily. He described places of employment, education, and appearance. I listened in awe when he told me about my two sisters, Linda and Cindy, and my brother Timmy. I had an insatiable appetite for knowledge, and the information Johnny provided helped me transition from my childhood fantasies to reality. Many of the things he told me were eerily similar to my dreamy childhood images of a perfect family. Learning about my birth family was an awakening that gave me a great deal of satisfaction and pride.

"You have similarities in appearance and habits with your siblings and many of us cousins. Like you, everyone has smooth complexions and large, toothy smiles. We are a large, extended Italian family, including all the cousins, aunts and uncles, and grandparents, where everyone enjoys each other's company. We are physically strong and stick together to help and support each other. Your father is a restaurant and tavern owner. He has many friends. He is a tough guy who is proud of his Italian heritage, a marine veteran, and a patriotic American," Johnny boasted proudly.

Johnny had recently left a job working for a casino in Las Vegas notoriously famous for laundering money for organized crime families in Milwaukee before he accepted his current job in Denver.

"When I was young, my father was killed due to my negligence. I needed to distance myself from the family, so I chose Las Vegas as my home. Our family has had more than their share of tragedies and accidental deaths. Bruno owned a large apartment building that was recently burned to the ground due to arson, and Rebecca's birth father was murdered when he failed to pay his excessive gambling debts."

I became highly concerned when Johnny informed me with a curious grin that the police had questioned him recently about the accidental death of a man crushed to death where he had been working. The media had reported the gruesome details, including the fact the coroner was uncertain if it had been an accident.

His casual demeanor when reciting the circumstances surrounding the incident worried me a great deal. I had opened a connection with a virtual stranger who made me exceedingly nervous and leery about continuing our relationship. The objective of my adoption search had always been about finding my birth mother, not my entire extended family. I wasn't sure I wanted to continue after meeting Johnny. Rebecca had rejected my plea for clemency, rudely cuffed me on the side of the head like a big mother bear, and adamantly pleaded with me to keep her secret private. I felt bad knowing I was being disrespectful of her reputation by exposing myself to Aunt Annie and Johnny behind her back.

I wondered if some of my relatives led secret lives or engaged in covert activities. That would explain why Rebecca had adamantly refused to communicate with me. Shady characters made my blood run cold. Johnny was a strong, powerful man with a large chin; thick, black mustache; and wavy, black hair with a quiet, concealing nature about him. I was uncomfortable in his presence because he seemed of disreputable character with a hidden personality. His shifty character seemed suspect, as did his recollection of the details surrounding the accidental death of his co-worker. Johnny left me feeling weary of dark consequences associated with persons involved in unethical situations.

My adopted father Mario had a similar reputation of being extremely intolerant, which moved me to wonder if there were any shared allies or enemies between the Rossi and Romano families. Mario had a violent temper and short fuse. He carried a revolver under the front seat of his car, and he was adamant about protecting his honor, which lead me to wonder if I had done something terribly wrong by placing myself between two opposing forces and giving them a reason to clash with one another.

Jolted Awake

Dear Mom, I think about you often. I pray that my birth father Bruno has a successful recovery from his heart attack to assure a long, happy life. Johnny Fazio and I had an amazing reunion in Denver. He claims I look like you and some of my cousins. He told me many things about the extended Rossi family and the way everyone supports each other. I liked what I heard. I was raised as an only child, differently than the way you have raised your other children. I speculate in a positive way about what life could have been like if I had been raised by you. Love, Judy

I WAS SOUND ASLEEP when the telephone rang. The ringer sounded urgent and exceptionally loud. It was dark outside and much too early for a normal telephone call. My nerves were shaken. I knew Rosella must be having a medical emergency.

I stumbled out of bed and threw my tufted chenille housecoat over my shoulders. I could feel my heart racing as I rushed to answer the telephone before it stopped ringing. Only an emergency caller would be waking me up at this early hour.

"Hello, Judy. I'm sorry to call you so early," Bruno said apologetically.

"Good morning," I replied in dazed astonishment.

What a pleasant surprise to hear my birth father's voice. I shook my head forcefully from side to side and rubbed my eyes to increase my alertness.

"I had a quadruple heart bypass, Judy," Bruno stated, unaware I had already been informed about his condition.

"I have been praying for you. I hope you are on the road to a full recovery," I said compassionately.

"Yeah, my chest hurts me a little bit, you know." Bruno understated the importance of his own welfare and the severity of his recent open-heart surgery.

"Rebecca had a vision last night. She saw God in her dream, and he told her that she should tell our children about you. She has completely changed. Rebecca wants to tell you about her dream," Bruno said, first addressing Rebecca and then me.

Flabbergasted by his statement, I was left speechless and astounded about what to expect next. Bruno had caught me completely off guard when he diverted the topic from his open-heart surgery and chest pains to Rebecca. I was acutely stunned by his remarks and unprepared to respond. I listened attentively as Bruno quietly summoned Rebecca to the telephone and handed her the receiver.

"Good morning, Judy. This is your mother speaking," Rebecca said contritely in a meek and humble voice.

Her change in behavior amazed me. She was calm and subdued and very unlike the person I had previously contacted.

"It is noble of you to call and wonderful to hear your lovely voice." I rejoiced wildly.

"My change in thinking happened as the result of a very powerful event, something I had never experienced before," Rebecca said with conviction still recovering from her life-changing apparition. "I dreamed the Lord was standing at the foot of my bed talking to me. His presence was very strong. When he told me to change my ways and tell the truth, I paid attention. I was semi-awake, but I evidently needed to hear his voice to clarify my choices and give me direction," Rebecca said, somberly reaching out to me with certainty.

"You experienced a remarkable event this morning. God works in mysterious ways. Thank you for sharing your vision with me. What does this mean for us as mother and daughter?" I asked with an air of startled amazement. "I visualize you wearing a radiant golden halo, breathing an enormous sigh, and smiling toward heaven as the awful burden of guilt and the shackles of secrecy are removed from your shoulders. I never stopped believing in you. My spiritual connection with you was never broken, even when you rejected me. What happened is forgiven. God has granted us serenity and brought us tranquility by bringing us together in harmony because the essence we share as mother and daughter is spiritual. We must celebrate this glorious day of reunification and peace," I rejoined calmly while allowing my sentimental thoughts to flow freely.

Rebecca agreed. "This is a divine day. I feel very devout and religious today. Someday, I will tell you a long story about myself, Judy, to help you understand why all this makes sense. I don't have many things that really belong to me, except my family. You belong here. It has been a long time." Rebecca extended a warm invitation to join her in spirit.

I was ecstatic. Rebecca had finally admitted the truth. Her change in temperament, from nauseatingly cold and rigid to passively warm and friendly, was a stunning reversal from her previous position dominated by fear and secrecy.

"I am glad you feel more decorous toward me now. I have always carried a torch for you and looked forward to a time when we could be reunited." I repeated a mantra I had been practicing for many years, inwardly hoping Rebecca would accept my suggestion for a personal reunion.

"The three of us should meet first, honey. After our initial meeting, Dad and I will sit down together with our other children and explain how this whole situation came about," Rebecca explained, giving her concurrence.

Our conversation had evolved into a friendly dialogue. Bruno and Rebecca had confessed to being my birth parents and resolved to treat me with the dignity and respect as their oldest child. My secret was candidly out in the open. My homecoming as their prodigal daughter was going to be a magnificent experience to be wholeheartedly celebrated, but they were now faced with the awkward task of telling their other three children.

"You sound strong. How is the healing process coming along?" I diverted my attention to Bruno.

"I am getting stronger day by day. I'm not as energetic as before, but I am making a good recovery. Thanks for asking. I enjoyed the pictures you sent. You have such a beautiful son," Bruno replied flatteringly.

Apprehension and hesitancy were suddenly gone as we mutually crossed a communication threshold. Interaction became spontaneous, and the exchange of ideas flowed freely. I could feel the blood circulating to my extremities and the color returning to my cheeks as my initial feelings of timidity and faint-heartedness were replaced with spontaneity and delight.

"Our daughter Linda will be twenty-nine in February. She is getting married next June." Rebecca eagerly volunteered to share the most recent family news.

Bruno interrupted, "When do you think you will be coming our way?"

"We are planning to spend Thanksgiving in Milwaukee."

"Oh, beautiful. Let's get together then. It was pleasant talking to you. Love you, honey," Bruno and Rebecca said in unison.

"I love you, too. Thank you for calling. Good-bye," I said elatedly.

I was absolutely euphoric. My energy level was sky-high. My fast-streaming consciousness had broken the sound barrier. In my mind's eye, I was euphorically standing high on the summit of a rugged mountain. The panoramic view of the wilderness landscape was spectacular.

A miraculous intervention of the Lord had inspired a turning point in Rebecca's life. God had intervened in a small way and given her hope for a better future. His image at the foot of her bed was the catalyst and turning point in her decision to confess and openly welcome me into her heart. He had encouraged Rebecca to be devout and friendly and penitently talk to me of her own free will. I thanked God for being so great and not forsaking me, as I had feared. I had been dreaming about Rebecca at the exact time she was having her spiritual vision, and I continued to marvel at the significance of the mysterious lingering image in my mind and the extrasensory method of communication that seemed to spiritually and biologically connect us.

I could feel the tension leaving my shoulders as the ever-increasing heat from the warming rays of the morning sunshine pierced the windowpane.

Today was the first day of a fresh new life. I had a warm sense of belonging and a new self-identity that I had been so passionately seeking. My childhood dream had come true. Fate had brought us together thanks to the spiritual bond that we shared. I looked forward to my new uniquely distinctive celebrity status and hoped the change would improve my personality and make me more stalwart and whole. My head was filled with pleasant dreams, and my sentimental heart was spilling over with ecclesiastical joy and ecstasy. I daydreamed about my siblings and thought about what I would say to them if I had the chance.

"My lovely sisters and dear brother, I am your prodigal older sister returned from a life of isolation in the wilderness. Abandoned and left alone to independently find my own way in the world, but now I have found you and recovered my true identity. My childhood cannot be recaptured, and my youth is history, but, in my new life, I serendipitously look forward to the highest achievement that anyone can ever experience, belonging with you because we are of the same blood. I send my fondest regards and all my love, your oldest sister, Judy Ann."

My mind gradually drifted back to reality. Other things were going on in the world, and I had been paying little attention to them. My adopted father Mario recently had back surgery. He was in pain and recovering slowly. He was disappointed I was not paying more attention to him. Rosella was lobbying for me to visit her because she was certain her cancer had returned. Martin's father had injured himself when he crashed his mountain bicycle. His mother had miraculously survived an enormous propane explosion that blew her through the roof of their cabin like a circus performer shot out of a cannon. Cut and bruised and receiving emergency medical attention in the hospital, she was in dire need of moral support and assistance. All of these unfortunate events had taken place at the same time, and it was important Martin and I extended our love and showed our support to all of them.

Aunt Frieda, who had been instrumental in providing me with so much pertinent information, had also been put on hold, so, as a token of appreciation, I sent her a dozen yellow roses with no return address with a sentimental note thanking her for her kindness.

Everything was in place. The clock was ticking. A reunion date with Bruno and Rebecca had been set for Thanksgiving Day in Milwaukee. I dreamed about the kind of people I might find and cautiously speculated about the future. I closed my eyes and contemplated about what Aunt Annie had meant when she said, "You are our blood." I was wondering if she were speaking figuratively, as in biology, or culturally, as in Mafioso.

The Reunion

Dear Mom, I am looking forward to our planned mother-and-daughter reunion with great anticipation as an amazing opportunity to obtain closure for the past and create new beginnings for the future. We have both suffered humiliation resulting from circumstances that were difficult to overcome. You were forced to harbor shame and be shackled with feelings of guilt. I was forced to endure the consequences of abandonment and loneliness resulting from the traumatic effects of childhood separation and lack of bonding. The opportunity to meet you in person will be a climactic end to a fairy-tale story, the fulfillment of my greatest and most enduring childhood aspirations. Love Judy

I T WAS THE DAY before Thanksgiving. I was jittery, high-strung, and nervous. To avoid the embarrassment of getting lost or showing up late, I had elected to do a dress rehearsal the day before the reunion to be certain I had the correct address. As we approached our destination, I became panicky thinking about getting a flat tire or running out of gas. Nervously, I slid down in the seat to avoid being spotted as we drove past my birth parents' house.

The Rossi house was an attractive, Midwestern country–style home located on a tree-lined street with healthy green lawns, large, mature shade trees, concrete curbs, and sidewalks. All houses faced the street, and garages were only accessible from the rear alley. Dark green evergreen shrubs, bright red and pink impatiens, white alyssums, and colorful hanging flowerpots enhanced the view of the front entrance from the street. A small leprechaun with a red stocking hat, a long, white beard, green jacket, and short brown pants guarded the front door.

On our way home, I noticed a big box music store called Peaches and impulsively suggested we stop to look inside. Martin complied by brashly jerking the steering wheel to the right and whipping the car into the parking lot as if he were avoiding hazardous debris on the racetrack.

Aunt Frieda had told me that my brother Timmy worked at Peaches, and he had been wearing a Peaches T-shirt in one of the photos Aunt Rosie sent me. I thought it was a good idea to familiarize myself with the store so we would have something in common to talk about. I wasn't worried if he saw me because Rebecca wasn't going to tell her children that I existed until after our initial reunion.

Martin and I strolled randomly up and down the aisles like a tandem detective team on a stakeout, trying not to look suspicious while vigilantly casing the place. I discreetly examined every male employee nearby to seek a familiar resemblance. Studying others was a personal behavior I had acquired long ago, searching for clues in body language, hair color, skin tones, faces, profiles, height, weights, and voice inflections.

I continued this process until I was certain I had thoroughly analyzed every male employee and customer. If someone returned a glance, I casually looked down to avoid eye contact while pretending not to notice.

The appearance of one of the female clerks who was briskly cleaning and straightening merchandise intrigued me. I studied her random movements without making eye contact. She was very feminine and attractive. When she glanced up, I quickly glanced down. When I moved to the left, she moved to the right. When I paused, she paused. I was right-handed, and she was left-handed. When she turned her back to look the other direction, I continued the process of observation. I sensed a strange connection due to our striking similarities of body language. She had dark hair and eyes and an attractive smile with white teeth. I was immediately suspicious and curious to know if she were my sister, but in a dilemma because I couldn't ask her without exposing myself.

Martin gently whispered into my ear, "Papa loves mambo, mama loves mambo; he goes to, she goes fro; he goes fast, she goes slow; he goes left 'n she goes right; younger than spring again, feeling that zing again, wow." From his perspective, the female clerk and I looked like two vaudeville mimes pretending to be looking at a mirror image. He elucidated excitedly that our mannerisms, posture, and facial expressions were remarkably animated and similar, but opposite.

Martin reasoned she might recognize me if I bought something with a credit card and showed her a picture ID with my name on it. I liked his idea. I selected "Mother and Child Reunion" by Paul Simon before casually easing into the checkout line, carefully timing my purchase to be certain she would be the clerk who waited on me.

"Excuse me. I'll handle this one," she said assertively and shoved an unsuspecting male clerk to one side.

She processed the transaction and mundanely handed me the receipt for signature. When I leaned over the counter to sign the receipt, she bent at the waist, placed her elbows on the counter, propped her chin up with her hands, and intentionally leaned forward until our foreheads were almost touching. She looked me directly in the eyes and smiled.

"Are you my sister Judy from Colorado?"

"Yes. Are you my sister Cindy?"

My heart skipped several beats as we instinctively reached across the counter and hugged tightly. We held hands, stared in amazement, and smiled radiantly at each other. Oblivious to the long line of impatient customers behind us, we stood catatonically speechless and faced each other until Martin summoned us both outside. He glanced around for a quiet place with intimate surroundings where we could talk and guided us toward the restaurant next door, astonishingly named the "First Connection."

We sat at a small table for three, gleefully sipping wine and chatting freely, as if we had known each other for a long time. The interior ambience was subdued, and an intimate feeling permeated the space. Our conversation flowed back and forth, and, like a good fireworks display, many ogles and awes filled it. We laughed, giggled, and bonded easily. I was thrilled to have my youngest sister Cindy as my first connection. It was a perfect day.

Martin was enchanted by the experience and astonished by our similarities in body language, habits, mannerisms, ways of thinking, and speaking. Even our voices were alike. He could see firsthand the obsession that had inflamed my passions to seek my true identity and why I had never given up. My reward was a lovely sister. I was thrilled.

Cindy explained what had happened. "We all gathered for a family powwow a couple nights ago. Our family had never had a formal meeting before, so we were all curious to know why we had been formally summoned together. After everyone was sitting down, Dad and Mom explained in a very sensitive way what had happened to them thirty-two years ago. Mom explained how she had accidentally become pregnant without any jobs or home of their own and why she didn't keep her first child. They were only minors. They had no standing in court or control over the situation. There was a prejudicial cultural clash between the families. Mom's mother had refused to allow her daughter to marry an Italian boy and forced her baby into adoption. This critical incident permanently tore apart the Rossi and Meyer families. We kids were wide-eyed, speechless, and flabbergasted when we learned you had contacted Mom and Dad recently. We were dumbfounded and bowled over in amazement when we heard you were coming to meet the family."

We squeezed each other tightly, hugged good-bye, and promised to continue our conversation tomorrow during the reunion. I was swelled with pride and feeling confident that meeting my birth parents would go just as smoothly and wonderfully triumphant as meeting my sister Cindy.

Thanksgiving Day was relaxing. We sipped Sangiovese wine from Tuscany, Italy, swapped stories, and enjoyed an excellent turkey dinner with Rosella. Martin's parents were visiting from Michigan and aware of my situation. They were aware of my secret plan to meet with my birth parents and willingly agreed to entertain Rosella during our eventful rendezvous. I explained to Rosella that we had been invited to meet with old friends and excused ourselves. She was perfectly content with the idea as long as Martin's parents and Michael stayed behind with her.

Embarking on a trip to meet my birth parents for the first time left me feeling hot and cold, alternating between feelings of apprehension, trepidation and alarm, and high spirits, exuberance, and cheerfulness. It was the journey of a lifetime, the culmination of an event I had been seriously planning and fantasizing for over two years. The closer we got to their house, the stronger my emotions became. My hands and feet were numb, my heart was racing, and I thought I was going to faint. I even considered backing out altogether and canceling the meeting.

To appear calm and perform naturally, everything had to be choreographed perfectly without a single flaw in my appearance, clothing, posture, or way I spoke. To boost my confidence, Martin had coached me on what to say and how to conduct myself so I would project a positive image. First impressions were very important. For that reason, he encouraged me to practice in front of a mirror to evaluate my body language, voice inflections, facial expressions, and choice of words. I practiced psycho-cybernetics and rehearsed my lines before the big event. I pretended I was an actress preparing for a stage performance because everyone would be judging my presentation and watching me from every angle. The door to my future was about to open into a completely new world, and I felt like a canary about to fly from its cage for the first time.

Martin successfully parallel-parked the car next to the curb, and I trembled slightly as I walked up the sidewalk to the front door. The feeling was eerily reminiscent of our wedding day when I had choreographically walked up the aisle with trepidation one slow step at a time. I rang the doorbell, and Rebecca immediately swung open the big, red door exactly on cue. She welcomed me into her home with a warm, ambassadorial greeting with open arms, a big smile, and a warm heart.

In my hands, I was carrying a small package of Italian candy—coated almonds as a hostess gift and token of appreciation. They were a symbol of friendship in the Italian community and ever present at weddings, birthdays, festivals, and special celebrations. They were an icebreaker that everyone could enjoy.

"You must be Judy?"

"You must be my mother, Rebecca?"

Rebecca smiled broadly as she leaned forward to welcome me with open arms and a big kiss on the cheek. Both of us loosely handled the exchange of Italian candies in our clumsy nervousness, and the handoff was somehow botched. The container broke open and dropped onto the tile floor in apparent slow motion as we both grasped at the air. Individual pieces of candy flew in all directions. They tumbled and bounced off the tile floor all over the foyer, onto the living room carpet, into the den, under a chair, and under the coat closest door, and one of them even landed in Timmy's pants cuff. A few of them continued making tiny noises as they continued spinning and rolling around like gyroscopes on the ceramic tile floor for quite some time.

Impulsively, Rebecca and I simultaneously stooped down to our hands and knees, almost cracking our heads together, and began gathering up the candies one at a time. The unexpected act of watching the candies accidentally rolling and spinning around on the tile floor triggered pandemonium, broke the ice, and triggered hearty laughing and casual discussion. Any stiffness of the introductory greeting had been instantly shattered as we crawled back and forth on our hands and knees to pick up pieces of candy. Formal introductions were over. There was no more rigid body language or social awkwardness to overcome. Rebecca and I had spontaneously burst into informal conversation as we chuckled at our unique situation. We laughed and crawled around on the floor like two children happily gathering up Easter eggs.

"Whoops! There goes another one under the chair." Timmy chuckled.

"Oh! Three more rolled under the coat closet door."

"Watch out for the dog. I think he has one in his mouth." Rebecca giggled as the dog rapidly wagged his tail, cuffing her in the face.

By the time we finished picking up all the candies, we found ourselves completely relaxed and laughing out loud until someone finally realized that Martin had been abandoned and ignored outside on the porch, where he was still standing gawking at our rear ends and waiting to be let in the front door. The entire group had completely ignored him after the front door had accidentally closed in his face. The fact that he hadn't even made it inside the house seemed hilarious to everyone, and we all broke out in raucous laughter at his expense. I laughed twice as hard as everyone else, knowing how diligently he had coached me to appear prim and proper. Here I was, crawling around on my hands and knees and laughing hysterically.

Between chuckles, Rebecca and I agreed that our handshake was like a scene from a comedy movie and the most unusual introduction we had ever experienced. When we had picked up all the visible pieces of almond candy off the floor, we stood up and held hands. Rebecca finally introduced me to my father, Bruno. We hugged, and he told me how glad he was that I had come so far to meet them. Rebecca then turned to introduce my sisters, Linda and Cindy, and brother Tim. I felt welcomed as we hugged and smiled and stared bewilderedly at each other even though we seemed to have an instant connection.

We sat comfortably in the living room and talked endlessly while Rebecca served cheese and crackers and diet drinks. There were no pauses in conversation. With so many things to talk about, several unrelated conversations burst out at the same time. Everyone was so eager to say something that we all kept accidentally butting in, interrupting, or talking at the same time.

Linda said my voice sounded exactly like Rebecca. Tim said I looked like Aunt Pat. Rebecca and Bruno both agreed that my voice sounded like my sister Cindy. The one thing everyone agreed upon was the fact that I definitely had common physical features and facial expressions similar to theirs.

I was unaccustomed to this much activity and attention from so many people at the same time. It was exhilarating, but difficult to hear what everyone was saying when more than one person talked instantaneously. Everyone had a gentle aura, and all of them were very kind and unconditionally accepting of me.

Our time together had passed quickly, and, before long, it was nearly midnight. Yet I still didn't want to leave. I wanted to stay all night, but, like Cinderella, needed to hurry home. We hugged and shared our mutual appreciation for each other.

On the drive home, I tried to re-create the entire reunion experience in my mind. It had been a perfect evening, their warm welcomes, the ambiance of their house, and the way they had made me feel. We all had toothy smiles and dimples and many remarkable similarities and things in common. I had a craving for peanut butter cups, and Rebecca had the habit of spreading peanut butter on bars of chocolate. Everyone had an appearance similar to mine with brown hair and smooth, attractive complexions. When they smiled, their dimples and white teeth were exposed. They looked like movie stars to me. I tried to memorize everything about them and remember everything that had been said.

Our connection was genuine and natural because I felt in harmony with them. Their house was bright and cheerful and filled with laughter, pleasant cooking smells, interesting conversation, lighthearted teasing, and constant activity, whereas Rosella's home was quiet, somber, dimly lit, excessively warm, and stuffy.

I left with happy feelings of camaraderie, belonging, and togetherness. I liked being part of a warm, friendly atmosphere and the indisputable closeness exhibited by everyone. My heart had been touched. I was content and satisfied because the experience of meeting them was joyous because it had wildly exceeded my expectations. Believably thrilled, I was infatuated and in love with my new family.

Before going to sleep, I contemplated the many tears and years that had quietly slipped through the cracks of time in life's big, lazy hour-glass and realized how fortunate I was to have had such a successful reunion with the Rossi family. My journey to find them had been long and arduous, but, because of perseverance, good fortune, and the intervention of the Lord, I had followed my instincts and found my way home to the special niche where I was born, my natural cultural surroundings, and the true place in the world where I belonged.

I thanked God for helping me put the pieces of my adoption puzzle together and allowing the passing of this wonderful unforgettably beautiful day. My prayers had been answered, and I felt incredibly blessed knowing my birth parents had validated my presence by expressing so much warmth and unconditional love.

My heart was glad knowing that my wandering soul had finally found peace. But would I ever see them again?

Reconciliation

Dear Mom, You are a spiritual beacon of hope for my soul. I was compelled to find you because my heart had a preeminent void forever longing to be filled by the love of you. There were many obstacles in my path and mental barriers to overcome along the way, but I never lost hope that we would be reunited some glorious day. The journey to find you was intensely thought-provoking and emotionally challenging, but, now that I have found you, I find myself perpetually in high spirits and content. Our reunion has nurtured healing through understanding and given rise to a beautiful friendship resulting in an uncommonly serene sense of peace and harmony. Your smile makes me feel alive. The sound of your voice makes my spirit soar and elevates my feelings of self-worth and well-being. Your mere presence gives me comfort. Getting to know you has inspired a positive transformation likened to a featureless, cocooned orphan miraculously transformed into a beautifully adorned adult butterfly vibrantly purified by sacred rays of sunshine. Reconciliation allows me to feel spiritually healed from the austere primal wound caused by the unnatural separation from you after I was born. Your unconditionally accepting me as your daughter generates delightful feelings of distinction and worthiness. The sacred benedictions we share were put there to mend our wounded hearts and restore our faith in God. Thank you for accepting me into your life again. Love, Judy

"WHAT DO YOU SAY after you say hello?" I kept asking myself. I had met my birth parents, sisters and brother, aunts and uncles, and cousins. But now what? What life script should I be following? I was at a turning point in my life and needed time for evaluation and self-analysis. Should I exert myself to create a continuing dialogue and friendship with my birth parents, or should I end the pretense that I would ever be a member of their family and withdraw to my former identity as a lonely, forlorn, pitiful wallflower? The answer was a cauldron of adult reasoning, intuition, logic, and emotions, depending if I were thinking like a parent, adult, or child. The answer to my question pleasantly arrived as an invitation to attend my sister Linda's wedding, which I immediately accepted.

Rebecca greeted me on the steps of the church with a big smile. We hugged and exchanged greetings before moving quickly inside to avoid a few misty raindrops. Dark rain clouds outside created a quiet, dimly lit, subdued atmosphere inside the church.

Rebecca and I squeezed into the first pew in the back row to watch the wedding rehearsal. Rebecca broke the silence by softly whispering some of her thoughts and recollections about my birth to me, followed by reminiscing about her own wedding. We were sitting close together, and our conversation was intimate. I listened attentively to everything she had to say. Her words had a spiritual healing effect. I felt very dear to her, and I was appreciative for this breakthrough. It was the reconciliation I had always wanted. Her words were an avowal and disclosure of all that had happened in the past. She acknowledged my birth was a very unfortunate experience for her, as well as for me, and admitted it was too bad things worked out the way they had. I was unaccustomed to the mutual feelings of closeness we were sharing, and I was amazed she was being so open with me.

"At the time, there were no alternatives other than adoption. Bruno and I were two poor young kids, and my parents were unwilling to offer any blessings, empathy, or financial assistance. It was a terrible time for me when I was pregnant because my mother steadfastly refused to allow me to marry Bruno. I had no support to keep you and only received condemnation from my parents and clergy," Rebecca said sadly, woefully recalling her nightmarish experience of being an unwed teenage mother. "It was a very miserable and sorrowful time for Bruno and me. We held hands and lamented again and again, 'How did this happen?' It was as if we were expecting a miracle from God."

Sitting side by side in the silent atmosphere of a church seemed entirely appropriate for reconciliation of the past. Rebecca felt ashamed and guilty for what had happened to me, but circumstances had been beyond her control. I felt no animosity toward her. I was only anticipating mending through conciliation. Rebecca acknowledged the truth by divulging her innermost thoughts, disclosing her most private memories, and admitting she was sorry that her baby had been given up for adoption. Out of kindness and love, she was saying *mea culpa*, and I unconditionally forgave her.

I was feeling the love she was offering, and I only wanted the chance to love her in return. It was a remarkable encounter and the first intimate bonding session we had ever shared as mother and daughter. She didn't need to confess all of these things to me because they were already understood, but hearing them in person was mystically healing, and her honesty and openness provided emotional relief. I could tell immediately we had reached a new plateau in our relationship. There would be no more secrets or uncertainty between us in the future. I viewed her candid openness and honesty as the catalyst for the beginnings of a true friendship.

"Bruno and I had an enduring love for each other ever since we met. We loved each other when you were born and rekindled our love when Bruno was discharged from the marines two years after you were born. We still loved each other when we were married, regardless of all the obstacles we had chanced upon earlier in life."

I thought about what Rebecca was saying, and I somehow wondered if I had always intuitively known that my parents had always loved each other. Her positive comments about Bruno made me feel good about myself. I listened carefully to every word she said and reserved them in my heart. Before this happened, I never realized how important it was for me to hear these things. I was like a sponge soaking up her truthfulness, which was filling the empty voids in my heart with gladness. Her sentimental words soothed my soul. I was sitting side by side with my birth mother, and the positive connection I was feeling with her after so many years of grave emptiness was too complex for words.

I was grateful we had our conversation in a church because, over a period of many years, I had been inspired by stories of the blind and crippled who, by accepting a spiritual faith in Christ, were able to lay down their crutches and be healed. Perhaps today was my day to be healed. I believed it was. It was my turn to raise my hands to the heavens, proclaim the miraculous healing of my lifelong primal wounds, and thank God for this opportunity and the positive change in my life he was allowing.

Martin sat down beside us. I grasped his hand tightly. I was glad he was there to share my happiness with me. I thanked God for allowing me to meet my birth family and the happiness they had brought me. I was finally healed. The conciliation was over, and I felt good about the outcome.

After the wedding rehearsal, we returned to Rebecca's home to relax and continue our conversation. Cindy stared at me in wonderment and commented how fantastic it was that I could be there with them on this day. I shared the same awed inspiration and respect as the fulfillment of my strongest reoccurring childhood dreams. I was elated to be participating in a friendly, casual conversation with my mother and sisters. We hardly knew each other, yet we all seemed so familiar with each other. My life really had become a fairy-tale story with a happy ending.

Rebecca was intrigued and curious to know what had happened to me after I was born and why I had been so strongly motivated to search for her. She had already confessed everything in detail to me. It was my turn to reconcile with her.

"God set the path," impulsively slipped out of my mouth.

Rebecca relaxed and smiled contentedly because this was a sentimental statement she had often expressed. I took a deep breath and a sip of tea before settling into a conversational position.

"Why an adoptee searches the past for hidden secrets is a mystery that is better understood by psychologists. The answers are complicated and esoteric and found primarily in the mind. The answers are complex, but I will try my best to help you understand the force that propelled me forward and justified my motives." I set the stage for a serious dissertation.

"Reaching out for you was a survival mechanism that was automatically turned on when I came out of the womb. The doctor symbolically cut the umbilical cord, physically disconnecting us, but my primal survival instinct to be with you remained intact. I was simply a wee life impulsively longing for my mother's breast to preserve itself. The physical, psychological, spiritual, and emotional roots that connected me to you were torn, and the separation in time and space that I was forced to endure was disorienting, but your spiritual beacon was strong, and it never stopped broadcasting. Even though you may not have been aware of my presence, I never stopped receiving your signals because I instinctively sensed a sacred bond with you."

I glanced around the room to see if everyone was listening. Cindy was leaning forward on the edge of her seat, and Linda's eyes were wide open.

"I cried without tears for something inborn that was lacking. When I finally found you, I realized that, ever since the day I was orphaned, I had been grieving on the inside. A strong force to survive was released that caused me to continually seek the security of my mother's embrace, but this instinctual need for security was never fully satisfied. The pleasure of being loved and comforted was not truly achievable due to our forced separation. I was lost in a spiritual wilderness and felt detached from the true place where I belonged, but, now that we were reunited in mind and spirit, I suddenly feel healed and connected with you and Bruno, Linda, Cindy, Tim, and all my family in a natural way. Being part of a real family is heartening because a visible connection to my ancestry is a core value for all humans, but an experience that I had never fully developed as an adoptee," I explained from the heart.

Our hearts were beating in unison, and a wonderful inner peace that I had never experienced before was being awakened while I spoke.

"Certain things were intuitive to me because, even as a small child, I felt something was wrong or missing in my relationship with my adopted parents because they could never completely substitute for the loss of you. My adopted parents were good providers, but, whenever they did something embarrassing, I was quick to distance myself from them by pointing out to others that I was adopted as my way of rationalizing their behavior and separating myself from them," I said philosophically, trying not to sound excessively dramatic.

"Martin wanted practical, analytical facts in advance before methodically analyzing each issue, whereas I was not always compelled to prioritize alternatives and analyze my actions using deductive logic according to his masculine way of thinking. From that standpoint, I have always wondered if male and female adoptees searching for their birth parents might approach an adoption search differently. Our routine conversations about my adoption were insightful and beneficial for our marriage. Our communication skills improved, and discussing a common topic was good for both of us," I added.

Everyone was listening intently so I continued speaking. "In the beginning, I was motivated by curiosity, much like others when they engage in ancestral searches, but my motives evolved into something much greater. In the hierarchal scale of human needs, it increased from a whimsical desire to a deep, primal, psychological need. The more time I spent thinking about you, the deeper the childhood void in my heart became, so I pressed onward. The closer I came to finding you, the stronger my sixth sense became. The internal forces that were motivating me continued growing stronger until meeting you in person became the definitive objective. I assume that other orphaned children around the world have been inspired to seek the same answers to the same ancient questions for as long as civilization has existed." I took a deep breath.

Rebecca agreed. "I think you are right. It is natural for adults to put more effort into nurturing their own biological children. That is why, as an adoptee, some emotional needs were never met. You inherited genes from your father and me, who provided the ingredients for your cake, or your fixed genetic code. Your adopted parents and certain environmental factors altered your behavior and made active certain traits, but only within the limitations of your genes. For example, you can put lemon frosting on a carrot cake to change its flavor, but you can't turn a carrot cake into a lemon meringue pie." Rebecca smiled.

I concurred. "Biologists provide the simplest answers to questions because they are unencumbered with the complications of emotionally driven behavior and psychoanalysis of diversified complex individuals. For survival purposes, many animal species are driven to reunite and reconnect with their own kind. Finding the right niche, forest habitat, and migration pattern is all part of the mystery of life, and those who are most successful at finding the niche into which they were born are more likely to survive."

It was difficult for me to express myself with words, but everyone still acted interested. "Rosella instructed me to believe in the power of prayer. Perhaps God does answer our prayers, if our thoughts are pure and sincere and our ideas have merit. The windows of opportunity to find you were extremely narrow, and the timing of my search was truly miraculous. I was either extremely lucky, or the hand of fate showed me the way because, if I had started a few days earlier or later, I never would have found you. I was blessed, and I have never denied that a spiritual force lit my path." I explained my good fortune and exultant outcome.

"My explanation may sound silly to you, but I always had a feeling that you were signaling to me with some form of telepathic energy.

I never professed to know anything about extrasensory perceptions, sixth senses, or paranormal communication, but the idea was always lurking in the back of my consciousness. Your spiritual essence was the life force that fueled the beacon of hope that lit my path and gave me the confidence to stay on course. I was driven by a noble instinct much grander than a simple image of you. Despite the great distance between us, your beacon haunted me because I was naturally drawn to find you, like a firefly to the light. Your brainwaves were transmitted unconsciously and may have resonated from your dreams when you were sleeping. Maybe we shared the same intangible thoughts or possessed extraordinary, invisible forms of mental telepathy, generated by an unknown force that spiritually connected us. Whatever the mysterious forces were that compelled me to find you, the result left me with very powerful mind-set and positive thoughts of you," I said, spiritually reaching out to Rebecca with a smile.

Our formal reconciliation was over. My highest ambition in life had been fulfilled, and the conclusion of my story scripted for a glorious ending because I had known what to say after saying hello after all.

PART 3

Epilogue

Choices, Relationships, and Conclusions

"Ancestral recovery was a peak experience, an extraordinary moment that took my breath away, liberated my spirit, and gave me the confidence to soar like an eagle." –Judith Land

Epilogue

ESTINY IS NOT PREORDAINED. It is about making choices. Our lives are the sum of all the choices we make, the bridges we cross, and the ones we burn. Our souls cast long shadows over many people, even after we are gone. Fate, luck, and providence are the consequence of our freedom of choice, not the determinants. When justice is served by following our principles, making good decisions brings us inner peace.

We must learn to do what is right, not what is acceptable, because life is very good when we make the right choices. Happiness does not depend on wealth or world traveling. It comes from following our own free will, finding the beauty of the environment, and building positive relationships with significant others.

Adoption is a familiar theme among all people that encourages group reminiscing about romantic fairy tales, fables, mysteries, historic legends, shaggy-dog stories, and tragic folk tales. The worldwide popularity of stories such as *Oliver Twist*, *Little Orphan Annie*, *Anne of Green Gables*, and *Heidi* transcend all ages, cultures, and languages. These tales are popular universal themes because an adoption story has inspired nearly everyone. Each personal story is unique, but the theme is universal. Children are separated from their parents due to war, pestilence, accidents, and natural disasters, but, most often, they are willfully abandoned due to inconvenience. Perhaps fewer adoptions would take place if more individuals understood the consequences and ramifications of their actions.

MY STORY DID NOT end when I found my birth parents. Another grand adventure took place when my husband and I teamed up as true adoption detectives to launch a serious effort to locate my foster parents, William and Priscilla Engelmann. The search to find my foster parents ended up being just as captivating, technically challenging, and convoluted as the original search for my birth parents, and the rewards were just as great. Coming together with them for a reunion in Tucson, Arizona, was a treasured experience and a major highlight of my life. They were wonderful people. It made me very happy to know I had been collectively remembered on special occasions and never forgotten in their prayers long after I had been forcibly torn from their arms. The warm welcome and hugs I received from Priscilla and William was priceless. Priscilla presented me with my original baby book filled with photographs I had never seen and numerous mementos from my short time with them. She was warm and good-natured and endowed me with precious lingering memories and insight into my early childhood. Barbara had carried a picture of me in her wallet for over thirty years, correctly assuming we would be reunited again someday, and Mary and I became friends for life. I am indebted to the Engelmanns for their generous spirits and nurturing strength of character. They were there when I needed them the most and will forever be grateful for their generous spirits and hearts of gold. I pray that the peace of the Lord will always be with them.

My youth was spent quietly wondering and longing for something intangible that I perceived was missing in my life. In the end, I found what I was looking for and much more. My senses were greatly heightened during my adoption search. When finally in the presence of my biological family, I cognitively recognized that which was intuitively familiar. The greatest and most important lesson learned during my journey was, "If a parent can love more than one child, then a child can love more than one parent." It's a simple parable and the most endearing way of addressing the idea of choosing between birth parents and adopted parents (which really isn't necessary at all and no adoptee should ever be forced to do so) because it is possible for an adoptee to love everyone equally, just as parents love all of their children.

In the end, I learned that family is much greater and more complex than simply a birth mother and birth father. I admired the way the multigenerational members of the Rossi family gathered at the annual cousins picnic each summer to honor the entire extended family, unconditionally welcome new babies and spouses into their inner circle, and openly express genuine care for each person.

When I was a child, I was unstable and lonely, but, now that I had found my clan, I felt whole, steady, and confident. I had been uncertain how to view my tentative relationship with my adopted mother Rosella as a child, but, now that I had discovered my birth family, our relationship was greatly improved, and I was more grateful than ever before for everything she had done for me.

I only had one mother to love as a child, but my personality was significantly brightened as an adult when it occurred to me that I had gained four new mothers to love in addition to Rosella. The gratitude and appreciation I felt toward her increased as I reflected on our shared memories and the important role she had played in my childhood.

Rebecca was the newest and most important mother in my life. I felt at ease with her and optimistically looked forward to being with her. I had a wonderful new companion in Priscilla and truly loved my new foster sisters, Mary and Barbara. I was exceedingly fond of my classy mother-in-law Grace, an excellent cook and entertainer, professor, artist, and writer, with whom I had many things in common and tremendous respect. Even my relationship with my father's new wife Vivian turned positive. She was an excellent companion for my father, an avid golfer, and a practical individual with an exceptional talent for keeping informed and understanding business issues.

ATTENDING THE WEDDINGS OF my sisters and brother were benchmark social gatherings that provided many lingering precious heartfelt moments because participation in these private events allowed me to actualize my fairy-tale dream of visualizing myself as a member of a closely bonded, loving Italian family.

Rebecca and Bruno were unconditionally accepting of me as their oldest daughter, and the wonderful relationships I gradually developed with them was cause for many joyous celebrations. The love of my parents for each other and the unconditional love they showed toward me inspired me. Familiarity increased our understanding and appreciation and satisfied my motivational drive to establish interpersonal relationships with them.

Their fiftieth wedding anniversary was a coming-out party and a dream come true. They honored me with an invitation to sit at the head table and be included in a formal family portrait for posterity, which I was thrilled to accept. I viewed them as an ideal couple when I saw their smiles and radiating love for each other while they glided across the floor holding hands and dancing to "Too Young" by Nat King Cole. They were childhood sweethearts, and their youthful longing for each other had blossomed into a lifelong love affair. They were an inspiration to everyone. The words to the song were clear, "Their love has lasted throughout the years, even though everyone said they were too young to be in love."

Before the wedding anniversary, I had purchased a small commemorative anniversary gift for my parents. My enthusiasm and excitement encouraged me to tell the clerk about my epic tale of reunion with my birth parents. The clerk listened in awe to the entire story without interruption until pent-up tears of joy suddenly burst forth, and she spontaneously leaped forward to give me a heartwarming hug of friendship. I found these types of incidents happening again and again because my personal story of achievement seemed to touch the heartstrings of men and women everywhere. Whereas I had kept my adoption search entirely secret from strangers in the beginning, I now found myself eagerly sharing my tale of success with anyone who asked, and these incidents eventually gave me the confidence to speak to church groups, service clubs, sororities, and newspaper reporters and permanently record the details of my life story in a manuscript for publication.

Each family celebration I attended was a marvelous success that established me as a true and legitimate member of the Rossi family. My parents' love for each other and the wonderful relationships I gradually developed with them inspired me. In my mind, there was no doubt I had chosen the right path by listening to the mysterious voices in my head leading me back to my roots. Being the lead adoption detective on my own case had been a rewarding experience that had left me celebrating life and pondering the joyous lingering feelings of contentment and belonging.

MY ADOPTED FATHER MARIO was an enigma. For much of my young adult life, I had no idea what his mental condition was, where he was living, or how he spent his time. His desire for privacy was extreme, but I chose not to interfere in his affairs because he owned an expanding grocery empire with many employees, and it was easy to rationalize his need to stay focused on business. When he divorced Rosella, he also elected to shut me out of his personal life and left no way to contact him directly, even in an emergency. He demanded perfection from everyone in his presence, something I often failed to deliver in his eyes. As a result, he eventually stopped communicating with me altogether for more than three years, leaving me feeling like one of Harlow's hapless rhesus monkeys, grasping for a ghostly surrogate father of coiled wire.

Rosella's accusations of his transgressions roused my imagination and fueled my nightmares that eventually triggered a complicated search to find my adopted father. In the third phase of my adoption quest to find the truth, I was shocked to discover that he had remarried, possibly before divorcing Rosella, and bought homes in other states under an assumed name.

Mario was devastated when his eyesight unexpectedly deteriorated due to macular degeneration, which abruptly changed his lifestyle. He could no longer peruse complex financial spreadsheets or track his favorite stocks or sports teams. He couldn't read legal documents, medical prescriptions, or dinner menus. He couldn't drive a car, play golf, or bait a fishing hook, and he no longer recognized his best friends. At the peak of his professional career, he had been forced to curtail nearly every enjoyable activity that mattered to him. His only consolation was his sympathetic and loving wife Vivian, who did everything she could to support him.

Only after he began to lose his eyesight did we restore our friendship. He was more relaxed and patient with me than before, but our best years of peace and harmony passed quickly. My emotions were numb when he died because he had been such a dominant force in my life. He had been my most important advisor and mentor in all serious matters in my early life. He was my father, and I loved him. He was like a rock to me. I greatly respected his strength and authoritative personality. Despite his contrary secretive nature and the never-ending verbal abuse he piled on me in his quest for perfection, I never stopped loving him or lost perspective of his positive attributes that made him a successful business leader. He was still my father and childhood hero for all the constructive influences he had imposed on me as a child. He was an excellent provider and intelligent man. I had always solicited his

good advice and counsel whenever he was available. Through perseverance and prayer, I had eventually worked my way back into his good
graces before he died.

I felt sorrow knowing he was gone forever and concentrated on
all the good traits I had learned from him. I was thankful for the encouragement and good work ethic he demonstrated and will always
appreciate the important lessons of life he taught me. He encouraged
me to be strong and independent, to look out for myself, and to know
how to be a survivor. Ironically, those personal characteristics gave me
the strength to find my birth parents.

Mario was a major philanthropist who gave his entire estate to
charity. He believed that helping the blind was the most important
contribution to the world he could make with his wealth. His legacy
will live on through achievements in research, education, and eye care
by many of the organizations he supported that are devoted to the
treatment and cure of macular degeneration and blindness.

SEARCHING FOR MY BIRTH parents, foster parents, and adopted
father had unexpectedly evolved into a trilogy, three separate mysteries to solve where the solution to one riddle was followed by another
conundrum inside of another. All three discoveries were equally rewarding. I eventually imagined myself as a female detective in a mystery novel whose mission never ended because it seemed as though
my life had been perpetually unsettled and characterized by a series
of significant events resulting from my incessant ambition, followed
by major breakthroughs during the long tedious process of detection
and exposure. My destiny became a work in progress as my mission to
uncover the truth evolved into a never-ending state of fluctuation. The
conclusion of my journey was reminiscent of a rousing classical orches-
tral ending with the round percussion cymbals making three satisfying
crash-bang-wallops in succession.

THE DAY I TOLD Rosella about my adoption search was eerily similar
to the memorable day she had asked me to sit beside her on my eighth
birthday and informed me I was adopted. She said she had picked me
because I was special. When the moment was right, I explained that
she was special, too. I was glad she was my mother and appreciative of
all the things she had done for me over the years. She had raised me

with positive values and set a very good example to follow. We lived in a comfortable neighborhood, and I had many enjoyable experiences as a child and teenager. I thanked God that she was my dutiful mother, knowing things could have been much worse if someone else had adopted me. Rosella smiled, and she was highly receptive and appreciative of my compliments because she had received very little positive feedback from me over the years.

Now that I was aware that a parent could love more than one child and a child could love more than one parent unconditionally, I became a much better person. With that thought in mind, I debated if I should tell Rosella about my successful search to find my birth family. After much deliberation, I reluctantly unburdened my secret by informing Rosella what I had done two years after my reunion with my birth parents and entire Rossi family. Learning about my birth parents did not seem to bother her, and she eventually agreed to meet them in person. The inaugural affair between my adopted mother and birth mother was concluded successfully. Bruno and Rebecca were excellent hosts and did their best to create a positive celebration reuniting the old with the new.

When her cancer returned, as she had been predicting for many years, Rosella turned to God to make her peace. She was very pleased with her hospice care, knowing her caregivers were nuns. Visits from Father Hennen relaxed her, making it easier for her transition into a life with God. When she died, a deep, melancholic sadness overwhelmed me. I sorely missed her, and it was difficult to choke back my tears. The reality of knowing I would never see her again was depressing. Her dying process had evolved slowly, and I had many weeks and months to prepare myself for the emotional loss, but there was no way I could have prepared myself for the way I felt after she was finally gone. The experience of burying my mother at the cemetery was the inevitable culmination of a tragic loss, and I was not prepared for the concentrated emotional trauma and potency of this terrible event. Thinking about the unpleasantness of death made me uncomfortable and stirred feelings of despondency. Her death created uncertainty about the future and left me feeling horrifically grim.

Rosella had painted over five hundred oil paintings. They were her legacy. Her entire estate and all of her paintings were donated to Catholic charities. Many of her religious paintings hang in churches throughout the world today. Her contribution as an artist will be treasured for centuries.

SOME OF THE MOST multifaceted and difficult choices to make in life pertain to the nurturing of children. Telling my son about my adoption was the most intricate and challenging topic I ever had to face as a mother. Perceptions can last a lifetime, and, for that reason, I consciously planned an appropriate time and setting for this discussion and chose my words carefully. Honesty brought us together, and I was thankful that God blessed me with his existence. It was comforting knowing that my young son was accepting and understanding of adult issues and aware of how important parents are to every generation.

BRUNO HAD PRIDE IN his grandson, but the travel distance between them made communication and personal contact difficult. Bruno was proud of his service as a United States Marine, but much of his military service was too painful to talk about with others. The sheer terror and horror that he had experienced was a private matter that he kept to himself. He never bragged, boasted, or published his biography, and he seldom talked in depth about his experiences. He was strong and willing to make the ultimate sacrifice for his country. He was proud of his Sicilian-Italian heritage, as well as his American citizenship. He enjoyed flying the American flag and proudly wearing red, white, and blue clothing with patriotic themes. My fondest memories of him were images of him wearing his marine hats and patriotic attire, especially during Fourth of July celebrations. His pride in his country and family was contagious. Thinking about him inspired me to think about the flags, lapel pins, wristwatches, jewelry, and other mementoes he had given me when celebrating special American holidays.

Bruno had a generous spirit, and he was very popular. He was the leader of his family and the individual who cemented them together. Many years later, when it was finally time for him to die, he was conscious and accepting of his condition. He made peace with everyone and said his tearful good-byes. He turned his Italian music up very loud and lay there in his bed with a peaceful smile on his face until he quietly closed his eyes and went to sleep forever. He was at peace with God, who granted him his wish to simply fall asleep when it was his time to go. His angels were there to take him to heaven, and that is all there was.

WHEN I STARTED MY journey to find my birth mother, I had no idea it would be the beginning of a grand and glorious voyage affecting so many individuals. It was impossible to survive the journey without forming many conclusions about life, parenting, and enduring relationships because the consequences of adoption are cumulative and wide-ranging. I was surprised by the number of acquaintances encouraged by the success of my search who wanted to discuss the mysteries of their origins or heartfelt loss of their own missing child, often with teary eyes, sad hearts, and melancholic sense of bewilderment. When advice was requested, I offered my sympathy and encouragement and, in a short period of time, became successful at helping others launch their own adoption searches. For that reason, I became known as Judith Land, the "Adoption Detective."

THE NEGATIVE CONSEQUENCES OF early separation are well researched, exposed, and documented by psychologists, social scientists, pediatricians, medical doctors, school counselors, mothers, and adoptees. By its very nature, the separation of an infant from its mother is a violent act that traumatizes children, leading to a weakened immune system that compromises health, learning, and behavior. The effects on behavior are subtle and lie deep in the personality. Children separated from their birth mother are likely to progress through various stages of fright, protest, despair, denial, and detachment. In the beginning, the child may be visibly distressed and cry and call for her mother. When children give up hope, they are likely to lose heart and become withdrawn, sullen, and quiet, as happened to me. Eventually, their relationships with others may become shallow and untrusting with little concern or interest projected toward any surrogate mother.

No infant would ever willingly choose to be raised by strangers. He would never agree to be lied to, nor have his real identity and name falsified and permanently concealed in secrecy. Severing the connection with the birth mother causes a primal wound that manifests itself as a sense of loss, depression, mistrust, anxiety, and trouble in relationships with significant others. A loving set of adopted parents can help to heal the wounds of adoption, but the psychological scar will always remain. Unfortunately, this large encyclopedia of information is seldom thoroughly researched or understood by panicky unwed mothers and fathers whose selfish reactions are to place their own welfare ahead of their child.

To be an adoptee in the twenty-first century does not carry the same stigma that it did a generation ago, but many adoptees are still prone to act out their frustrations and hostilities through destructive antisocial behavior. A consequence to society is the abnormally high number of adopted children involved in crime and drugs, which is strikingly higher than the average population.

Adoption provides some options that, on the surface, appear highly beneficial to the child. Adopted parents are typically older, emotionally stable, and better educated and often possess more material wealth. They can provide a larger home, financial assistance, a better education, more stable family life, and trips around the world, but, for adoptees, the lack of a connection with their biological parents is still something they feel they are lacking. Life is not about money. It is better to love your own than to live a false life with sorrow, secrets, and lies. Material possessions and surrogate parents can never replace the void created by separation or heal the psychological wound of knowing your biological parents did not want you or love you.

Adoption is inherently difficult even in the best of homes. Concern about the character, weaknesses, afflictions, and instability of the birth parent may paint a negative portrait of the adopted child. Parental frustrations may lead to increased hostility and provoke the child's separation anxiety.

From a positive standpoint, parents with the highest number of things in common with their adopted children may have the best chance at successful bonding, but even the strongest and healthiest adoptees will understand that something is wrong and missing in their lives. The most secure and healthiest children may be best at dealing with their afflictions, but all adoptees subconsciously experience the pain of biological separation and abandonment. They need to be more cautious, watchful, and ever-vigilant for intangible threats to their personal security. Adoptees may be characterized as lacking confidence and timid. The Santa Claus syndrome raises their fears that their parents will not bring gifts and get rid of them if they perform badly.

Mothers who are contemplating adoption should be aware of the possible ramifications and repercussions that may occur to their infant if they allow strangers to bring up their children. Social workers, medical doctors, political progressives, and even clergy often tout the material benefits of adoption. They seldom inform birth mothers that their children, if given to strangers for adoption, will have a high possibility of exhibiting selective mutism, oppositional defiant disorder, separation syndrome, and other unstable qualities. They are also more likely to exhibit antisocial behavior. The world is littered with social misfits, criminals, alcoholics, and chronically afflicted persons who began their lives as adoptees.

If more women followed the natural way, they would accept responsibility for their babies. They would rely on their own female instincts and not mindlessly give their children away to strangers. They would seek positive spiritual guidance. They would exhibit more self-confidence and be less self-centered, egotistical, and selfish, and they would consider the long-term fate of their child their highest priority.

Giving a biological child to strangers is a dangerous step to take. It is a shattering experience that leaves birth parents prone to emotional instability, insecurity, and psychiatric problems. Grieving birth mothers may suffer from depression and chronic bereavement the rest of their lives. The mother may spend the rest of her life secretly regretting her decision. Unresolved grief may lead to overcompensation in the future by being unnaturally overprotective and clinging to subsequent children. Unmarried birth fathers may suffer guilt and grieve long after the child is adopted. They are not as strong as they could be, and they are more susceptible to the negative effects of alcohol and other vices.

Parents with good, old-fashioned, traditional family values who work hard to achieve long-term commitments have sustained modern civilization for a very long time. They are better suited for understanding the consequences of adoption and prepared for working through the difficulties of childrearing. Persons of faith with positive moral values are better at dealing with the stress of raising children because their standards are more consistent. When these basic values are ignored, the entire society suffers from the effects of an unstable, disconnected population.

My wish is for all mothers to cherish, love, and stay close to their children forever and always. The stigma imposed on adopted children leaves many to wander the world, forever searching for their true identity. To understand one's biological roots is a natural human instinct, but, for adoptees, it is a troubling need that is never resolved. If it is true that blood is thicker than water, then the bonds of family and common ancestry are stronger than relationships between genetically unrelated individuals. Perhaps that is why children from open adoptions are better adjusted and more secure than children in closed adoptions are.

BEFORE LAUNCHING MY JOURNEY of self-discovery, I was like a little butterfly flitting around in the air, accepting whatever life gave me. I relied primarily on ever-changing ephemeral wind currents for direction. My uncertain state of genealogical bewilderment gave me stress. I was more prone to rebellion because I had no roots or foundation from which to judge my potential.

Now I found myself to be more self-directing, emotionally stronger, mentally wiser, and significantly more self-confident with fewer doubts and insecurities. Knowing my true identity makes me feel like an eagle. I'm full of confidence, mature, and skilled, and I'm able to soar in the direction of my choosing. My new sense of well-being was liberating and gave me a spontaneous will to live life to the fullest. Like Anthony Quinn in *Zorba the Greek*, I also feel like dancing for joy on a sandy beach in the moonlight.

I TURNED THE VOLUME on the car stereo as high as it would go until I could hear it echoing off the canyon walls and listened to "I am Woman" by Helen Reddy.

I am woman, hear me roar in numbers too big to ignore ... oh yes, I am wise, but it is wisdom born of pain. Yes, I've paid the price, but look how much I've gained. If I have to, I can do anything. I am strong. I am invincible. I am woman.

I WAS DAYDREAMING ABOUT the good times Martin and I had shared as husband and wife and secretly wondering if I would ever be this happy again. I was thankful he was there with me because, without his emotional support and assistance, I never could have discovered my genealogical roots or true inner being.

"I love you, honey!" I grinned from ear to ear and looked at Martin sitting in the driver's seat as we raced through Glenwood Canyon in our red convertible.

The combination of clear mountain air, beautiful Colorado landscapes as a scenic backdrop, blue skies contrasted with white, rugged, snow-tipped mountains and green forests, the wind in our faces, and sunshine on our shoulders, as John Denver was so fond of singing, gave me euphoric feelings of joy. I love the mountains and fresh air and find the gold-quaking aspen trees in the autumn, especially at Maroon Lake in the Maroon Bells Wilderness, irresistible. I love warm summers and campfires, and I become excited whenever the snows are deep and the skiing challenging in Vail and Aspen.

As the crimson rays of sunlight fade into darkness, my final thoughts will always be about how glad I am to be alive.

References

Abraham Harold Maslow (April 1, 1908–June 8, 1970), an American professor of psychology, founded humanistic psychology. A visual aid he created to explain his theory, which he called the hierarchy of needs, is a pyramid depicting the levels of human needs, psychological, and physical. When a human being ascends the steps of the pyramid, he reaches self-actualization. Beyond the routine of needs fulfillment, Maslow envisioned moments of extraordinary experience, known as peak experiences, profound moments of love, understanding, happiness, or rapture, during which a person feels more whole, alive, self-sufficient, and yet a part of the world. He is more aware of truth, justice, harmony, goodness, and so on. Self-actualizing people have many such peak experiences. Ancestry recovery was a peak experience for Judith Romano in *Adoption Detective* (http://en.wikipedia.org/wiki/Abram_Maslow).

Maslow, Abraham. *Towards a Psychology of Being*, 3rd ed. Wiley, 1998.

Harry Frederick Harlow (October 31, 1905–December 6, 1981), an American psychologist best known for his maternal separation and social isolation experiments on rhesus monkeys, demonstrated the importance of caregiving and companionship in social and cognitive development. The first love of the human infant is for his mother. The tender intimacy of this attachment is such that it is sometimes regarded as a sacred or mystical force, an instinct incapable of analysis. Harlow's experiments offered irrefutable proof that love is vital for normal childhood development and revealed the long-term devastation caused by deprivation, leading to profound psychological and emotional distress. Harlow's work helped influence key changes in how orphanages, adoption agencies, social services groups, and child care providers approached the care of children. Along with child analysts and researchers, including Anna Freud and René Spitz, Harlow's experiments added scientific legitimacy to two powerful arguments: against institutional child care and in favor of psychological parenthood. The permanence associated with adoption was far superior to other arrangements when it came to safeguarding the future mental and emotional well-being of children in need of parents (http://en.wikipedia.org/wiki/Harry_Harlow).

Harlow, Harry Frederick and Clara Mears Harlow. *From Learning to Love: The Selected Papers of H. F. Harlow (Centennial Psychological Series)*. New York: Praeger Publishers, 1986.

Nancy Verrier, an American psychotherapist, author, lecturer, and adoptive parent, is perhaps best known for work in the areas of adoption and adoption reform. She has published two books concerning the psychopathology of adoption, *The Primal Wound: Understanding the Adopted Child* (1993) and *Coming Home to Self*. The core premise of the primal wound theory is that a child separated from its mother at the beginning of life, when still in the primal relationship to her, experiences what she calls the primal wound. This wound, occurring before the child has begun to separate his own identity from that of the mother, is experienced not only as a loss of the mother, but as a loss of the self, that core being of oneself that is the center of goodness and wholeness. The child may be left with a sense that part of oneself has disappeared, leaving a feeling of incompleteness and lack of wholeness. In addition to the genealogical sense of being cut off from one's roots, this incompleteness is often experienced in a physical sense of bodily incompleteness, a hurt from something missing (http://en.wikipedia.org/wiki/The_Primal_Wound).

Verrier, Nancy Newton. *The Primal Wound: Understanding the Adopted Child*. Nancy Verrier, 1993.

Gail Sheehy (November 27, 1937), an American writer and lecturer in Mamaroneck, New York, is most notable for her books on life and the life cycle. Her fifth book, *Passages*, has been called "a road map of adult life." Several of her books continue the theme of passages through life's stages. Judith Romano in *Adoption Detective* used this information to cope with life's tribulations through understanding of normal changes in human perspective and performance based on age and experience (http://en.wikipedia.org/wiki/Gail_Sheehy).

Sheehy, Gail. *Passages: Predictable Crises of Adult Life*. Ballantine Books, 2006.

Genealogical bewilderment refers to potential identity problems that could be experienced by a child who was either fostered or adopted. Psychologist H. J. Sants, referring to the plight of children who have uncertain, little, or no knowledge of one or both of their natural parents, coined the term in 1964. He argued that genealogical bewilderment constituted a large part of the additional stress that adoptees experienced that is not experienced by children raised by their natural parents. Sants wrote in the journal *Mental Health*:

> *Knowledge of and definite relationship to his genealogy is ... necessary for a child to build up his complete body image and world picture. It is an inalienable and entitled right of every person. There is an urge, a call, in everybody to follow and fulfill the tradition of his family, race, nation, and the religious community into which he was born. The loss of this tradition is a deprivation, which may result in the stunting of emotional development.*

Sorosky, Pannor and Baran drew upon the work of Sants in a number of publications during the 1970s, including a book entitled *The Adoption Triangle*, thus exposing the concept of genealogical bewilderment to a larger audience (http://en.wikipedia.org/wiki/Genealogical_bewilderment).

O'Shaughnessy, T. *Adoption, Social Work and Social Theory: Making the Connections*. Brookfield, Vt.: Ashgate Publishing, 1994.
Sorosky, Arthur D., MD. *The Adoption Triangle*. Triadoption Publications, 1978.

Jean Paton, founder of Orphan Voyage, is regarded as the grand-mother of adoption reform and reunification efforts. In a book written under the name Ruthena Hill Kittson, one of many that she used during her life, adoptee and visionary search activist Jean Paton presented her rationales for adoption search: the equality of all citizens, the self-determination of individuals, and adoptees' emotional need for a curative and breakthrough reality that would finally make sense out of their disrupted life stories. Her vision of an independent, voluntary adoption registry through which natal relatives might be reunited dates to an article she wrote in 1949, making it one of the earliest such suggestions in the documentary record. Mutual consent registries proliferated after 1975. Late in life, Jean Paton was a supporter and mentor to Judith Romano during her quest to discover her birth family in the book *Adoption Detective* (http://pages.uoregon.edu/adoption/archive/PatonOV.htm).

Kittson, Ruthena Hill. *Orphan Voyage*. Arvin Publications, 1980.

Betty Jean Lifton, acclaimed author of several books on the psychology of the adopted that have helped open the field, tells her own story of growing up adopted in the closed adoption system. Calling *Twice Born* both an autobiography and a psychological journey into the past, Lifton takes the reader with her as she describes the loneliness and isolation of an adopted child cut off from the knowledge of her heritage. She explores the ambivalence and guilt that she feels toward her adoptive parents when she awakens as an adult to her need to ask, "Who am I?" With the mounting suspense of a detective novel, *Twice Born* explores not only the difficulty of searching for one's past when records are sealed, but also the complexity of trying to reunite with the birth mother from whom one has been separated by social taboos and time. More than a vivid and poignant memoir, Lifton has given her a story of mothering and mother-loss attachment and bonding, secrets and lies, and the human need for origins (http://www.goodreads.com/book/show/2487022.Twice_Born).

Lifton, Betty Jean. *Twice Born: Memoirs of an Adopted Daughter*. Mc-Graw-Hill Book Company, 1975.

Helen Schucman and **William Thetford,** authors of *A Course in Miracles,* are the creators of a self-study metaphysical thought system unique in teaching forgiveness as the road to inner peace and the remembrance of the unconditional love of God. The book is published by the Foundation for Inner Peace. It consists of preface, text, and workbook for students, manual for teachers, including clarification of terms, and two supplements. Two million volumes have been published and disseminated worldwide. The book has been translated into nineteen different languages with eight new translations underway. This course is helpful for adoptees dealing with the high stress common to most adoption searches (http://en.wikipedia.org/wiki/A_Course_in_Miracles).

Schucman, H., and W. Thetford. *A Course in Miracles.* Tiburon, Calif.: Foundation for Inner Peace, 1985.

Linda Dillow, author of *Calm My Anxious Heart,* encourages the reader to imagine what life would be like without worry in a world free of the burden of fear. Filled with encouragement and practical help for overcoming anxiety, this book includes a twelve-week study to help the reader discover contentment and ways to apply it to daily life that comes from trusting God. Traveling backward in time to find the truth during an adoption search can be invigorating but stressful, and this book provides a method for finding inner peace (http://www.navpress. com/images/pdfs/9781600061417.pdf).

Dillow, Linda. *Calm My Anxious Heart: A Woman's Guide to Finding Contentment.* Navpress, 1998.

Denny Sargent, author of *Your Guardian Angel and You,* establishes the goal of making an internal connection to a spiritual being that exists solely to help you find your way, your path, your true will, the purpose of your plan, and your place in it. Your whole life is simply a search for what it is you are supposed to do in this life and do it to the best of your ability. Guardian angels exist to patiently guide you every day through the divine plan that you embody. If you follow the path God has provided for you, you will find real happiness, peace, and freedom, the universal goals of life. For as long as human beings have been recording their thoughts, dreams, and ideas on stone, wood, or paper, there have been accounts of guardian angels. Across many different religions, the accepted views are remarkably similar and show us examples of divine intervention at moments of danger (www.amazon. com/Your-Guardian-Angel-You-Signals/dp/1578632757).

Sargent, Denny. *Your Guardian Angel and You.* York Beach, Me.: Red Wheel/Weiser, LLC, 2004.

Maxwell Maltz wrote the classic self-help book, *Psycho-Cybernetics*, published by the nonprofit Psycho-Cybernetics Foundation. Motivational and self-help experts in personal development, including Zig Ziglar, Tony Robbins, and Brian Tracy, have based their techniques on Maxwell Maltz. Many of the psychological methods of training elite athletes are based on the concepts in psycho-cybernetics as well. The book combines the cognitive behavioral technique of teaching an individual how to regulate self-concept developed by Prescott Lecky with the cybernetics of Norbert Wiener and John von Neumann. The book defines the mind-body connection as the core in succeeding in attaining personal goals. Maltz found that his plastic surgery patients often had expectations that were not satisfied by the surgery, so he pursued a means of helping them set the goal of a positive outcome through visualization of that positive outcome. Maltz became interested in why setting goals works. He learned that the power of self-affirmation and mental visualization techniques used the connection between the mind and the body. He specified techniques to develop a positive inner goal as a means of developing a positive outer goal. This concentration on inner attitudes is essential to his approach, as a person's outer success can never rise above the one visualized internally. Millions of people have benefited by putting these ideas to work (http://en.wikipedia. org/wiki/Psycho-Cybernetics).

Maltz, Maxwell. *Psycho-Cybernetics.* New York: Pocket Books, 1960.

Jim Suhr, author of *Choosing by Advantages (CBA),* states that one of the greatest of all human aptitudes is the faculty for making intelligent choices. All human performance is based on a decision-making process. Use of a sound method is among the most important decisions ever made. People can significantly improve the quality of their lives by skillfully applying sound methods for weighing alternatives and making the best choices. Judith and Martin Land, co-authors of *Adoption Detective*, used the CBA method of decision making as a rational technique for weighing alternatives, estimating collateral effects, and making important choices to accomplish their goals (http://www.enlignconsultants.com/ChoosingByAdvantages.htm).

Suhr, Jim. *Choosing by Advantages Decision making System*. Westport, Conn.: Quorum Books, 1999.

The **Minnesota Twin Family Study** seeks to identify genetic and environmental influences on the heritability of psychological traits; academic ability; personality; interests; family and social relationships; and mental and physical health to determine prevalence of psychopathology, substance abuse, divorce, leadership, and other traits, and behaviors related to mental and physical health, relationships, and religiosity. Thomas Bouchard studied twins separated at birth and raised in different families. He found that an identical twin reared away from his or her co-twin seems to have about an equal chance of being similar to the co-twin in terms of personality, interests, and attitudes as one who has been reared with his or her co-twin. This leads to the conclusion that similarities between twins are due to genes, not environment. Judith and Martin Land, co-authors of *Adoption Detective*, considered this scientific research enlightening for understanding genetics as a character determinant, and weighing the effects of environment versus inheritance issue for adoptees.

Rick Warren author of *The Purpose Driven Life*, is a devotional book on the New York Times Best Seller list for one of the longest periods in history, while also topping the *Wall Street Journal* best seller charts as well as *Publishers Weekly* charts with over 30 million copies sold by 2007. *The Purpose Driven Life* was the most frequent response in a May 2005 survey of American pastors and ministers asking Christian leaders to identify what books were the most influential on their lives and ministries.

Warren, Rick. *The Purpose Driven Life: What on Earth Am I Here For?* Insdirio, Zondervan, Running Press, Philadelphia, 2003.

Dr. Laura Schlessinger, author of *Bad Childhood Good Life: How to Blossom and Thrive in Spite of an Unhappy Childhood*. With her characteristically pointed advice and take-no-prisoners attitude, Dr. Laura's tackles one of the most basic questions of therapy: How can a person effectively move past the injuries of a bad childhood? Her answer will be familiar to her fans—look at your current behavior and modify what you can change rather than simply venting your anger or allowing yourself to ever be victimized again. Forget about simply accepting or forgiving your parents for their errors—Dr. Laura extols the virtues of conquering. Through excerpts from her radio show, she illustrates her points about guilt, anger, and fear in personalized accounts from individuals. References and her website provide all the additional information you could want. Faith is a subtle component.

Schlessinger, Dr. Laura. (2006) *Bad Childhood---Good Life: How to Blossom and Thrive in Spite of an Unhappy Childhood*. Harper Collins.

Khalil Gibran, (1883 – 1931), a Lebanese American, is the third best selling poet behind Shakespeare and Lao-Tzu. Many of his writings deal with Christianity and spiritual love. His poetry is notable for its use of formal language, as well as insights on topics of life using spiritual terms. Since it was first published in 1923, *The Prophet* has never been out of print. Having been translated into more than forty languages, it was one of the bestselling books of the twentieth century in the United States. The letter addressed to Mom in chapter one of *Adoption Detective*, was inspired by his writings.

Gibran, Khalil. *The Prophet*. Borzoi Book published by Alfred A. Knopt, New York, 2001.

Sophie Anderson (1823–1903), a French-born British artist, specialized in genre painting of children and women, typically in rural settings. *The Time of the Lilacs* oil on canvas painting used on the cover of *Adoption Detective* is a file from the Wikimedia Commons. The painting represents Judith Romano, an adoptee and main character in *Adoption Detective* and the First Lilac Club (FLC), an international women's organization. This work is in the public domain in the United States and those countries with a copyright term of life of the author plus one hundred years or fewer. Above all, Sophie Anderson is known for pictures of overly sweet little girls. Her depiction of nature is almost photographic, with the flowers and leaves in her paintings most naturalistic. Her depiction of fabrics and drapery and often the light effects in her pictures are of great merit.

Susan S. Morris, is a Utah born American artist devoted to painting an intimate view of simple things and days gone by, exposing the beauty and nostalgic spirit of the past. Her illustration in the book *Adoption Detective* depicts Judith Romano and friends sharing intimate secrets.

> *"The compact space under the lilac bushes provided a secure environment where the girls felt relaxed and comfortable. The proximity of the seating arrangement facilitated intimacy, whispering, and the sharing of secrets—only then did Judith Romano decide to tell her girlfriends she was adopted." –Judith Land*

Her pen and ink drawing commemorates the initial meeting of the *First Lilac Club*, an international women's organization founded by Judith Romano, Milwaukee, Wisconsin, 1956.

CPSIA information can be obtained at www.ICGtesting.com
Printed in the USA
266771BV00003B/1/P